BLOCKADE
BUSTERS

BLOCKADE BUSTERS

RALPH BARKER

W · W · NORTON & COMPANY · INC ·

NEW YORK

Library of Congress Cataloging in Publication Data

Barker, Ralph, 1917-
  Blockade busters.

  Bibliography: p.
  Includes index.
  1.   World War, 1939-1945—Blockades.   2.   World War,
1939-1945—North Sea.   3.   World War, 1939-1945—Supplies.
4.   Binney, George, 1900-   I.   Title.
D771.B28   1976   940.54'52   76-49446
ISBN 0-393-05609-0

1 2 3 4 5 6 7 8 9 0

CONTENTS

AUTHOR'S NOTE

Through the courtesy of Lady Binney and her son Marcus I have had access to all the late Sir George Binney's manuscripts and papers, and these have been a valuable basic source, filling out the material gathered from official documents and in the course of interviews and correspondence with those who took part in the blockade-running operations or had some responsibility for them.

The enthusiasm and spontaneity with which so many of Sir George's wartime comrades and associates responded to appeals for help and personal reminiscence provided convincing proof of the esteem and affection in which he was held.

Many of the people listed at the end of the book (*Sources*, p. 213) have helped at considerable length, and it does not detract from my indebtedness to them to say that I must single out here four for special mention. They are Harald Meltzer, of Oslo, who was my guide and host when I made a research visit to Scandinavia; J. C. 'Jack' Aird, whose translation of Norwegian documents was an essential preliminary to that visit; Stina Siberg, widow of Ville Siberg, of SKF, who undertook important research work for me in Sweden; and Captain R. W. 'Bob' Tanton, who organised and led me in a tour of the men of the little ships in and around Hull.

R. B.

ILLUSTRATIONS

ACKNOWLEDGMENTS

The copyright in the photographs is acknowledged as follows: 1 and 12b, Popper-foto; 2a, 3a, 3b, 4c, The Imperial War Museum, London; 2b, Henriksen & Steen A/S; 4a, Royal Norwegian Government; 4b, Captain W. J. Escudier, OBE; 5a, Captain Henry Denham, RN (Retd.); 5b, Leif Blücker; 5c, 5d, C. W. Kjellberg; 6a, John V. G. Mallet; 6b, Reportabild, Stockholm; 6c, 8a, 9b, 10a, 11b, Captain E. B. Ruffman, DSC; 7a (inset), Colonel Björn Egge; 7b (inset), F. Wessel Berg; 8b, Mrs. A. Whitfield; 8c, Mrs. Constance Jackson, ALCM; 8d, Mrs. M. M. Holdsworth; 9a, 10b, Associated Newspapers; 11a, Curt Wards; 11c, 12a, SKF, Gothenburg. The maps (on pages 23 and 104) were drawn by Edgar Holloway.

INTRODUCTION

A Man Called Binney

GEORGE BINNEY had never quite got over the accident of birth which had caused him to miss the First World War. Born on 23rd September 1900, he had been accepted for a commission in the Scots Guards soon after his eighteenth birthday, but the date of acceptance had been 11th November 1918—Armistice Day. Then, when he went on to university, he found himself surrounded by young men very little older than himself who had distinguished themselves on war service, and although he was not a person who easily developed a sense of inferiority, the gap in his experience rankled.

Of any healthy Englishman born in the early years of the Twentieth Century it might be said, adapting Oscar Wilde, that to have missed one World War might be regarded as excusable, but to have missed both looked like cowardice. This was the prospect facing George Binney when, on the outbreak of the Second World War on 3rd September 1939, he volunteered at once for the Navy, only to be told that he was too old to be commissioned to go to sea.

Civilised in the true sense of the word, and enjoying both sensual and aesthetic pleasures, Binney played squash to keep himself fit; but nevertheless he bore the marks of good living. Short but well-built, he was written down by the naval authorities (so it is said) as a man of unmilitary aspect who looked more like a stockbroker than a seafarer and who at close-on 40 could offer them little. But when he protested that he was fitter than many men ten years his junior, his blue eyes sparked with such stubborn refusal to accept outright rejection that the interviewing board recognised him as a fighter.

'We'll put you on the list for later consideration,' they told him.

Sentimental, but with few illusions, Binney was nothing if not resourceful. What was he best fitted for? How could he find some facet of the war for which he was uniquely equipped? The reaction of the authorities, he feared, would be to find him a desk job. That was something he was determined to avoid.

On his seventh birthday the young George Binney had been taken by his father to see Eton College, partly as a treat, partly to give him an appetite for the things it offered. At that time it was a distant prospect indeed. His father, Rev. M. F. B. Binney, was then Vicar of Richmond, Surrey, and with four sons to educate he couldn't afford to send George to Eton or anywhere else without a scholarship. But he believed that a good education, and good health, were by far the most important things any parent could bestow on an offspring, and he encouraged the boy to try for a King's Scholarship to Eton. In July 1914, after six years at Summerfields School, Oxford, the young Binney was duly taken by his headmaster to Eton to sit the scholarship examination. When it was over he was sent home to await results.

'On the appointed day,' wrote George Binney many years later, 'my father stood in the hall in his frock coat, anxiously pacing about and peering through the window across Richmond Green for the telegraph boy. Suddenly he shouted "Here he comes!" Hurriedly donning his top-hat, he leapt down the front steps, shot across the road, vaulted over the railings, and dashed across the Green towards the slightly alarmed messenger boy who was carrying the telegram. Snatching it from him, he tore it open and devoured its contents. Then he threw his top-hat into the air, danced with joy, and waved and shouted at me in a frenzy of excitement. "George sixteenth on Eton list," read the telegram. "Scholarship certain."' Binney attributed his scholarship to the luck of being set for his Latin verse paper a Walter Scott poem he had worked on two weeks earlier.

The boyish enthusiasm which the father had retained into his fifties was equally characteristic of the son at 39. A bachelor, but no misogynist, he believed in experiencing life to the full. Allied to this were qualities of ingenuity, tenacity, a disarming ingenuousness which was almost naïvety, and old-fashioned virtues of integrity, enterprise, self-reliance and patriotism. Where might these qualities now best be applied?

From Eton Binney had gained a scholarship to Merton College, Oxford, attributing his luck this time to writing an essay on Joachim, the violinist, only to be examined in the oral by Joachim's nephew. In his second term he had succeeded Beverley Nichols as editor of *Isis*. Then a chance visit from Julian Huxley, at that time a fellow of New College, had set him on a fresh course. Huxley and other scientists were keen to organise an expedition to Spitzbergen, and they wanted *Isis* to help them launch the project. Binney soon found himself first a member of the expedition committee and later organising secretary. 'This involved the raising of funds, the charter of a Norwegian sealing-sloop, the finding of suitable stores and equipment, the selection of personnel and the sale of press rights,' he wrote afterwards, 'for none of which I was qualified. But as I have never been discouraged by my ignorance, I entered into my duties with zest.' Here further characteristics were revealed, for wartime adventures perhaps the most important of all: cheek, and luck. However boldly planned such adventures might be, they often depended as much as anything on luck for their ultimate success.

Having organised and led three university expeditions while at Oxford, Binney wrote two books on his experiences: *With Seaplane and Sledge in the Arctic* (1925), and *The Eskimo Book of Knowledge* (1931). The first of these books brought him to the notice of Sir Charles Sale, governor of the Hudson's Bay Company, who rightly judged Binney's exploits to be exceptional for a young man of 25. He gave Binney a job in the Fur Trade Department of the company, which meant that Binney divided his time between winter in London and summer in the Canadian Arctic and around Hudson Bay. Sale, a stern taskmaster, inculcated into Binney a strict Edwardian concept of business methods, together with a respect for precision in verbal negotiation and in the wording of documents. But in 1931 the company had to be reshaped following the Wall Street crash, and Binney was facing dismissal when his second book was published and noticed in a *Times* leader. He was at once offered a transfer to the Canadian headquarters in Winnipeg. But nearly all his friends were in London, and he was a man who set great store by his friends. So he resigned. Next morning, quite fortuitously, he was offered the job of forming and developing a Central Export Department in United Steel.

Nine months' training at the works at Sheffield, Scunthorpe and Workington did not turn him into a metallurgist, but it gave him the necessary background. What they wanted was his patience, humanity and persuasiveness as a negotiator. Binney never tried to impose his will on anyone, and he was never arrogant. But his gentle approach concealed a mind that knew exactly what it wanted to achieve and generally did so.

At his house in Porchester Terrace, Bayswater, waited on by a manservant and surrounded by the collection of antiques which was one of his few conceits, Binney let his mind drift back to the Arctic, and to what now seemed the next best thing, Scandinavia. It was the obvious choice. Britain had vital interests there in ferro-alloy, iron-ore, Swedish iron, special steels and ball-bearings, and these interests, of paramount importance to the planned expansion of key British industries in wartime, might well be threatened by German competition. At the same time the background of a neutral country might give opportunities for some form of Intelligence work. Both before and after Munich, Binney had had contacts with Military Intelligence, but his lack of a specialised language had gone against him, and he still hadn't found his niche.

'Do you know the Norwegians, George?' asked Robert Hilton, managing director of United Steel, when Binney approached him, and Binney reminded Hilton that he had spent many months with Norwegian sealing crews in the Arctic and if his Norwegian wasn't exactly fluent it was colloquial and to the point. And Sweden? 'We've got the best agency in Stockholm of any of the steelmakers,' replied Binney. 'Carl Setterwall and Co., and their chief Adolf Fagerland. They've got long-standing Sheffield connections and I couldn't wish for a better foundation there.' Binney's schemes, however imaginative, always had a sound logical basis. 'I'd like to meet your Intelligence friend,' said Hilton. 'If he satisfies me, I'll discuss it with Sir Andrew Duncan.' Duncan, a Glasgow-trained lawyer, was the government-appointed chairman of the British and Iron Steel Federation. Duncan agreed that there was work to be done in Scandinavia; already, in October 1939, he had sent a representative with long family connections with Swedish steel, Edward Senior, to order materials. 'Both the special steel industry and the bearing industry,' writes Senior, 'were dependent at the beginning of the war on Sweden.' Now Duncan appointed Binney to represent Iron and Steel Control in Sweden and Norway. 'You'll have all our support,' he told Binney. In the months that followed Binney was to need it.

For the next few weeks Binney was busy preparing the ground and establishing contacts, of which the most important were those with the Ministry of Economic Warfare; the Special Operations Executive (when it was formed); and the Ministry of Supply. But Binney was a man for personal rather than impersonal relationships, and his real support lay in his friendships with the men he would be dealing with in these departments—Charles Hambro, a fellow Etonian from the banking family then in the Ministry of Economic Warfare, later to become head of the Scandinavian section of SOE; Harry Sporborg, a humane and practical lawyer in MEW who was also destined for SOE; and C. R. 'Mike' Wheeler, a deputy steel controller at the Ministry of Supply. Taking the first three letters of their Christian names, Binney was to christen them the 'Chaharmiks', and it was on them that he chiefly relied, when the going got tough, to keep him afloat on the stormy seas of Whitehall.

These men told Binney of Britain's requirements for Scandinavian iron, alloys and steels, and of their plans to pre-empt and frustrate the Germans wherever possible through a campaign of economic warfare. But for the present Binney's brief was simply to renew and establish contacts in the Scandinavian steel industry and smooth the way for existing contracts. Germany and Russia had already divided up Poland, and on 30th November 1939 Russia had invaded Finland, but Norway, Sweden, Denmark, Holland and Belgium were still unviolated and the Scandinavian ports were open to both sides.

On 9th December 1939, with a roving commission to report anything which might be of interest to Military Intelligence under cover of his steel appointment, Binney flew by DC2 from Perth to Oslo, and four days later he reached Stockholm. These two cities, capitals of what still remained neutral countries, had rapidly become centres of espionage and intrigue, as Binney was to discover.

Binney's first interview was with the Jernkontoret, the Swedish equivalent of the British Iron and Steel Federation. This was the authoritative body of the Swedish iron and steel industry, where problems were discussed and policies formulated. Here, as with all the leading Swedish steelmakers, Binney found he was the inheritor of a friendly trading relationship that had already lasted for centuries. But it was soon made clear to him that the appearance of strict neutrality must be maintained.

His next call was on Adolf Fagerland, senior partner of Carl Setterwall and Co., agents in Sweden for his own firm, United Steel. Fagerland had been a frequent visitor to Sheffield since 1905, was basically Anglophile, and had been Edward Senior's choice to undertake the wartime commercial representation of British steelmakers and the Ministry of Supply. Quiet, shrewd and imperturbable, he was pleased at the prospect of being able to help his English friends; but he too reminded Binney that first and foremost he was a Swede and must respect his government's policy of neutrality. Within that limitation, however, he was enthusiastic. The fact that the Germans, when they heard of his appointment, hinted to him that there could well be a day of reckoning, did not seem to disturb him. Black-listing by the Nazis was something he regarded as a compliment.

Britain's imports from Sweden in wartime were governed by the Anglo-Swedish War Trade Agreement, negotiated two months earlier, in October 1939; under this agreement the volume of permissible exports was based on the 1938 figures. A parallel agreement between Sweden and Germany restricted their imports in the same way. Binney learned from the Jernkontoret that this agreement would work out unfavourably for Britain, reducing the volume of iron and steel exports attained over the first six months of 1939. Another limiting factor was the Russo-Finnish war; in view of Sweden's treaty commitments to Finland, exports to both Britain and Germany might be affected. In addition, a French Supply Mission had recently arrived in Stockholm, and since the French had done little business in Sweden before the war, the Mission was seeking to buy its way in by offering higher prices. These were some of the problems to which Binney addressed himself.

In order to gain first-hand knowledge of the Swedish steel industry he travelled 500 miles north by train from Stockholm to Lulea, the port near the head of the Gulf of Bothnia which the Germans used for their ore shipments to the Baltic during the ice-free summer months. Continuing by train north-west parallel with the Finnish frontier to Kirkuna in Lapland, he was shown the ore-fields from which the bulk of the annual Swedish iron export of about 15 million tons originated. Then he travelled another ninety miles north-west to Narvik, the Norwegian port on the North Sea used by the Germans in winter and by the British all the year round. This was Britain's steel lifeline, and it was Binney's job, in the weeks that followed, to nourish and preserve it.

Visiting Oslo in March 1940, Binney found the capital still humming with the excitement of the rescue, off the Norwegian coast, of nearly 300 prisoners taken by the German pocket-battleship Graf Spee from the ships she had sunk during her Atlantic foray. These prisoners had been transferred to the German fleet auxiliary Altmark when the Graf Spee was herself cornered and destroyed. Then in her turn the Altmark had been boarded by the crew of the British destroyer Cossack in Norwegian territorial waters and her prisoners reclaimed. Arguments about violations of neutrality by both sides raged; but for Britain the operation was vindicated by success. It was an incident, however, which was later to have repercussions for Binney.

The Nazis were operating quite openly in Oslo, and they had their Norwegian sympathisers; now Binney had the opportunity of meeting, through his business contacts, a German steel agent named Eugen Lenkering who was known to be a prominent Nazi. The conversation that took place between them was one that Binney was to reflect on afterwards.

'How do you like the climate here?' asked Lenkering.

'I find it very exhilarating. I love Norway.'

'So—we also like Norway.'

Binney was in Trondheim on 9th April 1940 when he received a long-distance call from Oslo. The German fleet was in Oslo fjord, a German naval contingent was heading for Trondheim, the German invasion of Norway had begun and the fighting had started. 'You must escape to the frontier,' he was told. 'Good-bye.'

So that was what Lenkering had meant. Forty minutes later Binney was on board a train bound for Sweden.

If the Germans took Norway and Denmark, the North Sea iron-ore trade would be controlled by the enemy, and the Skagerrak would be finally closed to Allied shipping. Even if Sweden herself retained her independence, it would be no more than nominal. All Binney's spadework over the past few months in maintaining and increasing Britain's share of the Swedish steel output would be frustrated by the total impracticability of transporting the product to Britain. Sweden would become totally dependent on Germany, and to the Nazi victors would fall the spoils.

BLOCKADE
BUSTERS

PART I

OPERATION RUBBLE

Escape through the Skagerrak

ALTHOUGH Britain began the war with the undoubted sympathy of the Swedish Government and people, her inability to defend the frontiers of small nations, demonstrated ever since the Italian conquest of Abyssinia and the German occupation of Austria, had led to the conclusion that neutrality was the better part of valour. The main objective of Swedish foreign policy inevitably became to maintain independence while avoiding war. But German reliance on imports of Swedish iron-ore for her steel industry, and British plans for a stricter economic blockade, meant that Sweden was bound to find herself in conflict at various times with one or the other or both. Whether or not the Germans, when they had consolidated their hold on Norway, would decide to secure their ore supplies by occupying Sweden, was uncertain, and was to remain so for many months; meanwhile they exerted a political pressure on Sweden fully proportionate to the implied threat. At first the Swedes resisted all German demands that would have constituted infringements of neutrality; but in mid-June 1940, following a hysterical outburst from Hitler, they began to allow the transit of German troops and materials to and from Norway via Swedish Railways.

In the First World War the Swedes had been largely pro-German; all Swedes in those days learnt German at school before any other foreign language and thus received an early injection of German thought and culture.* But after the First World War, Anglo-Saxon influence became predominant, and when the Second World War started only a small proportion of the 6 million Swedes were Nazi sympathisers and probably 90 per cent of them leaned towards the West. An exception was that certain leaders of the armed forces, and particularly a majority of the Board of Admirals directing the Navy, retained their pro-German outlook. This outlook was largely inherited from the traditional belief that Sweden's integrity was dependent on a strong Germany to counter-balance the hereditary enemy Russia; but in the Navy the belief was fortified by the friendships formed

* *Diplomat*, by Gunnar Hägglöf (The Bodley Head, 1972).

17

between the officers and men of the two navies when they mixed, as they were accustomed to do, on cruises and exercises in the Baltic and the Gulf of Bothnia.

The special relationship between the two navies did not imply any hostility towards the British on the part of the Swedes until an incident on 2nd June 1940, when four second-hand destroyers bought by the Swedes from Italy for coastal defence were seized by the British when they reached the Faroes, although conforming to an itinerary agreed by the British Admiralty. The British feared that if they didn't seize the ships the Germans would. The destroyers—the Romulus, the Remus, the Puke and the Psilander—were eventually allowed to continue, but not before some over-zealous searching and indiscriminate looting while the ships were in British hands had justifiably angered the Swedes. Their Government and press showed remarkable patience and forbearance, as did Admiral Fabian Tamm, head of the Swedish Navy and one of the many influential Swedes who had come to accept the inevitability of a German victory; but for the destroyer crews, already well indoctrinated in Nazi propaganda, suspicion and bias were intensified into hatred and contempt. The subsequent payment by the British of nearly a million kröner in compensation could scarcely do more than alleviate the blow to Swedish *amour-propre*.

The German naval attaché in Stockholm reported somewhat disappointedly to Berlin that the Swedish press had played down the incident, which thus made little public impact; but like the Altmark affair, it was to have repercussions later.

The Germans had anticipated from the start that one of the fruits of their Norwegian campaign would be that Swedish exports to Britain would cease and the Anglo-Swedish War Trade Agreement would lapse, leaving the Swedish economy at their mercy. In London, too, the implications were fully realised. It had taken the whole of the 'phoney war' period for the Swedes to manufacture the goods ordered by British industry on the outbreak of war, and now Britain couldn't get her hands on them. Binney warned that with exports to Britain for the moment impracticable, the Swedish Government might soon be pressed by Swedish exporters to allow increased quotas to Germany over and above the war trade agreements, to compensate them for the stalemate with English contracts. He asked that all such contracts, which amounted to approximately £1 million, be confirmed, even if the British Government had to take them over. 'You will, I venture to think,' he wrote on 4th May, 'agree that now our only line of defence here (and incidentally of offence) is the maintenance of our Swedish War Trade Agreement, which automatically binds the Germans. It is the Verdun of our position, but it is untenable unless we can establish entirely new routes of export within a very short time. I venture to go further in saying that however unpractical those routes may appear at first sight from the geographical and economic standpoints, we MUST establish them, cost what it may. . . .

'I submit that we can still fight an extremely important rearguard action here and that we may even succeed ultimately in retrieving much of the ground that we shall be forced to give way, if we act promptly and decisively.'

Binney envisaged the trade campaign with Sweden in terms of a military and/or naval operation, and in this he had the full support of the Ministry of Supply and the Ministry of Economic Warfare, who at once approached the Treasury for the money. All materials delivered by the Swedes, it was agreed, should be sent to suitable storage points, there to be held until an opportunity occurred for onward despatch to Britain; the priorities were stated to be hollow tubes for both tube making and the manufacture of roller-bearings, steel strip, wire rods, alloy steel for aircraft, pig iron, bar iron, and certain machine tools. Cited as a specially urgent requirement were the roller-bearings being made by Skefco (SKF) at Gothenburg for a new strip mill at Ebbw Vale operated by Messrs. Richard Thomas & Co.; this mill, the first modern strip mill in Europe, was rolling half to three-quarters of a million tons of sheet steel annually and had the biggest capacity in Britain. It was equipped with Swedish roller-bearings, and no alternatives were available to replace them when they wore out. (At that time, Swedish thick walled tubing was of better quality and more reliable than British or Canadian, and the need was urgent.) Other priorities were special steels for the Sheffield steel industry, and for the building of tanks, for gun forgings and armour plate for the Navy, tube steel for the Skefco works at Luton, and bearings for aircraft engines. About 20 per cent of the bearings for the engineering industry as a whole were imported even in peace-time, and with the increased demand, serious shortages were threatened. Pressurised by the Chaharmiks, the Treasury authorised the taking up of outstanding contracts to the value proposed.

The Swedes reacted favourably, but they feared that any long-term storage of goods ultimately destined for Britain would attract protests and threats from Germany, and they wanted all goods removed to Finland, Norway or Russia pending shipment. Binney had already begun negotiations with the Finnish Government for the granting of facilities which would enable him to use the ports of Petsamo and Kirkenes via the Arctic Highway, but from his own Arctic experience he realised the vital importance of close supervision of any such transport plan, and in this he had the support of the French. 'On the assumption that our Governments require us to prosecute the war with efficiency,' he wrote on 6th May, 'we can hardly leave so important and difficult a task to the goodwill of countries now very much subject to German domination . . . The fact that we are desperately at war *per se* stimulates our efforts. Automatically we meet exceptional difficulties with exceptional measures.' The Swedes and the Finns, warned Binney, tended to be rather complacent people, and in any case they could hardly be expected to share Allied conceptions of urgency. In nine years' experience of Arctic transport he had discovered how easily the phrase 'exceptional severity of conditions' could be made the excuse for human inefficiency. 'The Arctic is fertile with little except excuses,' he wrote. Here was a man who, to use a phrase soon to be coined by Winston Churchill, had the root of the matter in him, and who was determined to get things done. Four days later, on 10th May, when the main German blitzkreig began, the value of men like Binney increased tenfold.

By 22nd May, at the suggestion of the Foreign Office, Binney had been put in charge of all arrangements for the transport of goods for shipment via the Finnish ports. But for once he was not optimistic. The route, he found, was still in the experimental stage, facilities at Petsamo were inadequate for Finland's own requirements, and Kirkenes was inaccessible owing to the destruction of a vital bridge. The Finnish Government were taking the view that they could not risk antagonising Germany by shipping goods destined for the Allies, and the political barriers began to look insurmountable. The Ministry of Economic Warfare, however, kept up the pressure. 'Please ask Binney to do everything possible to ensure maximum supplies urgent material available at Petsamo,' they cabled. And Sporborg wrote: 'Some of these special steels cannot at present be replaced for aircraft manufacture, and since we are really starting to build aeroplanes, stocks are vanishing at an alarming rate. In what could be a disastrous situation, to get one cargo back safely would go a long way.' Binney eventually succeeded in getting a small load away from Petsamo via North America and a much larger one by rail through Russia and down through the Caspian Sea to the Persian Gulf; but these were tediously circuitous routes, and it was many months before either consignment reached Britain. Meanwhile the Finnish settlement with Russia, and the completion by the Germans of their conquest and occupation of Norway, closed all possible outlets.

Sweden thus became a small island of neutrality in a sea of enemy-occupied territory; and her isolation was completed by the collapse of the Allied armies on the Continent in May and early June and the evacuation at Dunkirk. Britain still had friends in Sweden in high places; but Sweden seemed doomed to become a vassal of Germany, her neutrality dependent on Hitler's whim, her industries tooled up exclusively to serve the Nazi war machine. British sea power might restrict the output of Swedish industry by blockade, but in doing so it could only throw Sweden more firmly into the German orbit. British diplomats, as jumpy as the Swedes themselves, saw their political aims restricted to encouraging the Swedish Government to resist German pressure where possible; and as for British activity, anything that ran contrary to the Nazi conception of what was meant by Swedish neutrality became a source of anxiety to the British Minister in Stockholm. It certainly did not occur to this official that the chief hope for maintaining a foothold in an effectively neutral Sweden might lie in the persistence, resource and imagination of a civilian named George Binney.

Binney's reaction to the appalling news from the battlefronts was to put a bold face on it. He assured both Adolf Fagerland and the president of the Jernkontoret that Britain would meet her obligations and would continue to order materials. With the collapse of France, the orders placed by the French purchasing commission were nullified, and the manufacturers faced bankruptcy; on Binney's advice, these orders were taken over by the British Government to prevent the materials being put up for resale. The Swedes, as Binney himself admitted, might well think the British were mad; but he judged that their legalistic minds would find it difficult to renounce the War Trade Agreement if Britain kept to her side of the bargain.

In all this, and in his faith in finding some means of shipment, Binney had the full backing of the Ministry of Supply, and on 9th June he received a staccato directive from Sir Andrew Duncan. *'It is of paramount importance that we receive all the war stores on order in Sweden (ball-bearings, machine-tools, special steels, Swedish iron, etc. etc.). You must repeat must at all costs get them to England.'* It was up to Binney to find a way.

Frustrated in his plans for using the Arctic Highway, Binney was looking as a last resort towards an outlet that had hitherto been dismissed as not remotely feasible—the blockaded Skagerrak. Arming himself with the appropriate sea charts, he called on Adolf Fagerland and showed him the telegram from Duncan. 'Look at this,' he said. 'They must be in desperate need.' What impressed Binney most, as they studied the chart, was the great depth of the main channel of the Skagerrak; both belligerents claimed to have blocked the Skagerrak with mines, but surely it must be difficult to lay effective minefields in such deep water and amongst such strong currents. Yet the Skagerrak, dominated as it was by enemy sea and air patrols, was closed to British shipping, even to the Royal Navy, who had learnt their lesson about steaming within range of German air bases during the Norwegian campaign. Indeed it was the *Luftwaffe*, strongly established astride the waters of the Skagerrak, that was now chiefly feared.

Binney decided there was one hope, slender though it might be: poor visibility due to thick fog or snow, when the German patrols would be less effective. Fagerland was inclined to agree. 'The sea,' he said, 'is a very big place.'

The Skagerrak, varying from sixty to ninety miles wide, runs north-east towards Sweden out of the North Sea, separating southern Norway from the Jutland peninsula. After 150 miles it narrows as it approaches the west coast of Sweden at right angles; and after rounding the Skaw, at the north-eastern tip of Jutland, it turns south and becomes the Kattegat. At the entrance to the Kattegat, on the Swedish side, a deep indentation more than ten miles in length leads by way of the Göta river and ship canal into Gothenburg, Sweden's chief seaport, her second largest city, and her gateway to the West. It was the port of Gothenburg, which had been brought to a standstill since the fall of Norway, that Binney had in mind as an assembly point.

Lying-up in Swedish ports were between twenty and thirty Norwegian vessels that had found themselves stranded in Swedish waters when Norway fell. At their last meeting in Tromsö on 18th May 1940 before going into exile in England, the Norwegian Government of King Haakon had promulgated a law under which they requisitioned all Norwegian ships which were outside Norway and whose owners were resident in an occupied territory, and placed them under a Norwegian marine directorate in London called Nortraship;* so in theory at least these ships belonged to the Allies. And an attempt by the Germans in August 1940 to transfer to Norway all Norwegian tonnage in Swedish ports was resisted by the Swedes on legal grounds, since Sweden still recognised the old Norwegian Government. Nine of these ships, all coal-burners, were employed by the Swedes for coastal traffic; but for the clandestine shipments that Binney was planning, steamships would be unsuitable anyway; they could not sail at less than twelve hours' notice, and in raising steam they betrayed their intention. He wanted the oil-burners, which left no tell-tale smoke. The Swedes had no use for these because of their own shortage of oil, brought about by the blockade. But most of the ships had more than enough oil on board to reach Britain.

For Binney the ships would serve a dual purpose. One of his most pressing needs was to take delivery of completed orders and find

* Norwegian Trading and Shipping Mission.

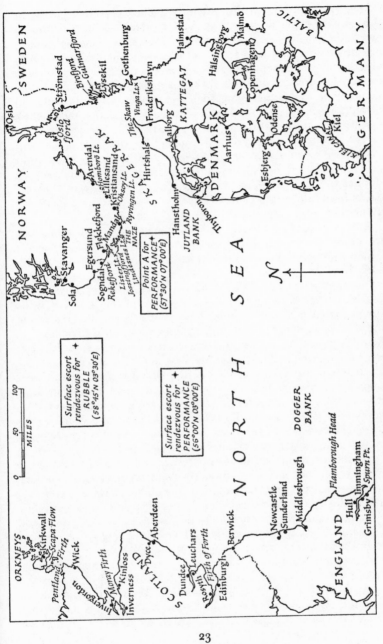

The North Sea, Skagerrak and Kattegat

storage space for them; the Swedes remained nervous of allowing Britain to stockpile goods in Sweden. One result of this nervousness, and of the general mood of uncertainty and loss of confidence following the French débâcle, was that factories were slow-timing on British orders, and even in some cases ceasing production altogether. So long as manufacturers could not fulfil the shipping terms of their agreements by delivering 'free alongside', they could not find the British in default, hence the go-slow. The obvious danger was that the Swedish Government might expropriate these goods, either for their own use or for re-sale, which meant to Germany. So even if it proved impracticable to sail the Norwegian vessels to British ports, they might be acquired from the Norwegians and used to store orders awaiting shipment. This would have the additional value of safeguarding the goods from falling into German hands if Sweden were invaded: any attempt at seizure and the ships could be scuttled.

Binney came to the conclusion that there was only one solution to the problem, and that it must be squarely faced: direct shipments to Britain through the Skagerrak and across the North Sea. On Sunday 16th June he confided this view to the recently appointed British Minister in Stockholm, Victor Mallet, and asked for his support. Mallet, well groomed and athletic, and a man of wide interests, was a career diplomat of considerable ability; but he was fully absorbed in the task of preserving what little influence the British retained in Swedish diplomatic circles, and the political implications of Binney's schemes disturbed him. In any case, he argued, any attempt to break out through the Skagerrak must certainly end in failure; and what ships was Binney going to employ? Binney replied that he was catching the train that night for Gothenburg, where he had arranged an appointment with the head of Wilson and Sons, the Swedish agents for the Ellerman's Wilson Line. He believed there were plenty of stranded Norwegian ships available, and he hoped to find Norwegian crews to man them. Mallet at once foresaw all kinds of objections to such a scheme, including Swedish embarrassment and German reprisals; but his principal reaction was one of extreme pessimism, and in this he was confirmed when he consulted his Service attachés. 'It's hare-brained,' he told Binney. 'I'm sure Steel Control and Economic Warfare will rule it out.' Binney, however, was determined to go ahead with his plans.

After travelling 250 miles across southern Sweden from Stockholm to Gothenburg, Binney met William Kjellberg, head of Wilson and Sons, in Kjellberg's office next morning. With Kjellberg was his assistant, Alva Henriksson, whom Binney was soon to assess as a remarkable woman, one who knew as much about freightage, stowage, stevedoring, and the handling and docking of ships, as any man. A spinster, aged 48, tall, blonde, soft-voiced and precise, she spoke with great deliberation, so that Binney could see her weighing each word before she uttered it. Kjellberg, who combined an old-fashioned conception of English virtues with an uncompromising hatred of the Nazis, agreed that there were plenty of idle ships in the port of Gothenburg—Swedish, Finnish, Esthonian, and of course Norwegian. But the port was paralysed and not a crane was working. The whole area, he told Binney, was infested with German agents and it would be impossible to load a ship secretly. Even in the Free Harbour, to which access was controlled, the news would very soon leak out, since cargoes had to be publicly declared by law. Armed with that knowledge, the Germans would redouble their precautions in the Skagerrak, making interception certain.

Binney wasn't unduly concerned about espionage. It was true that the Free Harbour lay in the middle of the town and was easily spied on; but he had no intention of making Gothenburg his final departure point. 'We'd keep to Swedish territorial waters and lie up in some suitable fjord until the weather was exactly right,' he told Kjellberg. Since he wouldn't know himself the precise date and time of any breakout beforehand, he could keep the Germans guessing until the last moment.

'Why don't you get the Royal Navy to convoy you out?' asked Kjellberg. 'Then you'd have no difficulty in getting volunteer crews.' This was the question most frequently asked by both Swedes and Norwegians, whose faith in the Royal Navy was boundless. Binney repeated what the naval attaché in Stockholm had already told him: the *Luftwaffe*, strongly established on both sides of the Skagerrak, made any sort of naval penetration unacceptably hazardous. 'The most we could hope for would be support after the first twenty-four hours' steaming when we were clear of the Skagerrak.'

Both the British and German naval authorities had advertised in the Gothenburg marine journals that they had mined the waters of the Skagerrak and that any ship proceeding through those waters did so at her own risk. But Binney had sensed an anomaly. 'How do you explain,' he asked Kjellberg, 'that the British and Germans claim in some cases to have mined the same areas? Could it be that both sides are bluffing, to some extent at least, and that the minefields are not so serious a hazard as they would have us believe?'

'You mean,' said Alva Henriksson, 'that it's a diplomatic minefield?'

'Precisely.'

A small Swedish vessel, the Nora, had recently run the German blockade of the Skagerrak and reached England safely with a cargo of timber, and this was a pointer. The passage of a small neutral ship with an unexceptionable cargo was entirely different from a blockade-running attempt by sizeable vessels operated by a belligerent and carrying vital war cargoes, sailing under continual German surveillance; but the minefields, at least, seemed not to be an insurmountable barrier. 'We need more proof,' decided Binney. 'Why not charter a small ship of about 600 tons and send her through to England in July or August? If she succeeded in getting through, it would help me a lot in my negotiations with London, and in collecting volunteer crews for a winter convoy. We could load her with small tonnages of special steels and machine tools, but only the sort of thing that could be replaced before our main venture if they were lost.' They agreed to plan a trial shipment on these lines.

That afternoon Binney discussed the availability of ships with the British Consul in Gothenburg, F. G. Coultas. Freddy Coultas, practical and direct, agreed that the ships were available, though not all of them were in Gothenburg. He believed they were fully manned, but his assistant, Peter Coleridge, would know all about them. Coleridge, despite a serious attack of polio which had left his right arm and shoulder paralysed, proved an energetic lieutenant. Coultas promised to send him up to Stockholm with all the relevant information as soon as possible.

The proposed trial shipment was agreed in London, and Binney hurried back to Stockholm. But in the meantime Paris had fallen, and soon afterwards France capitulated. When Binney got back to Stockholm he found an atmosphere at the Legation of unrelieved gloom. He might have shrugged this off had he not been shown a signal from the Ministry of Economic Warfare which indicated that the Minister, Dr. Hugh Dalton, had withdrawn support for all his schemes. It was conceded that Binney could remain in Sweden for the moment; but the British Government were looking for a way out of most of their Swedish commitments. Materials that could not be shipped safely to England, it was suggested, might be re-sold to the United States, Russia or Turkey. Binney's activities thus looked like being severely curtailed and eventually terminated altogether. 'You don't seem to realise, Mr. Binney,' he was told by Victor Mallet, 'that the war may be over in four or five weeks. That's what some of our friends in the Foreign Office are saying.' The date was now 21st June 1940, and the recent catalogue of disasters seemed to support what Mallet said. All British forces had been withdrawn from the Continent, Mussolini had declared war on France and Great Britain, and Norway, Denmark, Holland, Belgium and a large part of France were in German hands.

Nearly everyone in Sweden believed the war was over. Yet the attitude of the Minister left the patriotic Binney aghast.

From the start of his mission in Sweden, Binney had been aggressively intolerant of anyone who did not seem to him to be engaged in the all-out prosecution of the war. Although he knew there was a faction in the United Kingdom that might be ready to come to terms with Hitler, he thought they had been effectively silenced by the emergence of Winston Churchill as Prime Minister, and he was appalled to hear their opinions being voiced within a British Legation.

Four days earlier, on 17th June, Björn Prytz, the Swedish Minister in London, and himself a steel man, formerly Director of SKF in Gothenburg, had had a conversation with R. A. Butler, Britain's Under-Secretary of State for Foreign Affairs, which he immediately reported back to his Government. According to Prytz, during the course of this conversation Butler had been called away to see the Foreign Secretary, Lord Halifax. When he returned he had brought with him a greeting from Lord Halifax, and a message. 'Common sense and not bravado would dictate British policy,' was Prytz's version of the message, and to make sure there was no ambiguity he quoted the sentence in English in his subsequent telegram. The second sentence of the alleged message, similarly quoted by Prytz, only reinforced the impression that Britain might be ready to negotiate, whatever its intention may have been. 'This could not, however, be interpreted as peace at any price.' Although Churchill was making loud belligerent noises, it was not easy, in Sweden, to see how Britain could survive.

Binney could appreciate the possibility of Britain's being overrun, but he did not doubt that, if such a thing happened, Churchill would fulfil his promise of continuing the fight from the Dominions. He had absolute faith in ultimate victory, and he scorned those who got side-tracked from the principal object of fighting the war. He poured all this out to Mallet in an impassioned outburst, so that Mallet, the wily professional diplomat, was completely taken aback. 'Well, that's what I'm told unofficially,' he said limply.

The truth was not that Mallet was defeatist so much as that, by virtue of his appointment, he was geared to the rails of diplomacy. Men like George Binney irritated him. Attached to his staff, and even operating from the basement of his Legation, they plotted all kinds of schemes that the Legation itself couldn't countenance, they usurped the functions of his own commercial department, he had little or no control over them, and they roughened the surface of the smooth relations it was his brief to establish with the Swedes. Worst of all, they were amateurs. Mallet knew perfectly well that Churchill had promised unequivocally that Britain would fight and would never surrender; he himself had drawn Churchill's defiant speeches to the attention of Christian Günther, the Swedish Foreign Minister, when confronted with the Prytz telegram. But in the prevailing situation he had no intention of encouraging Binney in his wild-cat schemes.

All Norwegian ports, he reminded Binney, were closed to British traffic. The outlet via the Atlantic Highway was similarly severed. The Kattegat was under strict German surveillance, and the Skagerrak was dominated by German sea and air power. The Admiralty were advising that the breaking of the blockade was impracticable; the only ships that could pass in and out of Gothenburg would be those that were suffered to do so by the belligerents under the respective War Trade Agreements for Sweden's essential needs. Any attempt to smuggle Swedish goods through the encircling German forces was doomed to fail. Even if some measure of success were possible, it could only compromise Swedish neutrality, leading in all probability to the Nazi occupation of their country that the Swedes feared above all else. Britain's diplomacy in Sweden must be principally directed towards avoiding that outcome. Binney should pack up and go home.

With all he had worked for collapsing around him, Binney swiftly retaliated. Before definite arrangements were made to cancel all plans for stocking in Sweden, he told the MEW, he wanted them to know that pressure from the Swedish manufacturers themselves had induced the Swedish Government to grant the necessary export permits, to allow storage in Sweden in the meantime, and to give assurances against any future requisitioning of stockpiled materials. They had also promised not to hinder the processes of export or re-sale if either of these courses was eventually decided upon. In these circumstances, argued Binney, he could presumably continue with his shipping plans. As a means of coercion he reminded the Ministry that bulk tonnage repudiated by Britain would inevitably go to Germany, and that a British default would mean that the Swedish iron industry would be forced to work full-time for Germany.

Binney's anomalous position *vis-à-vis* the Legation urgently needed clarification, and to force the Foreign Office's hand he threatened to resign as representative of the British steelmakers in Sweden unless his advice was taken. One man in the Legation, however, understood Binney's value; this was the commercial counsellor, Jack Mitcheson. 'We feel,' said Mitcheson in a memorandum, 'that the question of the delivery of steel to the United Kingdom has probably passed out of the province of Civil Servants, and is possibly better adapted to the attention of the more adventurous, such as Mr. Binney. In other

words, the problem will entail more risks than the Legation are likely
to assume. But we need the steel, and Steel Control may be prepared
to take the risks. Therefore let Mr. Binney go ahead, the Legation
giving him all the co-operation it can. . . .'

Meanwhile, whatever faltering there may have been in Whitehall
at the time of the fall of France, Government departments, under
Churchill's leadership, soon recovered their nerve, and Binney's position was confirmed. 'Binney should urgently go ahead with his plans
for clandestine exports via Gothenburg,' said a signal of 28th June.

Having established the principle, Binney proceeded to consolidate
his position and to plan for the long term. What would be his situation
if Sweden were over-run? Although what he was planning was a
commercial operation, he wanted diplomatic status, and eventually
he was granted it, being given the title of Assistant to the Commercial
Counsellor. Next he wanted administrative help. For some time he
had been looking for someone to control all payments for goods, to
marshal the materials for shipment, and to keep a check on all
expenditure for shipping arrangements, leaving him to concentrate
on the operational problems of mounting the expedition. The man
he wanted was a qualified chartered accountant named H. W. A.
(Bill) Waring who had worked for some years in Oslo and who had
been conscripted to work for the British Legation, first in Oslo and
then in Stockholm. With his wife Anne and small son he had escaped
to Sweden when Norway fell, and he had tried to get back to England
via Petsamo to join up. Heavy tortoiseshell glasses, a black moustache,
and an engaging stutter, made him easily distinguishable, and Binney
judged that he had the ability to take all accounting and book-keeping
worries off his shoulders, and the character to act as his *alter ego* in
Stockholm or Gothenburg when necessary, and to withstand the
pressures that would result. Waring was enthusiastic, and the Legation
eventually gave way. In some respects Waring was more able than
Binney, in that he could find his way through administrative and
financial labryinths which Binney could not. He was also fluent in
Swedish and Norwegian. But Binney was the man with the flair for
capturing the imagination of others, and they made a formidable
team.

*   *   *

Having secured his base, Binney began to consider the Gothenburg
operation in earnest. But although he well knew the importance of
expediting shipments, he had no intention of rushing his fences.
Apart from the mooted trial shipment, he proposed to defer any
really substantial shipments until the longer nights and worsening

weather of autumn improved the prospects of success. Although others doubted his good sense, he had never underestimated the difficulties. 'Please transmit to me at once a three-months' programme covering your principal requirements from Swedish suppliers,' he cabled London on 30th June, 'bearing in mind that at least 50 per cent of materials shipped are likely to be lost *en route*.' And sensing that this grim warning might stimulate renewed opposition to his plans, he followed it up with a characteristic cable nine days later. 'We are left with two alternatives,' he told his friends the Chaharmiks. 'Either on the grounds of *force majeure* to leave everything in the hands of the Swedish steelmakers for them to dispose of as best they can, i.e. to Germany, or alternatively to settle with the Swedes on a reasonable basis and to stock that portion of the material at the bottom of the North Sea which we are unable to ship successfully to England.' Once again Binney, amateur or not, revealed himself as a man who understood the harsh brutalities of war. He was not afraid to contemplate failure, and he reminded the Chaharmiks that even if the stocks eventually became valueless to Britain because they could not be transported, the Swedes would be likely to delay turning over their industry to German requirements while the prospect of British custom remained.

At the beginning of July Binney crossed to Gothenburg again with two objects in view. He wanted Adolf Fagerland, whom he took with him, to work out with Kjellberg the freight-handling machinery that would connect the inland storage depots with the wharves of Gothenburg Free Harbour, where the goods could be loaded into the hatches of whatever Norwegian ships he could charter. And he wanted to meet a Captain Fuchs, commander of a small Finnish tramp steamer, the Lahti, who had signified his readiness to attempt a trial run.

Binney accepted that he must not expect too much of a man whose motivation was profit and who was running a blockade which was part of a war in which he was not engaged. Fuchs was a man of about 45, puffy in complexion, with a penchant for schnapps and whisky, rather too anxious, Binney judged, to give the answers he thought were wanted. He was obviously a bad security risk, and Binney was soon warned against him by the Gothenburg police. But no one but an adventurer could be expected to take on the job, and the Lahti was not going to be entrusted with an irreplaceable cargo. The head of the Harbour Police, Captain Ivar Blücker, who was to prove the staunchest of Binney's Swedish allies in the days ahead, reported that so far as was known Captain Fuchs was not in German employ; and on 5th July, laden with 300 tons of war materials, including another set of mill bearings for Ebbw Vale, the Lahti left Gothenburg and sailed northwards in Swedish territorial waters towards the approaches to Oslo Fjord. Short of Frederikstad, and under cover of darkness, she struck out westwards across the Oslo–Frederikshavn shipping lane and into the Skagerrak.

Although a moonless period had been chosen, it was mid-summer, the nights were short, and the Lahti was a slow ship making not more than nine or ten knots, whereas for his main attempt Binney would choose longer nights and faster ships. Nevertheless she reached the outer limits of the Skagerrak before she was seen by a German air patrol and shepherded with no show of resistance into Kristiansand. A more resolute captain, Binney believed, might have signalled an engine breakdown and waited for nightfall; but Binney was satisfied. For the loss of a small tonnage, valuable but replaceable, positive proof had been obtained that the minefields were not the obstacles that the Germans would have them believe. When it came to recruiting volunteers for the larger ships, the Lahti's voyage would serve as a powerful argument against fears of being blown up.*

*　　　*　　　*

It was not until early August that Peter Coleridge was able to collect full details of Norwegian merchant ships lying-up in Swedish ports and pass them to Binney; but he estimated that there were twenty-six of them, all legally requisitioned by the Norwegian Government before going into exile, and all now under the control of Nortraship, whose Director, Hysing Olsen, had already shown a readiness to co-operate. The Norwegian Government's prescience in passing this requisitioning law was to acquire increased significance as time passed.

Binney was appointed by the Ministry of Shipping (later to become the Ministry of War Transport) to represent them in negotiations for the purchase or charter of suitable foreign vessels. But to acquire ships outright would be a costly procedure, and there was no certainty that crews would be available to man them. Chartering presented similar difficulties, and owners, although not anxious to see their ships rotting in port, preferred waiting for better times to the prospect of losing their ships altogether in a problematical breakout. Thus the Norwegian vessels were the only hope. The trouble was that these vessels, although technically available, were subject to further inhibitions. Some of the Norwegian masters had managed to get their wives and families over from Norway, and they were living in comfort on their ships, in an atmosphere of prams, window-boxes, pets, and children. Their wages were being paid regularly, either by their

* When the Lahti's cargo came up for sale Bill Waring succeeded in buying it back.

owners in Norway or by Nortraship. Safely ensconced in a friendly neutral backwater, they needed to be imbued with a fanatical patriotism, not to mention a somewhat undiscerning confidence in Great Britain, to evince any enthusiasm for Binney's schemes.

Binney found, when he met some of the captains, that they were the victims of confused loyalties. First came an overriding loyalty to the safety of their ships. Complementary to this was a strong and understandable sense of loyalty to their owners. Binney could brandish and quote the Norwegian Government's requisitioning law as often as he liked, but the reaction was always the same: 'I must consult my owners.' These owners, in Oslo, Bergen or wherever their offices happened to be, were easy enough for the masters to contact, too easy in fact, since communications channels were open and no security obligations were recognised. German agents knew at once what was afoot, and opportunities for sabotage, and for the suborning of crews, were inevitably sought. The tendency of the Norwegian owners was to congratulate themselves on having good ships laid-up in neutral harbours rather than available where they would soon be put to work, standing a good chance of being sunk. The war wouldn't last for ever, and when it was over there would be an acute shortage of tonnage. The chance would come to recover the losses of the idle years.

One or two of the shipowners, those perhaps with Nazi sympathies, actively obstructed the take-over of their vessels by Nortraship, but in most cases they accepted the situation with a shrug. Since no one but a lunatic would attempt to sail out of the blockaded Skagerrak, control of the ships for the moment seemed to them little more than academic. But for Binney, the prospect was that Whitehall would be able to persuade Nortraship to charter to Britain as many ships as might be required. 'The best chance of success in running this blockade,' he told Wheeler, 'lies in regarding it as a venture rather than as an ordinary commercial voyage, and it will be necessary to infect the Norwegians with this spirit. They tend to be rather feckless as Allies and are very critical of our performance in Norway last April and May, and I think that by sharing the risk with them rather than by merely paying them to undertake an unpleasant voyage the chances of success will be increased.' Binney's hopes were fulfilled soon afterwards when the Ministry of Shipping secured the charter from Nortraship of five Norwegian ships in Swedish ports, of 4,000 to 6,000 tons each, ostensibly for the storage of materials delivered to Gothenburg.

The position of Norwegian subjects in Sweden was equivocal— indeed almost schizophrenic; they hardly knew where their allegiance

George Binney

George Binney with Captain Einar Isachsen (right), the ship's mascot, and members of the crew of *Tai Shan*, after breaking the blockade, January 1941

The flagship *Tai Shan*

Safely in a British port. Captain Andrew Henry with members of the crew of the *Elizabeth*

The *Elizabeth Bakke*

Captain Carl Jensen with
King *Bakke*

Captain Bill Escudier

One of the **volunteer** seamen with his bonus

lay. So it was perhaps unfair for Binney to describe them as feckless. On the one hand stood the Norwegian Government in exile, still operating a Legation in Stockholm and a Consulate in Gothenburg; on the other stood the *de facto* administration of Vidkun Quisling in Oslo. Norwegians could not easily forget that the British had abandoned the defence of their country after seeming to provoke an attack on it; thus their reaction to Binney's proposals fluctuated. Since the Consulate in Gothenburg was believed to have Quisling affiliations, a vice-consul was appointed to represent Nortraship, and business affecting the chartered ships was removed from the sphere of the Consulate and entrusted to him. The man appointed was a loyal Norwegian named Fred Fuglesang, Anglicised after many years in business in London and entirely trustworthy; but, although he worked tirelessly, he lacked the ruthlessness necessary for the conduct of operations of war. The Norwegian chargé d'affaires at the Legation in Stockholm, Jens Steenberg Bull, continually under fire from London and Oslo and subjected to intense German pressure, had already made one attempt to transfer the ships into German hands, but the Counsellor, Christopher Smith, or 'Frenchie' Smith as he was known because of his year *en poste* in Paris, was a notable ally. Short, red-faced and rotund, and bubbling over with good humour, he never faltered in his conviction that Norway was in honour bound to support the Allied cause.

It was now September 1940, and in the course of that month Britain's stock in Sweden received a timely boost from the performance of the RAF in the Battle of Britain. To take the tide at the flood, Binney leased a flat in Gothenburg in early October so as to concentrate on the task of interviewing and entertaining Norwegian crews and recruiting volunteers. He had been assured by an official of Nortraship that the Norwegian masters were all loyal to King Haakon and that the majority were anxious to get their ships to England, and his first task was to test this opinion. Fuglesang produced a brief outline of each captain's attitude and characteristics, and Binney met the captains and pledged them to secrecy. The most common subject of debate amongst them, Binney found, was the possibility of running their ships to England; but their general conclusion was that they would only be prepared to take the risk if they were assured of a convoy. They meant by that a Royal Navy escort, and in all honesty Binney had to explain at the outset that such protection would be impossible to provide, not anyway until they reached the North Sea. They must rely on speed and evasion. But Binney did not press the captains to an immediate decision; he did not want to be faced with a refusal at the start. He told them that their ships had been chartered by the British Government for the storage of iron and steel cargoes, that marine risks from now on would be borne by the British Government (insurance being of course unobtainable), and that they might eventually be asked to sail their ships to the UK.

The five ships Binney had in mind for the breakout were all well-found, reasonably fast ships, easily capable of carrying the 25,000 tons of special steels and ball-bearings which were now coming forward and which were urgently needed in Britain to maintain and increase the level of aircraft and tank production. The five ships he wanted were:

		gross tons	knots
M/V	Elizabeth Bakke	5,450	17/18
M/V	John Bakke	4,718	13
M/V	Tai Shan	6,962	14/15
M/V	Taurus	4,767	14/15
M/V	Dicto	5,263	14/15

Since he judged that the most dangerous period of the voyage would come in the first fifteen hours after sailing, Binney felt from the start that the initiative for making the attempt must lie with the ships' captains, who would be in the best position to judge the local weather conditions, rather than with the Admiralty in London. This was a point he insisted on. The ships could then skulk in some suitably remote fjord and await foggy or snowy conditions, timing their departure for nightfall and aiming to get into the North Sea if possible before dawn. The departure from Gothenburg could hardly be camouflaged, but there seemed a good prospect of achieving surprise in the actual breakout. All this Binney rehearsed for the captains in the course of many conferences at his Gothenburg flat; but he could see that they were unconvinced. The risks they were being asked to run, they felt, were out of all proportion to the guarantees being offered for their protection; and at a subsequent meeting Binney found they had banded together to oppose the scheme.

This set-back came just as the first cargoes were beginning to arrive at Gothenburg. And it was followed by further frustration. The captains of the five ships had not unnaturally taken other Norwegian captains into their confidence, while the captain of the Dicto, Captain Knutzon, had telegraphed his owners in Oslo to warn them of the plan, and the message had been intercepted by the Gestapo. The owners, Aabys Rederi Co., were ordered by the Germans to take all measures to prevent the ship from sailing, and to warn the Norwegian Legation in Stockholm that if any ship sailed it would be captured and confiscated or alternatively destroyed. Then, under relentless German pressure, Aabys Rederi issued a writ against the Norwegian Legation questioning the validity of their diplomatic status—a delicate point at that time. So far as the Swedish Government was concerned, their attitude had always been that they could not prevent whoever was rightfully in charge of the ships from sailing them without hindrance from Swedish ports; but they also held that the question of who were the legal owners could only be settled by a Swedish court. In this confused situation, with the possibility of a breakout common gossip, the whole question of blockade-running by Norwegian ships chartered to Britain came under further scrutiny in London at a high political level. Meanwhile Binney was instructed to mark time and to play down the urgency of the operation.

It was inevitable that the Norwegian Government in exile, faced with the possible defection of basically loyal crews of whom too much was perhaps being asked, and with the probable loss of their ships, should demur. And there were undoubted human problems. Many of the men had families or relations still residing in Norway who might be victimised for any action they took to support the venture. Visiting Stockholm by air on 18th October, Charles Hambro explained the political difficulties to Binney, and after consultations with Mallet a conclusion was reached that Binney could not well dissent from. The question of storing British goods on Norwegian ships in Gothenburg with a view to the possibility of running the blockade at some future date was to be shelved until the political situation was clarified. Binney was to continue with his preparations as a smoke-screen, but a hint was to be dropped to the captains that the whole scheme was in abeyance.

Back in London, however, the Ministry of Economic Warfare soon convinced Hysing Olsen that vital British industries would be brought to a standstill without the cargoes that the Norwegian ships might be able to deliver; and after the legal arguments had been thoroughly ventilated it was concluded that there was no reason why the breakout should not be attempted if Binney could assemble the crews. Nazi coercion of the owners of the Dicto would probably rule that ship out for the moment, but Binney was instructed to go ahead with his plans for the other four ships.

Enough had happened in the previous fortnight to discourage a lesser man than Binney. He had been faced with the resignation of his captains, the breakdown of security, and the probable cancellation of the operation. But the telegrams he had previously received from London exhorting him to get the materials to Britain at all costs sustained him during this period, and he had great faith in the younger Norwegians who formed the crews. As for security, he would have liked to keep his plans secret, but he accepted that nothing that was done in Gothenburg was safe from prying eyes. The one thing he resented was the loss of the Dicto. She was one of the biggest and fastest ships available, and quite apart from her cargo she would make a very acceptable present to the Ministry of Shipping. He did not entirely reconcile himself to losing her, nor to reducing his strength to four ships and their crews, though four ships were enough to cope with the available cargo. So in case he won the battle over the Dicto, he decided to go ahead with the recruitment of a fifth crew as planned. At the least it would form a valuable reserve against defections. There was the possibility, too, of manning a tanker at the last moment and taking her across in ballast, using her perhaps as a decoy.

The crew problem remained unsolved; but for some time Binney had been contemplating an alternative source of recruitment. Encamped at Hälsingmo, inland from Söderhamn, about 150 miles north of Stockholm, were the crews of five British ore ships that had been trapped at the first Battle of Narvik in April. Later, when the Germans were forced to evacuate the area after the second battle, they had been obliged to get rid of their prisoners, and they had force-marched the British ore crews, together with the survivors of the destroyers Hunter and Hardy, through deep snow and blizzards and along fjords and gorges, over the border into Sweden. Binney believed that he ought to be able to find volunteer masters and crews from among their ranks. They had not been treated as internees, since the Swedish Government had already allowed escaping German prisoners of war to return to Germany, and the Swedes, anxious to act in accordance with their neutral posture, were prepared to grant the same privilege to the British. No opportunity for returning these men to Britain had so far presented itself; but the men were free to find their own way home if they could. First, however, Binney felt it was politic to have one more go at the Norwegian masters.

The captains of the Tai Shan and the Taurus, Binney found, were lying doggo; he could not get to see them. But the mate of the Tai Shan, Einar Isachsen, was a man who had already inspired Binney with confidence; and Isachsen had been left in charge of the ship. Although he had never taken a ship to sea, he held a master's ticket, and he listened to all Binney had to say and quickly showed an ability to reason things out for himself. If the captain of the Tai Shan remained elusive, decided Binney, here was the man to deputise. Moreover, Isachsen had a close friend, Carl Jensen, who was mate of the Taurus; and although Jensen had only just gained his master's ticket and under Norwegian law was not strictly entitled to take charge of a ship, he was keen to go, and Binney thought he might overcome any technical difficulties through Nortraship.

The captains of the other two ships, Captains Fjärtoft and Tallaksen, were as proud of their vessels as they could be, so proud indeed that their attitude towards putting them at risk was lukewarm. The Elizabeth Bakke held the blue riband for the fastest merchant ship crossing of the Atlantic; and the John Bakke, although a lot slower, was also a fine modern ship. Fred Fuglesang reported to Binney that there was little hope of inducing these two masters to sail, and on 1st November Binney told them bluntly that if they wouldn't make up their minds he would have no alternative but to replace them with British masters from the Hälsingmo camp. This as yet was little more than a bluff, but he hoped it would stimulate the captains into acting positively out of pride in their appointments. Both men protested that it was against Norwegian law for British masters to sail Norwegian ships; and although Binney hoped to get round this one through Nortraship, he wanted Norwegian captains if he could get them. When he still couldn't bring them to a decision, he warned them that when the British masters he hoped to recruit arrived, they would have to leave their ships.

Isachsen and Jensen, however, remained enthusiastic, and they began a preliminary indoctrination of their respective crews. They approved of the alternative of appointing British masters to ships where no Norwegian captain was available, and they agreed with Binney that a joint Anglo-Norwegian venture was well suited to the spirit of the occasion. As yet they were not certain what part in the operation Binney himself intended to play, but one evening in Binney's Gothenburg flat, with charts of the Skagerrak spread out on the floor, Isachsen came out with it. 'Are you coming with us, Mr. Binney?'

It was an adventure that Binney had never for one moment intended to miss. In any case he was duty bound to go. 'I could hardly ask you to go,' he replied, 'and stay comfortably here myself.'

'Then will you come with me in Tai Shan?'

'Gladly. Tai Shan shall be the flagship.' Binney's only reservation was that if there were trouble on any of the other ships before sailing, he might have to transfer.

Isachsen thrust out his hand. 'I have a very good steward in my ship,' he said, 'and he'll look after you in the owner's suite. You will be very comfortable.'

It struck Binney afterwards that the Legation in Stockholm, with which he was still at loggerheads, might veto his active participation in blockade-running on diplomatic grounds. This was another hurdle that the Chaharmiks would have to clear for him.

*   *   *

The British crews at Hälsingmo had suffered some early privations, especially on the march and at their first camp. Ore ships were by no means the Rolls-Royces of the Merchant Service, the toughness and resilience of the crews had its attendant problems, and although the ships' masters took charge ashore and mostly maintained discipline, the British Consulate in Stockholm was put to a good deal of trouble. With all routes out of Sweden closed, the men felt frustrated and forgotten. However, as the Swedes grew to realise that their guests were normal human beings and neither rapers nor looters, a degree of integration took place. The men acquired bicycles to ride into Söderhamn to the cinema, the local girls responded, and some of the men were billeted out in the neighbourhood. There was a period when the men would have volunteered for anything; but that period was past.

The man directly concerned with the crews stranded at Söderhamn was Vice-Consul Jack Aird, who visited the camp two or three times a month and whose task was to help solve individual problems; in this way he got to know the crews fairly well. Binney told Aird his plans for a breakout. 'I want two or three English masters if I can get them. And some English crews. Is there anyone in Hälsingmo who you think might volunteer?' Aird was non-committal, but next time he visited the camp he tested the reaction and found it not unfavourable. 'I think you'll get a response,' he told Binney, 'but I think you must talk to them yourself. If you like I'll arrange it.'

After reporting to Victor Mallet that morale among the Norwegian crews needed a boost and that it might be necessary to get volunteers from Hälsingmo, Binney travelled by train to Söderhamn with Vice-Consul Aird. At the suggestion of the Consul, Kenneth White, he gave a dinner in Söderhamn that night for the masters, to explain the plan to them before broaching it to the crews.

Of the four masters, three had names of confusing similarity: there was a Nicholas, a Nicholson and a Nicolson. Their spokesman, Captain D. J. Nicholas, was a 'monkey-slinger' from North Shields, forthright and quick to react. Captain H. Nicholson was a stolid Welshman, Captain J. Nicolson a brawny Shetlander. The fourth master, mercifully, was a Captain J. Donald. There were also two chief officers whom Aird had assessed as out of the ordinary. First was the 64-year-old Andrew Henry, a retired master, born in the Shetlands but a Bristolian by residence, who had gone back to sea on the outbreak of war. The son of a crofter who was also a Methodist lay preacher, Henry had gone to sea with the fishing fleet at the age of 12, and later, like his three brothers, had joined the mercantile marine. He got his foreign-going master's certificate in 1907, and he had been torpedoed while in command during the 1914–18 War. Second was W. J. Escudier, a much younger man, born in Cardiff of English parents but of Huguenot stock, who also held a master's ticket. This made a possible six replacement masters. Out of respect for his seniority the masters had invited Andrew Henry to attend the dinner.

The man who impressed Binney most of all, in fact, was Henry. All the crews, it transpired, owed him a debt for the example he had set on the march from Narvik, when those who dropped out were left behind, their ultimate fate uncertain. Quietly religious, and a disciple of physical as well as mental fitness despite his age, he had stood up to the ordeal far better than many of the younger men, some of whom felt they owed their lives to him. Amongst his possessions in his ship the Romanby had been a hat-box belonging to his wife; and he had carried this hat-box, together with an old black Bible, throughout the forced march and kept them intact. If Andrew Henry got home, said the marchers, hat-box and Bible would go with him.

During the meal, Binney kept the conversation to general war topics. But when the coffee had been served and the tables cleared, Aird produced a bottle of whisky and Binney a box of cigars, and Binney outlined his plan. First he spoke of the paramount importance of getting the ball-bearings and special steels back to Britain, and he passed round a copy of Sir Andrew Duncan's telegram. He told them of the Norwegian ships lying up in Gothenburg and other Swedish ports, and of the disappointing attitude of the masters. With a chart of the Skagerrak spread out before him, he explained the impossibility of providing a naval escort before reaching the North Sea. And he enumerated the hazards with a frankness that the masters appreciated. These, he said, included minefields, patrol ships, submarines, aircraft and destroyers, four or five of which were believed by Naval Intelligence to be located at Kristiansand. There could be no way of concealing the loading of the ships or their departure from Gothenburg, and in any case the Germans already had wind of the plan and would maintain a continual surveillance. The one hazard that he did not mention, because he knew little or nothing of it himself, was detection by radar.

Then he gave them the brighter side. By lying-up in some quiet Swedish fjord, they could seize the moment when weather conditions allowed them to get away unobserved. It was true that they would have twenty-four hours' steaming before they could reach the rendezvous with the naval escort that was promised them in the North Sea; but if the weather was right—and that was the crux of the matter—the Germans would be unlikely to be able to round up all the ships, particularly if they sailed more or less independently. As for the minefields, Binney gave them his well-developed views on that hazard, citing the experience of the Lahti. 'I'm asking you,' he concluded, 'to take a risk—but no greater risk than that taken by our bomber crews every night of the week. Now let's have your views.'

The initial reaction was good : but as the hazards were reviewed there were a few demurs, particularly from the Welshman Nicholson. Then the masters sought the view of Andrew Henry. 'This is the first realistic proposition we've had for getting home,' said Henry, 'and I think we owe it to ourselves and to our country to try it.' This swung the meeting, and it was left to Captain Nicholas to sum up. 'I think we're all agreed that we ought to volunteer for this job—aren't we?' Approval was unanimous, even Nicholson acquiescing, and there were requests to 'sign on here and now'. Binney refused. 'I'd like you captains, and you too, Mr. Henry, to think it all out in the cold light of morning. We'll come over to your camp at about 11.30, we'll have a meeting with you and the other officers at mid-day, and after lunch we'll talk to the crews and see what they make of it.'

An hour's drive next morning through the snow-clad countryside brought Binney and Aird to the handful of wooden huts and outhouses that comprised the camp. A small wooden house was reserved for the four masters, and it was here that the car drew up. Captain Nicholas was there to meet them. 'Will you come in for a few minutes?' He clearly had something on his mind.

Inside the house Nicholas dropped his bombshell. 'We four captains have had a long and serious talk this morning and we've come to the conclusion that the risks are impossible. We wouldn't have a chance of getting through, and it just wouldn't be fair on the crews.'

Binney was not greatly surprised, and he reacted calmly. It was a chance he had taken when he allowed them to sleep on it. But his experience as a negotiator told him this was better than defections later. 'I think you're making the biggest mistake of your lives,' he told them, 'but all I'll ask is for an undertaking that you won't try to influence your officers either way. Also, for the record, I'd like to have your decision in writing.' A document was duly prepared in long hand by Captain Nicholas and signed by the four captains. *After very carefully considering your proposition from all possible angles, we are unable to see where it is at all possible for us to make a success of the venture and therefore we do not see our way clear to participate*

in this project.' It was much the same reaction as Binney had had
from the Norwegian masters in Gothenburg: interest and enthusiasm
at first, quickly evaporating when the implications sank in.

What would be the effect of this rejection on the ships' officers?
Some of them, Binney knew, were younger men, and he hoped they
might be more inclined to take the risk. 'I'd like you,' he told the
masters, 'to sit in with me when I talk to your officers in a few
minutes' time. I want them to hear the story exactly as you heard it,
and I want you to be witnesses that I omit none of the hazards. I
shall also tell them frankly that you're against it. Then they'll know
exactly where they stand.'

At this point Aird asked a pertinent question. 'Did Mr. Henry sit
in on your discussion this morning?'

'No. From what he said on the way back last night, we thought he
had already made up his mind on your side.'

They moved on to the central hut for the officers' meeting. Here
Binney found himself confronted by as motley an array of mariners
as it would be possible to assemble, some looking too old to be still
seagoing, others young and vigorous despite their castaway garb, but
the majority of indeterminate age and character, and varying from
the clean-shaven and spruce to the bristly and dishevelled. 'I wonder,'
began Binney, 'if any of you fancy the idea of being home for
Christmas?' It was an attractive bait, and there was an immediate
chorus of approval to break the ice. Binney went on to repeat all he
had told the masters the previous night; and at one stage he caught
Henry's eye and noticed him nodding approval of the various points.
The young chap sitting next to Henry, he guessed, must be Escudier,
the man Aird had mentioned in the train coming up. Finally Binney
indicated the four masters. 'I must tell you all now,' he said, 'that I
have been unable to convince your captains of the practicability of
this scheme, and I respect their honest viewpoint, much as it dis-
agrees with my own. They've obviously had greater experience of the
sea than I have. But I'm not asking anyone to undertake risks that
I'm not prepared to share with them. I shall be coming along.'

All eyes focused on Andrew Henry as he got to his feet. 'I've now
listened to Mr. Binney twice. If it's good enough for him it's good
enough for me. What do you think, Mr. Escudier? You've got a
master's ticket.'

For Escudier, the meeting had gone far better than he had expected.
Most of these chaps from the ministries and legations let you know
they were someone, subtly or otherwise. This man Binney was more
like an overgrown schoolboy, distinguished no doubt, but with the
gift of retaining the common touch. 'I think we can get away with it

if we have any luck,' said Escudier. 'I agree with Mr. Binney that the Nazi blockade may not be half as effective as it sounds, especially if we choose the right weather.'

For the next few minutes Binney answered their questions. 'I'm leaving a signing-on form here on the desk,' he concluded. 'I don't want you to sign it, though, until you've quite satisfied your consciences that it's the right course to take. Give the forms to Mr. Aird tomorrow morning when you've made up your minds.' The forms, which Binney had prepared beforehand, read:

1. We, being the officers of the ss Blythmoor, ss Romanby, ss Mersington Court and ss Riverton now stationed at Hälsingmo have been asked whether, if called upon to do so, we will volunteer to man Norwegian vessels now lying at Gothenburg and Malmö and to run those vessels through the German blockade of the Skagerrak to England with cargoes of steel, pig-iron and other materials urgently required by the British Government for war purposes.

2. Mr. Binney has explained to us in detail the risks entailed in the voyage, namely enemy submarines, destroyers, armed trawlers, aircraft and mines. He has also emphasised to us that we can expect no protection from the British Navy at any rate until we are in the North Sea clear of the Skagerrak. He has also warned us that the Germans are aware of the proposed attempt to run the blockade and will endeavour at all costs to sink or capture the vessels.

3. We are unanimously agreed that it is our special duty to uphold the traditions of the British Merchant Service at this time, and if we are given the opportunity to do so we shall put to sea in good heart in the capacities allotted to us whether as shipmates of our Norwegian allies or in the sole charge of vessels entrusted to us by the Norwegian Shipping Board and the British Ministry of Shipping, and we shall use our utmost endeavours to bring ships and cargoes safely to the United Kingdom.

Several of the officers insisted on signing the form there and then, and as Binney left the hut, four fresh-faced young men pressed around him. 'We're the radio operators,' said their spokesman, a man named Bell. 'You can rely on us. We're all coming with you.' Something about their confident enthusiasm caught Binney off his guard and it was only with difficulty that he concealed his emotion.

In the afternoon Binney talked to the crews. Aird had warned him that it would be a tough meeting and that some of the men would take the opportunity to air their grievances. But Binney had done

some electioneering in his time, notably at Gorebridge in the Mid-
lothian, and he knew how to turn heckling to advantage. 'I suppose,'
interposed an Irishman, after Binney had made his usual promises of
a tough voyage with the prospect of Christmas at home at the end of
it, 'that when we put to sea you'll be directing us from the Legation
in Stockholm.' 'No,' said Binney, 'I'm as keen as anyone to spend
Christmas at home. But I'll send you a Christmas card from London
if you prefer to spend your Christmas here.'

The fact that the four masters had turned the idea down weighed
with a good many, but to set against that was the quiet optimism of
the man they respected above all others—Andrew Henry—and the
approval of Escudier. Many of the men remained apathetic, while
others, reluctant to abandon their present comfort, seemed content to
stay in Sweden for the duration; but they took to George Binney,
and the response on the whole was not discouraging. Sensing that he
had stirred up emotions which the men might be too embarrassed to
acknowledge, Binney decided not to press them further, but to leave
Henry and Escudier to select the men they wanted and complete the
task of persuasion.

How was it, Binney asked himself on the train back to Stockholm,
that he had failed to convince a single master, Norwegian or British?
Was it the master's ingrained sense of caution based on his responsibility to his ship and his crew? Or was it that, in the months of
inactivity in Sweden, they had lost contact with reality, especially
with the realities of war? He wondered if their unanimous rejection
of a breakout might have damaging repercussions in Whitehall.
Nevertheless he now had four captains—two British and two Norwegian—for four ships, all of them volunteers. The enrolment of
deck officers and engineers could go ahead, and from one source and
another, Norwegian, British, and perhaps Swedish, he would get the
crews he needed. Loading, too, could soon begin on an operational
basis. The decision to store the cargoes in Norwegian hulls had been
a useful preparatory step, and most of the goods were already on the
water, safe from confiscation. In the next few weeks he would have
them transferred to the selected vessels.

That brought Binney up against another problem—protecting the
ships not so much from sinking as from capture in the Skagerrak,
where it might be more difficult to ensure effective scuttling. What
was needed was explosive charges, but under Swedish neutrality laws
it was strictly forbidden for foreigners to acquire or introduce arms
or explosives. The problem was solved by an ingenious device suggested by Mr. S. Townshend, the Lloyd's surveyor in Gothenburg.
Eight holes were cut in the side of each ship before loading, each

fitted with valves which could be manipulated from the 'tween decks by remote control levers. The holes were submerged when the ship was loaded. If after the cocks were turned on the levers were concealed, or flung overboard, nothing could stem the inrush of water. Nor could it be controlled from the engine room. Townshend calculated that once the valves were opened the ships would sink in about an hour. 'This must be the first time Lloyd's have been consulted,' said Townshend, 'on how to scuttle a ship.'

*　　*　　*

Returning to Stockholm, Binney was confronted on all sides by manifestations of the opposition and resentment he had aroused. Most serious was the hardening of attitudes which Bill Waring warned him was taking place at the Legation. Victor Mallet, already christened 'Windy Vic' by Binney and Waring (who of course did not have his problems) automatically frowned on anything which the Swedish Government objected to, disliked, or feared might make them appear even remotely un-neutral or anti-Nazi; and he also feared, reasonably enough, that failure would bring a disastrous fall in British prestige. A new naval attaché, Henry Denham, was with Binney in spirit, but he was bound, in his reports to the Minister, to admit that by naval reckoning the chances of success were slim, and to repeat the Admiralty's advice that the operation was impracticable. Mallet also knew by mid-November, from his diplomatic contacts with the Swedes, that the Nazis already knew of an intended breakout by at least three ships; they had actually named Dicto, John Bakke and Elizabeth Bakke.

It is fair to say that once Mallet was convinced that Whitehall was determined for Binney to go ahead, he did all he could to secure from the Swedes that assurance of goodwill and fair play without which the operation could not possibly succeed. But he continued to view Binney's activities with anxiety, and now, with the professional opinion of the captains of two seafaring nations starkly revealed, a strong tendency to backpedal became discernible in the Legation's cables to London. One of the cypher officers was Anne Waring, and she was so alarmed by Mallet's attitude that quite improperly she warned George Binney. The Minister's advice to London, she told him, was that the chances were extremely unfavourable. They should allow the loading of the ships to go forward and then call it a day.

In Gothenburg, too, matters were getting into a tangle, and Fuglesang sent an urgent call to Binney to come and sort things out. German agents were busy suborning captains and crews, and fears of sabotage were growing. So back Binney went to Gothenburg.

Fuglesang told him a woeful tale of the pressures being exerted on masters and crews to refuse to sail; he feared that if the captains walked off, key men amongst the officers and crews would walk off with them. Despite a curt reminder to the captains from 'Frenchie' Smith that they were acting disloyally to their country, they remained united in their attitude, and they asked again for specific guarantees that the British Navy would escort them from Swedish territorial waters to England. Binney repeated that such guarantees were out of the question, but he told the captains that British merchant crews were ready to share the risk of the venture with them and that Nortraship had agreed in principle to making it a joint Anglo-Norwegian endeavour. He read them the declaration that the British officers had accepted and signed, then closed the meeting so that the captains could make a final decision.

Next morning, with Smith and Fuglesang in attendance, Binney saw the captains of the Elizabeth Bakke and the John Bakke separately and told them that after waiting for them to make up their minds for so long, he had become convinced that they had no confidence in the plan. In these circumstances he could not, as representative of the charterers, place valuable cargoes in their charge, and he had made up his mind to man the two ships with British crews. The captains protested again that this was illegal; but Hysing Olsen, the Director of Nortraship, had agreed to the unprecedented step of allowing Norwegian ships to be commanded by British officers, and he had induced his Government to telegraph to Sweden to that effect. When the captains again demurred, Smith cut them short. 'You've had long enough.' The two captains then agreed to resign and hand over their ships.

The master of the Dicto, too, offered his resignation that morning. Binney was not so worried about the captains of Taurus and Tai Shan as he had capable deputies in Isachsen and Jensen.

Most of the chartered ships had now reached Gothenburg, and their arrival from their distant moorings provided electrifying news in a city whose normally busy harbour lay silent and still. But at a lunch given that day by a group of Gothenburg shipowners to mark a visit from Jack Mitcheson, commercial counsellor at the British Legation, Binney met open scepticism. Although there were exceptions, the sympathies of these men lay traditionally with Britain; but like most Swedes they had been deeply impressed by the swift mastery Germany had achieved in Europe and by the awful efficiency of the Nazi war machine. They related how the German naval attaché had roared with laughter at the mention of the ships. 'We've got the whole thing taped. If they dare to show their faces in the Skagerrak they'll be sunk or captured out of hand.' At this point Mitcheson, always an ally of Binney's, intervened. 'Never mind about the German naval attaché—what do you Gothenburg shipowners think?' 'We think,' was the reply, 'that you are underestimating the thoroughing of the Nazis if you think these ships can get through on their own. It would be another matter if the Royal Navy came in and fetched them.' Norwegian and British masters alike had thought the same way.

The only way to stop the rot, thought Binney, was to get the British crews down from Hälsingmo to help bolster morale, and to move the ships to some remote fjord away from the seductions of Gothenburg. There it might be possible to weld the expedition together and work up effectively for a breakout. He left that night for Hälsingmo. Arriving at the camp on 8th November, he called first for Henry and Escudier. 'I congratulate you,' he told Henry, shaking him by the hand, 'on your appointment as master of the Elizabeth Bakke.' Then it was Escudier's turn for a handshake. 'And I congratulate you, Mr. Escudier, on your appointment as master of the John Bakke. They are both excellent ships.' They were to select the men they wanted from the officers and crews in the camp who had volunteered. Henry, who was wanted in Gothenburg immediately to supervise the loading of his ship, travelled back with Binney. Escudier was to travel on the 14th, and the rest of the officers and men were to join them within a few days. Captain Nicolson, the Shetlander, agreed to supervise the collection and despatch of the men. Binney had again put the dangers squarely to them, and he warned them of their responsibility for keeping up the overall morale. The men were in high spirits at the prospect of being home for Christmas. Including Henry and Escudier there were thirty-one volunteers in all.

Returning to Stockholm in more optimistic mood, Binney found himself facing a fresh crisis. Sent for by Mitcheson, he learned that some of the Gothenburg shipowners he had lunched with had gone into the lists against him. They had sent a delegation to Victor Mallet and begged him to use his influence to bring about the cancellation of the breakout, on the grounds that it must certainly fail and in so doing cause the abandonment by the British of the Swedish market, besides the disastrous loss of prestige that Mallet had always feared. Mallet, Binney learned, had asked London for his recall, on the grounds that he was fulfilling no useful purpose and was an embarrassment to the Minister, and that the certain failure of his plans would bring ridicule to Britain and further reduce the Minister's waning influence with the Swedish Government. Then, following the visit of the delegation of shipowners, he had sent a cable to London without consulting Binney which repeated their views without comment, as though endorsing them. Mitcheson showed a copy of the cable to Binney.

Binney's reaction was immediate: the delegation could have been influenced by the Norwegian shipowners; or by Swedish politicians who feared reprisals; or even by the Germans themselves. 'Have you put that to the Minister?' demanded Binney. 'Surely you ought to be protecting him from his folly. Do you honestly think that the aircraft factories and the tank production units should be deprived of the supplies they're screaming for just for a bunch of prosperous business men who want to keep out of the war? I shall chase the Minister's cable with an immediate cable of my own.' Clearly every endeavour was being made to capsize the operation, on the grounds that it must end in fiasco or worse; and in a bitter exchange with Mallet Binney accused him of fighting a different war. Mallet, quick to anger but equally quick to repent of it, retaliated unworthily by hinting that Binney's determination to remain in Sweden owed something to the comfortable bolthole he had established there.

With one or two exceptions, prominent amongst whom was Peter Tennant, the press attaché, Binney had found himself a lone and often resented voice at the Legation ever since arriving in Sweden a year earlier, and now his relations with the Minister reached their lowest ebb. 'Do you realise,' he said to Mitcheson afterwards, 'that I spend 75 per cent of my time stopping other people from trying to stop me doing what has to be done?'

*   *   *

There was more trouble awaiting Binney at Gothenburg: two of the Norwegian engineers had resigned, and their specialised knowledge could not be replaced by the volunteer engineers from Hälsingmo, none of whom had diesel experience. Binney got in touch with the Götaverken shipyard, and they produced a competent Swedish engineer, Birger Lundhquist, who had been on the Elizabeth Bakke during her original trials. On 15th November Lundhquist accepted a sum of £100 in cash in return for signing a contract to act as chief engineer on this vessel for the voyage to Britain; this would be in addition to the payment of his normal salary and war risk allowance in accordance with Swedish rates, and to his share of the £1,500 bonus that each crew were now promised on safe arrival in the United Kingdom. He also agreed to provide a Swedish engineering staff— second and third engineer and motorman. That was one problem solved, and Binney described Lundhquist as worth his weight in gold. Lundhquist, however, proved to be equally aware of his value.

Binney had set his face firmly against the offering of extravagant inducements to British or Norwegian crews; they must regard the operation as part of their war service. A 20 per cent increment on their normal wages acknowledged the risk they would be running, and the share of the safe arrival bonus, although heavily weighted in favour of the captain (£500), brought even the lowliest super-numerary crew member £30. For men who were captured or drowned, compensation would be paid to their families at the going rate, using the most favourable yardstick available. But Swedes and other neutrals fell into a different category. It wasn't their war, and if Britain wanted their expertise she must expect to pay for it.

It was on this Gothenburg visit that Binney was introduced for the first time to Captain Ivar Blücker, head of the Gothenburg Harbour Police. Blücker was a man of medium build with fair hair to relieve an office-grey complexion, but his principal feature was a square, determined jaw. An ocean-going sea captain himself in his time, now in his early fifties, he had been an instructor in navigation at the Gothenburg Merchant Navy School before being appointed head of the Harbour Police. Shrewd, efficient, scrupulously neutral in the overt observance of the regulations, but secretly anti-Nazi, he spoke a good seafaring English with no more than a slight Swedish inflection.

Blücker's job was to maintain law and order in the docks and in the marine community at large, and since Binney's planned operations were based on legitimate wartime trading, it was perfectly consistent with the Swedish policy of neutrality that Blücker should seek to ensure the safety of the ships and their protection from sabotage while they were under his jurisdiction in Gothenburg. On the other hand, espionage and under-cover activities were a criminal offence, so Nazi agents could be rounded up and jailed. Blücker's work, and the background he brought to it, kept him well informed of everything that went on in Gothenburg and even further afield in the Kattegat and Skagerrak, and he warned Binney of the malevolent designs of the Nazis against these ships, and of their enticement of crews. Blücker was continually on the alert to prevent the Germans from planting Nazi sympathisers amongst Binney's engineering staff, and the ships and their cargoes were watched day and night by his men. All this he would have done equally efficiently for the Germans in a parallel case. But he gave Binney another, more confidential warning: the Swedish Navy remained indignant over the Faroes incident and might not scruple to take the first opportunity to get their own back. Such an opportunity might present itself during an attempted breakout.

Binney took Blücker fully into his confidence and was encouraged to find that the Swede believed the plan was practicable. Indeed as time passed Blücker's personal involvement in the success of the operation grew.

By mid-November Captain Henry and his largely British crew had taken over the Elizabeth Bakke, and when Binney first went aboard he noted two items in the captain's cabin—a hat-box and a Bible. The ship had her bottom scraped to improve her speed and was then loaded in the Free Harbour. The bridge was fortified against machine-gun bullets and bomb splinters by the erection of blocks of concrete six inches thick, and this became a standard fitting for all the ships. The transfer of crews was carried out smoothly, Captain Fjärtoft now conceding that although he himself had lost his nerve, there was a fair chance of success. But no security risks were taken, and on Blücker's advice Binney engaged special watchmen from the Seamen's Association to augment the watch by the Harbour Police, while Captain Henry also maintained a permanent watch on board.

With the John Bakke, however, there was a succession of delays which infuriated Binney. The good-natured Fuglesang failed to exert a strict enough control, and Captain Tallaksen and his family remained on board long after the ship had been chartered to Britain. Their continued residence delayed the work of reconditioning the engines, and it eventually took Götaverken three weeks to get the ship seaworthy. The final straw came when Tallaksen's daughter contracted scarlet fever the day before the family had agreed to leave, necessitating a thirty-six-hour stand-down while the ship was fumigated.

The captain of the Tai Shan, too, had withdrawn from the operation, believing it was doomed to failure, and before the ship sailed from Gulmarfjord on 15th November, Einar Isachsen was confirmed as master. So far as Binney was concerned this was a desirable outcome; and there was further welcome news when the Swedish Navy gave the Tai Shan the escort Binney had asked for. It looked as though bygones, so far as they were concerned, were bygones. A German armed trawler was sighted on the way down the coast, but it sheered off when it saw the escort. The Tai Shan's timber cargo then had to be unloaded and her bottom scraped, and the earliest she could be ready was 15th December. Taurus was still at Malmö, but doubts about her captain persisted as he failed to answer letters and was never to be found when Nortraship telephoned. His wife, who had been with him in Sweden, had gone back to Norway, and he was under domestic pressures not to sail. When Binney, through Fuglesang, ordered the ship up to Gothenburg under Swedish naval escort, he complied with the order; but when he learned of Binney's plans he handed in his resignation, citing family reasons.

As with the captain of the Tai Shan, the loss was an outcome that Binney was not only prepared for but saw as a blessing, since it made room for Carl Jensen to take over. And the departing captain was as much in the dark as anyone about the place and time of the breakout.

By this time litigation had forced Binney to reconcile himself to the loss, for the time being at any rate, of the Dicto. She had been scheduled to load 5,400 tons, and her absence meant loading the other four ships rather more deeply than he had intended, thereby slightly reducing their speed. But he reallocated the cargoes so as to give each ship an equal share of the most needed items; thus no single ship could take all the machine-tools or all the ball-bearings to the bottom. At the same time he caused Captain Henry to issue an invitation to Captain Nicolson, the Shetlander, to visit Gothenburg for the week-end from Hälsingmo; he wanted him for the 12,000-ton tanker Ranja, which he hoped to add to the breakout force. Besides being a valuable reinforcement to Allied shipping, she would be useful as a decoy during the breakout. 'Once safely ensconced in the captain's quarters of your ship,' he told Henry, 'sipping a tumbler of his national beverage, sniffing a ship's odours again, and sensing its rhythm, Captain Nicolson will be sunk.' Both men roared with laughter at the unfortunate choice of metaphor. But the forecast, metaphorically speaking, proved correct, although Nicolson was to find that the care-taker crew of the Ranja, angry at the prospect of losing their jobs, had carried out numerous acts of minor obstruction, and that an operation crew had still to be recruited.

That was five ships, complete with five captains. But the morale of the Norwegian crews remained uncertain. Unlike the British crews, they were not sustained by the prospect of a triumphant homecoming. And Binney had two other worries: he feared that further litigation might enable the Germans to secure some sort of embargo which might delay the ships from sailing: and he felt that, in the atmosphere of nervousness that pervaded the Legation in Stockholm, the initia-tive might be seized by Whitehall. He recorded these fears in a signal to London of 18th November, urging upon them how vital it was for the breakout initiative to remain with him.

Apprehensions of driving Sweden into the enemy camp, however, were more obsessive at the Legation than in London, where the possibility of a complete blockade of Sweden, as virtually a part of the German economic system, was continually under review. Against this course lay the old objection that the more Sweden were treated as a dependent of Germany the more she would become one; and during that month a programme of 'safe-conduct' traffic was agreed between the belligerents which allowed four ships per month to ply to and from the Americas out of Gothenburg. These ships carried incoming cargoes of fuel-oil and grain. For Britain the advantage of the agreement seemed twofold : it bestowed a lever in the implicit threat that the 'safe-conduct' traffic could be stopped at any time, together with establishing a *quid pro quo* to encourage the Swedes not to hamper Binney's shipping plans. Unfortunately exactly the same blandishments were available to the Germans, and they enjoyed the greater reputation for ruthlessness.

By the end of that month, the Elizabeth Bakke was loaded and ready to move to the chosen hideout farther north along the Swedish coast. Captain Blücker had selected an anchorage in an inner recess of Brofjord, some five miles north of the fishing port of Lysekil, which was itself about forty miles north of Gothenburg. Here they would be sufficiently remote to escape the embarrassing attention they attracted in Gothenburg, yet handy enough for regular access by road from the Gothenburg Consulate. Since under Swedish security laws no foreigners were allowed to visit any part of the coastline without special permission, inquisitive characters who appeared in the vicinity of this lonely fjord could be watched and if necessary arrested.

On 7th December the Elizabeth Bakke, loaded with 6,200 tons of cargo, and with Ivar Blücker accompanying Captain Henry on the bridge, left Gothenburg for Brofjord, keeping within the three-mile limit and escorted by a Swedish sloop. Soon afterwards, two Swedish naval officers of junior rank were arrested; they had tried to pass the course the ship had been ordered to take to the German naval authorities, presumably with a view to submarine attack. The fact that both these officers received an exemplary sentence of seven years imprisonment demonstrated the Swedish Government's determination to pay more than lip-service to the doctrine of neutrality.

The persistence of German agents, however, remained undeterred, and when Binney returned to his Gothenburg flat early one morning from a visit to Stockholm, Bill Waring greeted him by putting a warning finger to his lips, then led him to the dining-room fireplace. Craning his neck up the chimney, Binney recognised a microphone, suspended from a vertical wire. 'How long has that been there?' he asked, when they had left the room and closed the door. Waring shrugged his shoulders. Up till now they had relied on the central heating, but recently it had been cold enough to light a fire; the chimney had smoked so badly that he had investigated it and found the microphone. Characteristically, Binney saw the opportunity to have some fun at the agents' expense. After regaling the microphone throughout breakfast with the decision, attributed to 'Whitehall warriors', that the ships couldn't possibly sail because the German Navy was much too powerful—a decision which he said he had now been forced to accept—he made the point that they must nevertheless continue to load the ships and move them from Gothenburg to fool the enemy. A few pithy but unprintable comments on Corporal Schicklgrüber and others of the Nazi hierarchy led to a dramatic discovery of the microphone, more unprintable comments, and then silence as they cut it down.

A signal from London giving the operation the code name of 'Rubble' lent the plan a new status and encouraged Binney to hope that his cables had carried conviction. But meanwhile he was faced with a Legation plot to oust him as leader. The pretext was that Binney must surrender his diplomatic immunity if he was going to engage in blockade-running, leaving him unprotected if he were captured. 'If these nitwits insist on my relinquishing my diplomatic immunity I'll do so,' stormed Binney. 'But can you see me waving good-bye to my crews from the quayside?' That evening, closeted for over an hour with Mallet and some of his staff, he listened with mounting impatience to their arguments about the acceptable limits of diplomatic conduct. 'Can you explain to me in my ignorance,' he asked pointedly, 'the difference between the Minister flying to London through the air blockade, and my humble journey in a merchant ship sailing the high seas on its lawful occasions?' This interjection proved unanswerable, and the outcome was that Binney was allowed to retain both his leadership and his technical immunity.

Other problems that were solved in those early days of December concerned communications after the ships had reached Brofjord. Local weather reports and forecasts would be picked up on the ships' radio, while Admiralty bulletins giving the broader picture would be collated by Henry Denham in Stockholm. He in turn would pass the information to the Consulate in Gothenburg. The Admiralty would indicate when they thought conditions looked promising, and Denham, by means of a pre-arranged code, would authorise a courier to be despatched from the Gothenburg Consulate to the anchorage, where Binney would bring his ships to one hour's notice of sailing; but the final decision would remain with him. Denham estimated that this decision could be safely in the hands of the DOD(H) (Director Operations Department (Home)) at the Admiralty within fifteen minutes of its coded and telephoned despatch from Brofjord. The executive signal would then be sent to the naval force which was to meet the convoy in the North Sea.

The most important role in all this would be that of the courier, and since foreigners could not pass freely in coastal areas, it had to be played by a Swede. The task—this time clearly in excess of his duties—was undertaken by Ivar Blücker.

The necessary plans, then, were carefully laid. But they still depended on Binney's ability to man the ships. The Norwegian Consulate in Gothenburg had virtually been turned into a seaman's employment agency, but Fuglesang was meeting continual set-backs to recruitment, the greatest difficulty being engineering staff. Men would sign on one day only to quit the next, while natural misgivings amongst the existing crews were exploited daily by Nazi and Quisling infiltration. What Binney had always sought to avoid were last-minute defections, and he asked the Chaharmiks if King Haakon might not be prevailed upon to send some rallying message. In due course a Royal proclamation arrived. 'Do your duty by your country and good fortune will attend you,' it read. Binney believed that it tipped the scales for many waverers; but it did not deter three engineers and a motorman from walking off the Tai Shan next day, dissuaded perhaps by the pressures they were under. The problem was solved by Peter Coleridge, who secured a first-class Swedish engineer named Tage Mark who professed himself perfectly happy to take the Taurus to Britain with no more than an assistant engineer and three motormen if the need arose.

Recruitment of Swedish engineers and motormen thrown out of work by the blockade, indeed, was often easier than engaging Norwegians. Binney's method, worked out with Blücker, was to over-estimate rather than underestimate the risks and then to offer a generous cash bonus for signing on; the privilege of crying off was made dependent upon repayment of the bonus. 'They'll have spent the money within twenty-four hours and they won't be able to repay you,' said Blücker, 'so they'll have to sail.' In the circumstances Binney felt this was as near as he could get to fair trading.

Captain Escudier buttonholed Binney one morning to say that he was having trouble with his second engineer, a Norwegian named Hansen. The chief engineer had walked off when the captain resigned, and Hansen was a key man, being the only engineer on board with practical experience of the John Bakke's engines. 'I can't afford to lose him,' said Escudier. 'Will you see him?' Hansen told Binney that his wife, who was Belgian, and a stranger in a strange land, broke down every time he returned to the ship. He couldn't bear to leave her in this state, he was emotionally upset and his concentration was affected. 'Would you think it impertinent of me,' asked Binney, 'if I asked to see your wife at the Consulate? I'll be there at six o'clock tonight.' Mrs. Hansen duly turned up, 'a very nice little woman of about 36,' according to Binney, and she told him how devoted she was to her husband, and how impossible life would be without him. Binney described how her husband's work was deteriorating under the strain. The point had been reached when he needed a good chief engineer to control him, but the man had walked off. 'I'm thinking of offering the job to you. Would you take it?' The woman opened her eyes wide, but said nothing. 'Of course you'll have to be very strict with him, and keep him up to the mark,' continued Binney. 'Don't stand for any nonsense.'

'Do you mean that I can make the voyage with my husband?'

'Well, if you are to be chief engineer, and if you choose to employ your husband, I shall raise no objection.' A few more tears, this time of gratitude, and the bargain was sealed.

The shortage of engineers, however, remained acute, and Nortraship felt obliged to ask Binney to sign a document agreeing that the charterers would hold themselves responsible for any engine damage attributable to deficiencies in engine-room staff. The owners, they said, must be protected. Binney had no alternative but to sign.

Protection of the ships from capture, and the safety of the crews, were other matters which exercised Binney that month. The valves suggested by the Lloyd's surveyor were duly fitted, and each man— and woman—was provided with a standard Swedish life-jacket, a loose-fitting rubber overall tightly fastened to the neck by a zip fastener and incorporating weighted boots and gauntlets. Unsinkable, and watertight, it protected the wearer from exposure as well as from drowning. The only drawback was that it was too cumbersome to be worn in the engine-room. It was also expensive. The Swedish-Lloyd Shipping Company paid for all jackets issued to British seamen, loaning them on the understanding that on safe arrival they would be handed over to the Company in Britain, a gesture of confidence that delighted Binney; and Nortraship purchased jackets for the Norwegian crews.

Largely because of his crew problems, Binney's forecast of 'home for Christmas' could not be kept. But he was anxious to get the rest of the ships away from Gothenburg as soon as possible. 'Frenchie' Smith warned him that Norwegian shipowners in Oslo, pressurised by the Germans, were still seeking means of having their ships legally arrested, a process which might at least be hindered if the ships had already gone elsewhere. Thus as Christmas approached the tension mounted. On Boxing Day the John Bakke and the Taurus followed the Elizabeth Bakke to Brofjord, where they were painted grey and where blackout precautions were taken. With the success of the operation depending on evasion, the greatest attention was paid to the efficient darkening of the ships.

RUBBLE

Loading of the Tai Shan was nearly completed and she would follow in early January. Captain Nicolson's crew difficulties with the Ranja were still not resolved, but three more British apprentices had volunteered and they arrived from Hälsingmo shortly before Christmas.

Immediately after Christmas Binney made a final liaison visit to Stockholm, and there, after all the frustrations and personality conflicts of the preceding months, he found nothing but goodwill now the die was cast. 'So you are going to carry a Foreign Office bag for us direct to Downing Street,' beamed Victor Mallet. Binney was given a letter which established him as an accredited member of the diplomatic corps carrying official mail to London, and this was his protection in case of capture.

Victor Mallet gave a dinner party for Binney that evening at Henry Denham's apartment, the other guests being Counsellor Bill Pollock, Commercial Counsellor Jack Mitcheson, Consul Kenneth White, and Denham himself. Denham, Binney learned, had informed the Admiralty that the naval force which was to be despatched from Scapa Flow to meet the ships should look out for a white identification flag edged with blue, six feet by four feet, which would bear the letters GB prominently displayed in the centre. 'This indicates not only the destination of the convoy but also the initials of the commodore.' The flagship Tai Shan, added Denham, would fly a pennant at the masthead similarly coloured and inscribed. For the dinner, Denham had provided a table decoration of two flagposts, one flying the Union Jack, the other the 'Rubble' identification flag, home-sewn by his housekeeper. These and other spontaneous gestures showed that Binney's natural gift for inspiring affection had won the Legation over in the end, Mallet included, despite all the trouble he had given them.

During the dinner Mallet advised Binney to take plenty of books, in case he had to wait a long time in Brofjord for the right weather. 'I've been reading a wonderful new novel by Hemingway which someone brought over from America the other day,' he said. 'I'll send it down to Gothenburg for you.' Binney asked its title, and Mallet's eyes suddenly glazed. 'Perhaps the title is rather unfortunate.' But he had to answer Binney's question. 'It's called For Whom the Bell Tolls.' There was a moment's embarrassed silence, and then the party dissolved into laughter. 'On second thoughts I'll send you a much more appropriate book,' said Mallet. 'Captain Hornblower. You remind me of him.'

*　　*　　*

55

Next morning Binney took the train to Gothenburg, and later that day he boarded the Tai Shan, where he was soon brought down to earth. There had been more defections, though somehow the gaps had been filled. And Townshend, the Lloyd's surveyor, was waiting to instruct him on the operation of the scuttling valves. Isachsen had delegated this responsibility to Binney, who had gladly accepted it, electing to deal with the aft part of the ship while a naval rating from HMS Hunter, supernumerary to the crew like himself, acted as his co-scuttler forward. Then, at 07.00 hours on 30th December 1940, the Tai Shan sailed for Brofjord. Whatever legal action might follow, it was now too late, Binney believed, to stop Rubble.

It was still dark as they swung into the river, but Binney experienced a tremendous sense of freedom and release. This was the real beginning, and he could hardly believe he had got this far. He had said good-bye to his friends in Gothenburg in a daze, hardly hearing Kjellberg's emotional farewell: *They should never have let you take the risk.* Then, looking aft from the wing of the bridge at first light, he watched the town and port recede in a mist of wood-smoke—occasioned by the rationing of coal—that made the skyline look almost medieval. Fifty minutes later, after a blast from the siren as they passed the Götaverken and Eriksberg shipyards had acknowledged the skill and devotion that had got the ships ready for sea, they reached the island of Vinga, at the seaward end of the Göta ship canal. There they dropped the harbour pilot and took on a coastal pilot, swung the compasses, and dealt with various engine defects arising from the long stay in harbour. Thus it was not until dusk on the last day of the year that they joined the other three ships in Brofjord. The Ranja had been left behind in Gothenburg, but Binney still hoped she might catch them up.

On the way up to Brofjord, Binney saw several small German coastal vessels and knew their progress was being reported. But the Tai Shan kept strictly within Swedish territorial waters, and there were no incidents. Blücker, travelling with them, held a watching brief. And once inside Brofjord Binney realised what a splendid haven Blücker had chosen for them. When they anchored that evening they found themselves tucked away in an isolated cul-de-sac that was all but landlocked.

The Tai Shan lay in fourteen fathoms of water, ten cables' lengths from the other vessels and 400 yards from the shore, where a few fishermen's huts and a ramshackle jetty narrowed to a rough track winding over a hill. This track connected with the road to Lysekil, situated in the much larger Gulmarfjord to the south. There was a telephone line near the quay, which would be essential for their communications; and the Swedish police had made a thorough survey of the neighbourhood and all known Nazi agents had been rounded up and gaoled.

Binney had undertaken to be ready to sail any time after 1st January, and at the Admiralty Captain J. A. S. Eccles, DOD (H), had already warned Admiral Sir John Tovey, commanding the Home Fleet in Scapa Flow, that five Norwegian merchant vessels were contemplating a breakout from the Swedish coast when conditions were suitable, and that it would be his task to cover the ships when they emerged from the Skagerrak. Now, however, Binney was relieved to find that both Swedish and BBC weather broadcasts were promising clear skies for the next forty-eight hours. He still had many points to discuss with his captains, and he called a meeting for the following morning in the Tai Shan's dining saloon. Binney was particularly worried about the morale of the crews, some of whom had already been in Brofjord for three weeks; there had been work to do, but Binney feared they might grow restive. Many of the key men on all four ships were Swedes, and several of them earned a special word of praise at this meeting. The only Swede who was giving any trouble was Lundhquist, who was continually asking for more money; and Binney, still fearing last-minute defections amongst key men, sought to establish a pool from which essential transfers might be made. 'The voyage is short,' he told the captains, '480 miles at the most. In a dire necessity, one key man could keep going the whole time.' He distributed packets of dope to keep the crews awake; and for less subtle persuasion, in case it should be necessary, he gave each captain a Service automatic, together with fifty rounds of ammunition.

Binney then gave them their sealed orders, to be opened at their leisure, and divulged to their chief officers only. The meeting then discussed precautions against getting iced in; engines were to be tested and anchorages steamed round daily. They ruled that for security reasons there would be no shore leave, made arrangements for the censorship of mail, and agreed states of readiness, which varied from Red (no likelihood of the operation taking place within forty-eight hours, their present situation), to Amber (prospects within twenty-four to forty-eight hours), and White (under starter's orders). To save time, two blasts from Tai Shan's siren would confirm that the Admiralty had given the green light, and the captains would then make a collective decision, on the basis of the local conditions, a privilege that had been carefully preserved by Binney. After the meeting Binney noted with satisfaction that the Norwegian and British captains were talking and jesting together in an atmosphere of mutual enthusiasm and trust. The magic circle of the Rubble enterprise had drawn them together, dwarfing all differences of situation, temperament and race.

For the next few days a spell of cold, clear weather ruled out all prospect of moving; but it provided an opportunity to complete the work of blackout and camouflage. It also gave German reconnaissance planes the chance to spy out their anchorage, and this, from a height of 4,000 feet, they proceeded to do. But Binney had never really expected to escape notice in good weather. The conditions he intended to choose for the breakout would, he hoped, be as frustrating to enemy aircraft as to surface vessels. These conditions, however, continued to elude them right through to mid-January, and Binney began to fear that the impetus of the operation would exhaust itself, especially in London, leading perhaps to an order for its postponement or even for its cancellation. How long could units of the Home Fleet be kept on call to cover the breakout? Each day Binney thumped the barometer hopefully, but it wouldn't budge. Ice six inches thick was forming in the fjord, and there was a real danger of getting iced in. Binney could see the strain showing on the faces of the men, guess at their unasked questions: why didn't they make a dash for it? And when the Ranja arrived on 8th January the pressures on Binney increased. Condemned to live for much of the time in artificial light, with all windows and portholes blacked out even in daylight, and under regular air surveillance, the crews naturally felt that if they were going to go at all then the sooner the better.

Once or twice conditions justified an Amber warning and spirits would rise, but then would come a Red and signs of disaffection would return. On 16th January the monotony was relieved by the arrival in the fjord of an ancient Swedish battleship; but its presence made Binney uneasy. What was it there for? Binney had ample evidence of Swedish punctiliousness in keeping strictly neutral, and it occurred to him that they might have got wind of an Altmark-type operation planned by German naval forces and be seeking to prevent any such incident in Swedish waters. Or her task might simply be surveillance, in which case messages might be sent which the Germans would be sure to intercept. After the affair of the Italian destroyers, Binney was forced to regard the attitude of the Swedish Navy as an imponderable; but his only change of plan was to cancel the siren as a sailing signal and arrange to summon the captains by despatching messengers across the ice.

From Captain Nicolson, of the Ranja, Binney learnt of the weeks it had taken Peter Coleridge to beg, borrow and bribe a crew to sail in the tanker. Coleridge had even combed the gaols, and he warned Nicolson when he sailed that he could not swear there were no Nazi agents on board. Yet when Binney tried to issue Nicolson with a revolver he refused. 'I think I'm big and ugly enough,' said the Shetlander, 'to look after myself, and if they want to take the ship off me I can't see that a gun would stop them.' Fifteen of his twenty-six crew were Britishers whom he had recruited himself at Hälsingmo, including three naval ratings from HMS Hunter, and he had complete confidence in his first mate, a Swede named Nils Rydberg. Then, well into the third week of January, five of the Ranja's senior crew, two deck officers and three engineers, all Swedes, walked off the ship by fooling the watch into thinking they were visiting another vessel. They left a message that they would return after a week-end in Gothenburg; but would they do so, and even if they did, was it wise to take them back?

On the Elizabeth Bakke, Lundhquist was still playing hard to get and asking for more money; meanwhile he had gone into hiding in his cabin, announcing that he was indisposed. And amongst the British crews, a young apprentice on Tai Shan was sulking in his cabin and refusing to work. 'It's against my principles unless I'm paid,' was his attitude. Binney reminded him of his contract, which promised to feed him, take him to England, and pay him a bonus of £30 on safe arrival, in return for his undertaking that he would lend a hand if required to do so. But the boy persisted in his refusal to work without payment. These discontents, Binney feared, were the tip of the iceberg; without firm action morale might disintegrate. When the apprentice persisted in his refusal to work, Binney had him sent back to Hälsingmo. He was sorry to do this to a 17-year-old, one of only five Britishers on the Tai Shan; but he could not countenance the continued idleness of a British apprentice aboard a Norwegian ship. So far as the Norwegian crews were concerned, a gratifying feature of the move away from Gothenburg was that their enthusiasm was rekindled and, although impatient to go, they bore the strain of waiting as cheerfully as anyone.

With recalcitrant Swedes Binney was obliged to deal more leniently, since they were all key men impossible to replace. Nils Rydberg was so upset by the indiscipline of his fellow Swedes that he offered to go back to Gothenburg to recruit replacements; but when, on Monday 20th January, the five missing Swedes returned, shamefaced but willing, Binney instantly forgave them. Meanwhile he cancelled a letter he was drafting to Lundhquist and sent him a hamper containing chicken and ham sandwiches, crystallised fruits and champagne to help relieve his 'indisposition'.

Binney had never imagined that he might be confined in Brofjord for three weeks or more, and each day his troubles mounted. If the ships didn't get away soon he would have to think about revictualling. Some were also running low on the lighter oils used for auxiliary engines.

Sunday 19th January brought a slight change in the weather, but it was a curious sort of day, with a very light off-shore wind and a few snow flakes fluttering down from an overcast sky; it didn't really look very promising. Denham, Binney remembered, had distrusted off-shore winds, which, although they might bring fog and snow from the north-east, left calm seas in which submarines and small enemy surface craft could comfortably operate. He had recommended choosing conditions which indicated poor visibility with a rising south-westerly blow. The captains agreed with this diagnosis, but Binney was beginning to feel it might be as broad as it was long. A quick getaway in thick fog or snow and it would be several hours before the Germans could be on their track; by first light they could be well beyond Kristiansand. And if the cloak of snow or fog were sufficient to enable them to get away unnoticed an hour or two before dusk, they would be that much nearer the rendezvous by daylight.

The trouble was that the rendezvous point, the first point at which they could expect naval protection, was a long way out in the North Sea, some seventy miles off the Norwegian coast and seventy-five miles from Stavanger. The actual position given in the sailing orders was 58.45 North, 03.30 East, a revelation that dismayed the captains when they saw it. From the exit from the Skagerrak, heading as they would be north-west for Kirkwall in the Orkneys, they would still have over a hundred miles to cover to the rendezvous, much of which they would have to traverse in daylight, and for the whole of which they would be within range of German bombers based in southern Norway. It meant that having negotiated the hazards of the breakout itself and of the heavily mined Skagerrak, they would have the most precarious part of the voyage still to come. '*Naval and Air support has been promised on your emerging from the Skagerrak,*' said the orders. '*Do not think that you will suddenly be surrounded by British warships, for such is most unlikely, but you may feel something encouraging in the fact that Naval support will be at hand.*' This drew further caustic comment from the captains. '*Similarly aircraft have been promised, but again they may not necessarily be affording continuous patrol over your particular ship.*' The difficulties of providing a long-range air umbrella were known and appreciated, but the caution of the Royal Navy was not so easily excused. Once again Binney had to expound the Navy's problems. 'If it wasn't for the importance of our cargoes,' he told the captains, 'they wouldn't even come this far.' In this he was almost certainly right; but he had in

John Eccles a man who was always ready to encourage the unortho-
dox, and Eccles' support for Rubble had ensured a strong naval
escort.

For the first part of the voyage the ships were to choose the deepest
water of the Skagerrak, which meant keeping to the northern side, in
the hope of avoiding the minefields. Here they would get the
advantage of favourable currents which might add one knot to their
logged speed. They would continue in this northern channel until
they reached the meridian of 6 degrees East, at the outer rim of the
Skagerrak, where they were to turn north-west for the rendezvous
position.

On Tuesday 21st January Binney made his customary visit to the
chart room with Isachsen to discuss the weather reports which Bell,
the wireless operator, produced for them each day. An Amber warning
was in force, but the wind was still off-shore, which meant clear
weather unless heavy snow was in the offing. All that materialised
was the same gentle, aimless snowfall of the previous day.

That night, despite the sumptuousness of his surroundings in the
owner's suite of the Tai Shan, Binney could not rest. For hour after
hour, clad in pyjamas and dressing-gown, he alternated between
testing the pile of the luxurious beige carpet in his saloon and playing
Patience on the central mahogany table. Each game became inextric-
ably linked with their fortunes; if it comes out this time, we'll go
tomorrow. A few minutes later he would be smearing the cards across
the table and starting again. Yet he could not free his mind from a
succession of images which alternated between the triumph of safe
arrival and the disaster of five ships sunk. Eventually he climbed into
his bunk and tried to read. He chose a slim, blue-backed volume of
Bacon's essays. 'Men fear death,' he read, 'as children fear to go in the
dark.' Was that the reason for his restlessness? He did not need to be
reminded that the pressure was on him to make a decision whatever
the weather. Were they, as so many people believed, heading for
certain destruction?

A tap on the door brought him to the realisation that it was morning and that despite his restlessness he had slept tolerably well. It was
Isachsen's chief steward, Kristian Overland, with the morning tea.

'What's the weather like, Overland?'

'About the same, sir. Light off-shore wind, grey sky, occasional
flurries of snow.'

A few minutes later Binney was in the radio cabin. 'What do you
make of it, Bell?'' The local reports, said Bell, envisaged a little more
snow, but nothing spectacular. 'The wind will be from the same
quarter,' he added, 'but it may freshen a bit later on.'

'Bringing more snow, and plenty of it, from the steppes of Siberia?'
'They haven't said that.'

Back in his saloon, Binney sat down to draft a letter to Lundhquist. The persuasiveness of the hamper seemed to have failed; the Swede was still locked in his cabin. Perhaps it was time to get tough. Binney had just finished drafting the letter when he heard footsteps outside, followed by a tattoo on the door. Both footsteps and summons, he decided, could belong to only one man: Ivar Blücker.

Blücker handed him an envelope, and he opened it and recognised Bill Waring's untidy scrawl.

> Best of luck and thanks for letters. H.D. [Henry Denham] rather agitated about his masters who are considerably worried over 'skating' position and wanted to send their lads elsewhere. Stalled this for the moment but hoping for an immediate break.
>
> 'Rubble promising, Rubble promising' is the mid-day special from his boys.

Binney handed the letter back to Blücker. 'This is hardly the green light,' he said disconsolately. Then he did a mental double-take, grabbing the note back for a second look.

'I agree it's not ideal,' said Blücker, 'but Bill told me last night about the difficulties at the other end. I think he feels you should try to make a clean getaway if you can talk the captains into it. If you go on waiting for ideal conditions with a sou-wester you may find yourselves without support at the other end.'

The ultimatum was becoming clear : units of the Home Fleet could not be kept idle indefinitely. An Admiralty Intelligence report had warned of an imminent sortie into northern waters of an unidentified German capital ship, and they were anxious to get the Rubble convoy out of the way. They would have been even more anxious, and indeed would certainly have cancelled the sailing, had they known the truth: the battle-cruisers Scharnhorst and Gneisenau, which were planning to break out into the Atlantic, had sailed from Kiel *the previous afternoon*.

Binney knew nothing of all this; but he recognised that other operations must be pending and that the initiative might slip from his grasp. Once lost he might never regain it.

'O.K. Ivar. We'll call it the green light. Summon the captains.'

Soon after 11.30 that morning, 23rd January 1941, the five captains assembled in the dining saloon of the Tai Shan. Binney noted with satisfaction that their greatcoats were dusted with snow. One or two voices, however, were raised in demur—the wind was still off-shore, the snowfall might not last. Binney read them the message from

Waring. 'In view of the danger of a postponement,' he said, 'I ask you to accept the advice to sail today.' To his great relief the captains unanimously agreed that the time had come.

In order to get as far as possible in darkness, they agreed to start out in daylight if the snow continued. They were to sail at half-hourly intervals, starting with the slowest ship, the Ranja, at 14.30. If a U-boat were waiting for them outside the fjord and a ship was to be torpedoed at the outset, it was better to lose the salt-water ballast of the Ranja than a steel cargo. The Ranja would be followed by the John Bakke, the Taurus, the Elizabeth Bakke, and finally, at about 16.30, the flagship Tai Shan. Each ship would steer an independent course and make the utmost speed to the rendezvous. Wireless silence would be kept unless attacked or mined, and one ship was not to go to the aid of another. The delivery of cargoes was to be the paramount consideration.

Each captain shook Binney warmly by the hand, then left to spread the news aboard his ship. Captain Henry had good news of Lundhquist. 'Your prescription for his indisposition,' he told Binney, 'proved wonderfully effective in the end.'

As the crews jumped to the task of getting the ships ready for sea, Binney was left with time for reflection. He went to his cabin and wrote a final letter, giving instructions on business and family matters in case he should fail to survive the voyage. 'Zero hour is in about an hour's time,' he wrote. 'We've been waiting for twenty-three days for the right weather—and I think we've got it at last. It remains to be seen whether we can evade German mines, submarines, U-boats and aircraft. It will be a fairly exciting voyage. If the worst comes to the worst we are going to scuttle our ships, rather than let them fall into German hands.' In an earlier letter he had told his step-mother: 'The more I examined the possibilities in detail the more confident I became that with fast ships and determined crews it would be possible to outwit the Germans and bring our cargoes safely to England. Eventually I was able to persuade the Legation and the various Government departments in London of the soundness of the scheme . . . you will, I am sure, understand that I could not ask 150 men to take this risk without throwing in my own lot with theirs.'

Everyone on board the ships seemed to have taken special care with his toilet, as though a clean getaway were something more than a metaphor, and Binney followed their example, donning a starched white shirt and collar and selecting his best blue suit from the wardrobe. Then he went on deck and watched the Ranja manoeuvring in the ice until she swung slowly past the other ships, heading seawards to the accompaniment of enthusiastic cheering, which was repeated for each vessel. 'Our first ship has just got away,' noted Binney. 'We're going out last. It is blowing heavily with plenty of snow, so we shan't be bothered by aeroplanes tonight.' To escape from the fjord unseen would be half the battle.

Ivar Blücker had arranged for Swedish pilots to take the ships out of the fjord to the three-mile limit, choosing men on whose discretion he knew he could rely. (He himself was aboard the Tai Shan.) He had gone ashore earlier to originate the message that would be passed via Henry Denham in Stockholm to the Admiralty, warning them of the breakout.

John Bakke moved off next, a few minutes ahead of schedule, an action of which Binney, with the weather still deteriorating, thoroughly approved. Through the glasses he spotted the slight figure of the chief (supervisory) engineer, and waved at her cheerfully. Then he caught the eye of Captain Escudier and grinned. They were a long way from Hälsingmo now.

Carl Jensen was next to go in the Taurus; and then came Andrew Henry in the Elizabeth Bakke, the fastest ship of them all and therefore the least vulnerable. Henry had the advantage of nearly four knots on the others and might well reach the rendezvous soon after daybreak. In a very short time the ship's silhouette was blurred by the deadening pall of snow.

All but one of the Rubble flotilla had gone, and Brofjord suddenly looked deserted, only the old Swedish battleship looming out of the murk. There were signs of activity on board, and Binney feared they might haul in their anchors and accompany him to the three-mile limit, which was the last thing he wanted, as it would advertise their departure. But he could detect no such move. Equally serious would be a radio message to report their sailing.

'Let's get cracking, Captain Isachsen,' said Binney. Then he felt Blücker plucking at his arm. 'I want a few words with you privately.' Binney led him to the saloon.

Blücker, it transpired, had done his best, through his contacts in the Swedish Admiralty, to urge that strict neutrality demanded radio silence about the ships' departure, and no shore leave in Lysekil that evening for the battleship's crew. But he had gone much further than that. 'This heavy snowfall' —and his eyes flickered for a moment— 'This heavy snowfall is playing havoc with communications in the Gothenburg and Bohuslän areas. It is very inconvenient and we must never let such a misfortune overtake us again. They tell me the telephones should be working again soon. But not before morning.'

It slowly dawned on Binney what Blücker was saying. Messages reporting their departure had little chance of getting through. Not, anyway, before morning. Somehow Blücker had arranged for line communications to be interrupted. Unless some German vessel actually saw them leaving and reported by radio, they were virtually assured of many hours' start. Even if their departure were discovered early next morning, some further time must elapse before the Germans could react.

However much Blücker might pretend that he was only doing his job, Binney knew better. 'I'll say nothing about this to anyone,' he said, 'in case we get captured *en route*. Someone might blow the gaff under interrogation. I shall even try to forget it myself. But if we reach England, we'll find an appropriate way of showing our gratitude.'

As the two men went up to the bridge, the Tai Shan was just emerging from Brofjord. 'It's a clear passage from here, isn't it,' Blücker remarked and the pilot nodded. 'Then why don't we leave them here? The sooner they can extinguish their lights, the better for them.' The pilot nodded and signalled for the engines to stop.

The small pilot boat was brought round to the gangway, and Binney accompanied Blücker to the lower deck. As he turned to descend the gangway Blücker pulled out a small seaman's knife in a leather scabbard and handed it to Binney. 'I don't suppose you've equipped yourself with one of these,' he said, 'but if you should get tangled up in ropes or wreckage or anything, you may find it useful. Stick to deep water and I think you'll make it.'

It was dusk as Blücker gained the pilot boat, and the lights of Lysekil were vanishing astern. The time was 5.45. It was still snowing slightly, and visibility was less than a mile. Then the engine-room telegraph clanged, the engines rumbled into life, and with the amateur commodore of the Rubble fleet now in the chart room with the captain, the Tai Shan extinguished her lights and set course westwards into the darkened Skagerrak, navigating by dead reckoning, the last of the five ships to sail.

*   *   *

They needed the darkness now. They were crossing the Oslo–Frederikshavn shipping lane—the main German supply route between Norway and Denmark. To be sighted and identified in that shipping lane would be to undo all Blücker's work. And indeed just ahead of them the Taurus, as she cleared Brofjord, actually sighted a southbound vessel. Carl Jensen, who had intended to sail south along the coast for a time before leaving Swedish waters, quickly headed out to sea, trusting to his blackout to avoid detection. He did not know whether he had been seen or not.

The previous night, the Scharnhorst and Gneisenau had anchored in Kiel Bay prior to making the passage of the Great Belt and the Kattegat, and that morning they had been led through the Belt by an icebreaker. So they were nicely positioned to surprise the Rubble force next day. Fortunately such an encounter would have been just as much of a surprise to the Germans. That evening, as the Rubble ships were crossing the approaches to Oslo fjord, the two battle-cruisers, delayed by ice and awaiting their escort, anchored east of the Skaw, less than fifty miles away.

In the mined Skagerrak it was essential for the Rubble ships to take advantage of the 'Norske Renna'—the deep waters on the Norwegian side. This automatically kept them clear of the Skaw. But it brought them within twenty miles of the Norwegian coast, liable to detection from land. To their astonishment, they found that most of the main lights along the coast were functioning, and the crews were able to take bearings at regular intervals to verify their position.

The Tai Shan had started off at about thirteen knots, and the engineers were increasing revolutions cautiously, anxious to keep something in reserve for daylight. Binney stuffed all his secret papers into a canvas bag and weighted it carefully, then went down to the 'tween decks and wedged an electric torch by the side of each turn-cock to make sure he could carry out his scuttling task quickly in emergency. Then he dressed himself in his life-saving suit and joined Isachsen on the bridge. Apart from the men on duty in the engine room, everyone was wearing a similar suit.

On the Taurus, which was already making fifteen knots, all hands seemed to have elected to remain on continuous duty, and they peered blindly into the darkness for the expected minefield or enemy vessel. The sea was certainly calm enough for submarines and fast surface craft. The weather could hardly have been more favourable, however, a light wind astern bringing thick snow which made it difficult, from the bridge, to see the look-out man up in the bows.

Isachsen, like Jensen ahead of him, was now clear of the Oslo–Frederikshavn shipping lane and had begun to ease in towards the coast. He gave the bos'n the new course, then noted his position and asked Binney to deliver it to the wireless cabin. There Binney discussed the latest weather forecast with Bell. The prospect was little changed except in the most important detail: there was no mention of any more snow. 'Kristiansand is coming in very loud now,' added Bell, 'but it's all in code.' Binney could not help wondering apprehensively what these coded signals might be.

On the way back to the bridge he had ample confirmation of a change in the weather: the snow was petering out and the horizon had lengthened to half a mile. It was just coming up to midnight, and in nearly eight hours they had put over a hundred miles behind them; but they badly needed a recurrence of the snow showers by morning.

Shortly after midnight on Taurus, the man on look-out duty on the fo'c'sle reported hearing the noise of engines dead ahead. Soon they realised they were overtaking another vessel. After several minutes of tense uncertainty they recognised it as the Ranja. Later they passed the John Bakke as well. Tai Shan, too, passed both these vessels in the early hours, but saw neither. The Elizabeth Bakke, which had been making nineteen knots, was far ahead of them all.

By two o'clock it had stopped snowing altogether and the night was clear. There was a fitful, waning moon, and the canopy above the escaping ships was suddenly pinpricked with stars. On the starboard quarter the Homborö light was flashing off Lillesand. Thirty miles away on the starboard beam was the Oksoy light off Kristiansand, where the German destroyers were reported to be waiting for them. Forward was the Ryvingen light off Mandal. 'I shall alter course north-west for the rendezvous at about seven o'clock this morning,' Isachsen told Binney. By that time they would be emerging from the Skagerrak and daylight would be near. Already the Lindesnes light was showing up off The Naze.

The beams of the lighthouses grew paler, and by eight o'clock it was daylight, and the sun was shining on the snow-clad mountains of southern Norway from a cloudless sky. Where were the promised snowstorms? The weather had turned positively Mediterranean. From Tai Shan the Taurus was easily discernible several miles ahead, while the superstructure of the John Bakke was equally clear astern. They still had more than sixty miles to go to reach the rendezvous, the German air bases at Sola and Egersund must be stirring soon, and the sense of nakedness, with the Norwegian coast twenty-eight miles distant and clearly visible, was becoming obsessive. Binney tried to get what comfort he could from the fact that three of the Rubble ships, to his certain knowledge, had survived the night, while there had been no distress messages from the other two, which were presumably in their natural order as befitted the fastest and slowest ships. Yet the thought of five more vulnerable hours before they could reach the rendezvous appalled him.

Where was the promised air escort? That, surely, would venture far beyond the rendezvous point, right into the jaws of the Skagerrak. But the sky was empty. On the Tai Shan, Binney had to remind Isachsen of a phrase in the sailing orders: 'Aircraft . . . may not necessarily be affording continuous patrol over your particular ship.' They would operate where it mattered most—perhaps over the German airfields, harassing their movements. He would have been severely shaken had he known that not a single RAF plane had yet taken off: the first patrols were grounded by early morning fog. Fortunately, although the Norwegian coastline was clear, it was still snowing inland, and with runways to be cleared the German Air Force, too, was inactive for the present.

Most of the German patrol craft had been left behind in the night. Hampered by the weather, and let down by a warning system that had proved all too easy to interrupt, they had been preoccupied in any case with the sortie of the two capital ships. All that day, however, 24th January, the weather off the Skaw prevented the German torpedo boats from operating as a screen, and the two battle-cruisers remained at anchor.

Reports on the sailing of these two ships had not yet reached London. But an Admiralty message of 17.45 the previous evening had warned Jack Tovey that the Rubble ships were out, and at 22.00 that night two cruisers of the 15th Squadron—the Naiad, wearing the flag of the Rear-Admiral Commanding, E. L. S. King, with the Aurora in company—sailed from Scapa Flow and steered for the rendezvous at eighteen knots. Five ships of the 18th Cruiser Squadron—the cruisers Edinburgh and Birmingham and the destroyers Escapade, Echo and Electra, under Vice-Admiral L. E. Holland—followed them three and a half hours later in support.

Air escort was in the hands of three squadrons of Coastal Command, operating from airfields in Scotland and the Shetlands. Each squadron was to put up six aircraft, operating in pairs, one pair relieving another as the day progressed; and each squadron was assigned to a different task. Bristol Blenheims of 254 Squadron were to escort Admiral King's two cruisers. Lockheed Hudsons of 269 Squadron were to escort Admiral Holland's force. And Hudsons of 224 Squadron were to patrol to a depth of 250 miles, extending as far down the Norwegian coast as Lister, seventy miles south of Stavanger, covering the emergence of the merchant vessels from the Skagerrak.

At 09.50 that morning, 24th January, the Naiad sighted a merchant ship, and on being closed she proved to be the Elizabeth Bakke. She gave her speed as nineteen knots and reported that four other ships had sailed with her. In view of her speed, and the progress she had already made, King allowed her to proceed independently to Kirkwall; this enabled him to begin the search for the other ships.

First to get away of the escort aircraft, soon after 09.30, were two Hudsons of 269 Squadron from Wick. Although hampered by snowstorms and low visibility, one of these Hudsons found both the naval forces before eleven o'clock. It was a fine piece of navigation; but in the next half-hour, as the mist lifted and visibility became extreme, Admiral Holland had to accept that low visibility was no longer going to be a contributory factor to the success of the operation. Meanwhile every minute brought both escort and merchant vessels closer to the main German air bases.

On board the Rubble ships the morning dragged by with almost intolerable slowness, the sparkling sunshine lending an illusion of unreality that somehow made the tension bearable. The Tai Shan, steering a zigzag course as an anti-submarine precaution in accordance with her sailing orders, with alterations of 40 degrees every ten minutes, had now dropped so far behind the speedier Taurus as to be out of sight. But what still puzzled Binney was the absence of any sign of searching aircraft, either German or British. He could only conclude that the morning patrols on both sides of the North Sea had been grounded by the snow of the previous night. No doubt they had Ivar Blücker, too, to thank for the inactivity of the *Luftwaffe*. But surely the RAF must appear soon. He did not realise, because he had never been told, that two-thirds of the promised air escort had been briefed not to provide an umbrella for the Rubble ships but to protect the Navy.

Captain Escudier, on the John Bakke, last but one of the ships, ordered the doubling of the look-out for air and surface craft. No one knew how far the minefields extended, but he kept as far as possible from the coastline, though he knew that anyone with a powerful telescope could pick them out. Then, just as they were emerging from the Skagerrak, they burned out an exhaust valve, and there was nothing for it but to stop to repair it. Even more than before, they were now entirely in the hands of Hansen and the other Norwegian and Swedish engineers.

Butterflies in the stomach had afflicted them all from the start, but they had somehow worked off their fear. Now their extreme vulnerability threatened a momentary panic. No one did more to alleviate this than the chief steward, a Welshman named Banks, who came up with hot coffee and sandwiches for the men on watch and never rested. Steadied by such devotion, the engineers set purposefully to work, while Escudier called up his demolition squad to stand by. It was a two-hour job, yet somehow they got through it unharmed. The Ranja had almost caught them up by the time they got going again.

At 11.45 Captain Jensen of the Taurus sighted an unidentified warship approaching at speed from the west. Although hoping it was the promised escort, he altered course to prepare for the worst. 'Before long she started signalling not shooting,' he wrote afterwards, 'and to our great relief she was flashing the agreed identification signal G for George.' This was the Naiad.

Twenty-five minutes later, from the Tai Shan, a blob was sighted on the horizon. Through the glasses Binney could just discern the masts of three ships. Too far away to identify, they were in fact the Naiad, the Aurora, and the Taurus. Captain Isachsen ordered the recognition signal to be run up; but Binney hardly had time to savour the emotion of seeing his initials fluttering at the masthead before a reconnaissance seaplane appeared from the north-east. It was a Blohm and Voss 138.

Leaving the Taurus to the Aurora, Admiral King in the Naiad closed the Tai Shan. With hostile aircraft in attendance he decided to give the two merchant vessels the maximum protection of his squadron's guns, and both cruisers altered course to the north-west-ward to keep close astern of their charges. 'Well done, Tai Shan,' came the stentorian voice of the Admiral from a loud-hailer on the bridge of the Naiad. 'What is your speed? I am escorting you to Kirkwall Roads.' Binney's reaction was to gaze apprehensively astern. There was no sign of either the John Bakke or the Ranja.

At 13.45 the BV 138 moved in closer to the Tai Shan as though to attack it, and the Naiad at once opened fire. The seaplane retreated out of range, but not out of sight, and the convoy remained under surveillance.

The first two Blenheim sorties from 254 Squadron had failed to locate Admiral King's force in the poor visibility then prevailing, but the two relieving Blenheims, having taken off at 12.30, were now approaching the rendezvous. At 14.15 they were sighted, and the Naiad at once opened fire in the direction of the shadowing seaplane to put the Blenheims on the target. The Blenheim crews saw the gunfire and soon chased the seaplane out of sight.

For the moment Admiral King continued to provide close escort for the Taurus and the Tai Shan; but the two ships that had not yet been sighted were very much on his mind. Meanwhile a Hudson of 224 Squadron, one of those briefed to look for the merchant vessels, having made its landfall off Lister, sighted the John Bakke and the Ranja emerging at last from the Skagerrak. The time was seven minutes past two and the two ships had been exposed to full daylight, apparently undetected, for nearly seven hours.

The Hudson crew, captained by Pilot Officer H. G. Holmes, estimated the speed of the ships as ten knots and their course as 300 degrees—roughly north-west. They had turned the corner and were heading for the rendezvous. He flew back to the Naiad to report. But by that time the two cruisers were so busily engaged in directing their two escort Blenheims on to a growing force of hostile aircraft that the Hudson crew could not get their message acknowledged.

Two Me 110 fighter-bombers and a Heinkel 111 had been sighted from the Naiad and the two Blenheims had been directed on to them by gunfire. Both Blenheims were making beam attacks on the Me 110s when the Hudson arrived. One Blenheim registered hits, but it suffered considerable damage itself and was forced to dive seawards, the pilot relying on his rear gunner for protection. Pulling up clear of the enemy machines, the pilot examined the damage, decided that a cracked windscreen and other defects were superficial only, and closed the He 111. But both Blenheims were nearing the end of their endurance, and when their ammunition was exhausted they turned for home.

Absorption with the air battle meant that it was 14.41 before the Hudson piloted by Holmes was able to pass its message; one of the deficiencies of naval/air co-operation at this time lay in an inability to share radio wavelengths, and Holmes needed the attention of the deck crew in order to pass his message by Aldis lamp. With shadowing seaplanes still circling, King felt he could not abandon his charges, but shortly before three o'clock, when the five ships of the 18th Cruiser Squadron were sighted, he decided on a change of plan. As soon as the two squadrons came within visual signalling distance King asked Holland to take over close escort of the Taurus and the Tai Shan while the Naiad and the Aurora returned eastwards to close the John Bakke and the Ranja. According to Admiral Holland, King's action in returning to look for the missing ships at this point, knowing that he was under enemy air observation, 'gave evidence of the determination which is characteristic of his nature'.

Half an hour later, still on an eastward course, the Naiad asked one of the patrolling Hudsons if it could pinpoint the position of the last two ships. The Hudson searched but failed to find them. Meanwhile Pilot Officer Holmes, in the Hudson that had originally sighted them, was approaching the end of his endurance. As a parting shot he attacked one of the Blohm and Voss seaplanes, but the enemy got in the first burst and the Hudson was hit in the port engine. Nevertheless Holmes pressed home his attack and peppered the seaplane amidships. The German escaped into cloud, and soon afterwards Holmes, having briefly resumed his patrol, suffered an engine failure and was forced to jettison his bombs. He got back to Scotland on one engine.

There was action too, if not combat, in the skies above the John

Bakke and the Ranja. Still without protection of any kind, they were shadowed for much of the afternoon. At first they thought that the promised air escort had arrived; then the black Maltese crosses became clear for all to see. When no attack developed they began to realise to their astonishment that the German planes were actually *escorting* them; they certainly came in close enough to recognise the Norwegian flag.

It was not until four o'clock that afternoon that a fourth ship was sighted from the Naiad, but it proved to be the John Bakke, well to the south-eastward but with her engines now running close to full power. The sight of shadowing enemy aircraft was an unwelcome one, but the Naiad at once began to close the merchant vessel. Fifteen minutes later, still farther to the east, and also under air surveillance, the 12,000-ton Ranja hove into view.

Instructing the Aurora to protect the John Bakke, Admiral King began closing the Ranja at full speed. Meanwhile it was at last dawning on the *Luftwaffe* that something unusual was afoot, and they began to react in force. Blohm and Voss and Heinkel floatplanes, and numerous Ju 88 and Dornier 17 bombers, all appeared on the scene. Yet the hesitation of the German air crews was obvious, and to Admiral King it seemed that they were completely puzzled by the movements of the merchant ships. From the start the enemy planes had concentrated their attention on the escorting vessels, presumably trying to divine their intentions. German intelligence on the breakout, King felt, must have been minimal; and indeed the German C-in-C suspected at first that the British had got wind of his plans for the battle-cruisers and were engaged on a big mine-laying operation.

Now, however, as the last of the Rubble ships approached the bosom of the escort, Naval Group North sized up the situation correctly, and a determined attack was made upon them. The Aurora was close enough to the John Bakke to put the bombers off with her guns, but the Naiad was still some miles from the Ranja. From vanguard to decoy to straggler—that had been the unfortunate lot of the Ranja and her crew. The *Luftwaffe* crews who had mistakenly acted as escort now changed their cloth angrily and dived in from astern, dropping several sticks of bombs that straddled the ship. Fortunately there were no direct hits, and even the near-misses caused no casualties and only superficial damage. But one of the seaplane crews was not done with yet. Climbing and turning, the pilot lined up for a machine-gun attack.

Captain Nicolson and his Swedish mate Nils Rydberg were in the wheelhouse, but as the attack developed Rydberg sought the protection of the concrete bridge structure that had been specially erected for this purpose. Perhaps the seaplane crew spotted him as he ran for shelter. Anyway their guns opened up, and before he could reach the safety of the concrete structure Rydberg fell wounded. Nicolson, who had stayed in the wheelhouse, was unhurt.

The Naiad was too far away to keep these aircraft off, but before another attack could develop it had come within range, and Admiral King was relieved to find that the tanker was apparently undamaged. Five machine-gun bullets, however, had hit the Swedish mate. The second mate, Viktor Böstrom, another Swede, took charge of him and picked out several bullets from his body; but it was clear that he was badly hurt.

The Aurora had meanwhile closed with the John Bakke and was zigzagging astern of her, and now, eight miles to the south-east, the Naiad prepared to defend the Ranja. Three shadowing Heinkel 115 floatplanes and eight Dornier 17 bombers were sighted at intervals, but again the accent seemed to be on reconnaissance, and the determined attacks that King expected never materialised. Whenever an individual aircraft approached at all closely, a few rounds from one of the cruisers were sufficient to drive it off.

Even to the men of the Ranja, dusk seemed to come early, and as darkness fell the last sight the crews had of the Norwegian coast was the vertical searchlight beam at Stavanger, homing the German aircraft whose performance had been so surprisingly muted and ineffectual. Each ship was escorted individually through the night towards the Orkneys, and one by one, at longish intervals, they sailed triumphantly next day into Kirkwall Roads. Not until then did Binney have the satisfaction of knowing for certain that the essential supplies he had schemed for more than a year to deliver, together with the five ships and their crews, were safe in British waters.

Altogether 147 men and one woman had taken part in Operation Rubble, and the crews comprised fifty-eight Englishmen, fifty-seven Norwegians, thirty-one Swedes and a Latvian. The cargo totalled just under 25,000 tons and was valued at about £1,000,000, while the ships were valued at £2,500,000; but these figures bore no relation to the cargo's importance at that critical time, representing as it did a year's supply of Swedish materials under the War Trade Agreement.

*   *   *

For George Binney this was the beginning of a period of almost unbridled euphoria, in which personal satisfaction at having erased an involuntary and indeed imaginary youthful disgrace played no small part. The one distressing feature was the news of Nils Rydberg. He had been hit in the stomach, and there had been little that Nicolson and Böstrom could do except apply field-dressings, lay him on a mattress in the chart room, and keep him sedated. When the Ranja finally docked he was taken to the Balfour Hospital at Kirkwall and was at once assessed as gravely ill. Binney visited him there next day, finding him fully conscious and quite unrepentant at having made the voyage; but the Matron was soon signalling to Binney to leave. Before he did so, Binney told Rydberg he would personally be recommending him for a decoration, and that he would arrange for him to be flown back to Sweden as soon as he was well enough to travel; but this was in the days before the practical use of penicillin, and three days later Nils Rydberg died of septicaemia. Thus the only casualty aboard the five ships of Operation Rubble was a Swede. The Ministry of Shipping granted his widow a pension, and he was posthumously awarded the MBE.*

Binney was flown straight to London from Kirkwall, while the ships were moved south to the Clyde in the hope of escaping a German retaliatory raid. Harry Sporborg went to Glasgow to meet the crews, but he wasn't the man they wanted to see. 'Where's Mr. Binney? We want to see Mr. Binney.'

Reaction to Binney's unexpected triumph was uniformly generous, bringing a chorus of 'I was wrong' messages, not least from the Foreign Office. 'Congratulations,' said Gladwyn Jebb, Foreign Office adviser to the Ministry of Economic Warfare, 'I was all against your operation—I never thought it had a chance of getting through.' Jack Mitcheson wrote to say that Binney's constant optimism had been the key; but he added: 'I only really felt sure of success when it was definite that you were going too.' He and Waring were already preparing for 'your next triumph'. Victor Mallet generously cabled his masters : 'I consider the success of Operation Rubble largely due to Binney's initiative and determination.'

Production of several lines at SKF Luton had been held up through lack of machine tools and tubing, and although the joint managing directors, Ville Siberg and George Mead, had discussed Rubble with Binney many months earlier, and had built a bomb-proof shelter to house key materials following an air raid on the factory in 1940, the actual deliveries when they came staggered them. 'When the railway trucks rolled in one after the other, containing materials which we'd been desperately in need of for months,' Siberg told Bill Waring, 'I just couldn't believe my eyes.' Roy Fedden, of the Bristol Aeroplane Company, was another who took the trouble to express his relief and admiration in writing; but the most convincing evidence came from

* Member of the Order of the British Empire (similarly Officer of, Commander of etc., p. 75).

the minutes of the Ball-Bearing Panel of the Steel Sub-Committee of Iron and Steel Control, dated 18th February 1941. The windfall from Sweden, said the minutes, had been most welcome and with two exceptions had made up the deficiencies to everyone's stock.

Binney also appreciated the reaction of the Minister for Economic Warfare, Hugh Dalton. 'I hope you'll continue with the help of Hambro and Sporborg to break the blockade,' said Dalton. 'The Prime Minister is delighted with the results of the operation. Are you returning to Sweden to bring over further cargoes?' This was the 64-dollar question, and Binney had always hoped to be able to answer it in the affirmative. The success of Rubble must surely mean that he could do so, and he had already begun to plan an immediate repeat operation, before the nights shortened. But despite the impulsive reaction of Hugh Dalton, political objections to a second operation were already being canvassed behind the scenes.

The comment that pleased Binney most was that of Admiral Tom Phillips, the Vice-Chief of Naval Staff. 'Why didn't you sink the Scharnhorst and Gneisenau while you were about it?'

Binney travelled north to the Rubble ships to hand the crews their bonus in person. 'And no nonsense,' he told the Treasury, 'about deducting income tax.' The reaction of the crews was the one he enjoyed most of all; as Sporborg had seen, it was striking the effect Binney had had on them. 'Right from the time when you first spoke to us in Hälsingmo,' said radio operator Bell, 'I knew you'd get us through.' Binney was quick to disclaim any such personal victory; and he was well aware how fortunate they had been. For him the decisive contribution had been made by his captains, and he put each of them up for an OBE, and asked them to nominate two crew members from each ship for an award. Binney himself was recommended by Victor Mallet for a CBE.

The chief 'honours and awards' problem was Ivar Blücker; his contribution had probably been decisive, yet he could hardly be rewarded officially. Some private but felicitous expression of gratitude was needed, and Charles Hambro came up with what seemed the right sort of gesture. At an audience with King George VI to tell the monarch about the operation, he described the part played by Blücker and asked if he might be presented with a pair of gold cuff-links bearing the Royal cypher. The King took off the cuff-links he was wearing and handed them to Hambro. 'If Captain Blücker wouldn't mind a secondhand pair,' he said, 'you'd better take these.'

Postscript to Rubble

Rubble had bridged a serious gap in Britain's supply lines and averted a crisis in the steel industry; but it had never been visualised as more than a stop-gap—except perhaps by Binney—until alternative sources in America, Canada and the United Kingdom could be developed. Now, with many of these alternative sources either over-stretched or still embryonic, the need remained acute. Thus the impact and implications of Rubble were wide, far wider than the timely sustaining of a war industry to which the windfall of supplies seemed heaven-sent. First it seemed a pointer to the future; what had been done once might at least be attempted again. Second was the reaction of the Swedes, which was ambiguous, even schizophrenic: keen as they were to keep communications open with the West, and scrupulously as they had acted over Rubble, they were now facing mounting pressures from an angry Führer. Hitler had always suspected the Swedes of some plot to surrender their iron-ore deposits to the British; now he accused them of collusion, and alleged that the ships could not have escaped without Swedish connivance. Third, the Norwegian Government in exile also had serious misgivings about a further attempt. It was their ships which were at risk, and they did not believe that the Germans would be caught napping again. Fourth, the Foreign Office, anxious as ever to keep a footing in a neutral Sweden, and aware of the pressures being put on the Swedes by the Nazis, had their reservations. When Binney was offered a post with the British Supply Mission in Washington, it looked as though the diplomats would win.

There is ample evidence that the Nazis were furious at what they saw not only as a physical defeat but also as a threat to their influence in Scandinavia and a serious blow to their prestige. 'Immediately the success of the first operation became known in Berlin,' cabled Mallet on 17th February, 'the Swedish Government were accused of complicity and strongly pressed to take certain measures to prevent a recurrence.' They were soon persuaded to deny the ships the use of a fjord as a *point d'appui* from which they might break away on a subsequent operation. And presently the Germans announced that they were 'taking their own precautions'. A large number of Danish trawlers had been requisitioned, reported the Swedes, presumably to patrol the Skagerrak, and the German Admiralty and Air Force were believed to be laying elaborate plans to intercept blockade-runners. All this was reported to London by Mallet, who, so Waring told Binney, was 'trotting out all the old objections to this type of operation'.

The advantages enjoyed during Rubble had been cumulative, and it was certainly true that many of them might not recur. Preventive measures by patrol craft had been limited by the prevailing ice conditions, and in any case only a few seaworthy vessels had been available. The moment of the actual breakout, although enforced by circumstances, had proved to be well chosen; the Germans, perhaps, were looking for the 'south-westerly blow' that the British could wait for no longer. The breakdown of telephone circuits had paralysed the German communications system. The sortie of the battle-cruisers turned out to be adventitious. The iced-up condition of Brofjord seems to have deceived German air reconnaissance. And the Germans may well have believed not only their own propaganda but also the British: that the breakout had no chance of evading the German air and surface forces, and that the British had accepted this and were not planning to go through with it. All the evidence from the German side confirms that the enemy were caught completely off their guard.

Had Rubble been an isolated fluke, then—a large slice of the Binney luck—or could it be repeated? Although Binney realised that next time the Germans would be much more vigilant, he still believed that fog and snow were more than a match for anything they could throw at him in the Skagerrak. If the ships could somehow be armed against air attack, and if the rendezvous point could be brought fifty miles nearer, he thought the chances remained good. He still regarded a 50 per cent loss as likely; but he had every reason to believe that such a loss would be acceptable. The policy of ordering essential war materials and machine tools from the Swedish steelmakers was one he had always adhered to, and he believed that Rubble fully justified a continuation of it. Before leaving Gothenburg he had been careful to order nearly 900 tons of surplus fuel to be discharged from the Rubble ships, together with a suitable quantity of lubricating oil, as a reserve for future operations, and he continued to press for official approval.

A telegram from the Foreign Office to Stockholm of 26th February, however, informed Mallet that 'after most careful consideration we have decided against making any further attempt to run the German blockade from Gothenburg at present'. The reasons given were that Nortraship and the Norwegian Government were opposed to the idea, that the Germans were likely to be much more on the alert, that the shorter nights greatly increased the hazards, and that Rubble 'has given us approximately a year's supply of these Swedish materials', while there was little important cargo awaiting shipment.

Rubble, indeed, had scooped the pool. The Foreign Office still had in mind the possibility of another big operation in the winter, bringing out at least six ships with a large amount of priority cargo, and preliminary plans were laid; but then came a Cabinet decision that all work in connection with the preparation of the ships for a further venture must cease.

*   *   *

It was not perhaps surprising that after completing his report on Rubble, Binney should go down with jaundice; the strain he had undergone in the preceding months had been considerable. Thus it was not until March that he was able to fulfil an appointment with Sir Andrew Duncan, the man who had first sent him to Scandinavia in 1939 and who had since been appointed Minister of Supply. Duncan told Binney that Churchill had likened his exploit to those of the seafaring adventurers of Elizabethan times; he was going to recommend Binney not for a CBE but for a knighthood. As for the future, Britain's desperate industrial needs, he thought, would soon overrule all objections to a second operation, though its prosecution could now be entrusted to others. When Binney protested, Duncan reasoned with him. 'How old are you George?' 'Forty.' 'Then do the sensible thing and accept this job in Washington.' But Binney refused. He spoke with feeling of the letdown to those who had helped him if he failed to carry on the work he had begun, amounting he felt to dereliction of duty, and he argued with some truth that no one else had his contacts, either in Sweden or Britain. Duncan himself must have known that Binney was right, and when he saw how strongly Binney felt he gave way.

At a meeting with the Norwegian Government in London on 27th March, the problems of a second operation were thoroughly aired. Foreign Minister Trygve Lie led for the Norwegians, backed up by Hysing Olsen of Nortraship and several ministers, while Charles Hambro headed the British side, supported by representatives of the Foreign Office, the Treasury, and the Ministries of Economic Warfare, Shipping, and Supply. As Duncan had forecast, the argument of operational necessity won the day, and the Norwegians were somewhat mollified by British agreement that Norwegian masters would be employed in future, though as the operation would be mounted under the joint auspices of the SOE and the Admiralty, a senior British Merchant Navy officer would be appointed to each ship for liaison duties.

The Norwegians warned at this meeting, however, that the legal position was becoming critical, since the Germans were applying to the owners in Oslo and elsewhere in Norway, under threat of imprisonment, for powers of attorney which would place all Norwegian ships in Swedish ports under German control. It would then be up to the Swedish courts to decide whether the legislation enacted by King Haakon's Government before going into exile was valid or not. It was agreed that the British should select and charter the ships they needed and pay and feed the crews, and that, in the event of damage or loss, full compensation would be paid to the Norwegian Government. Those ships which succeeded in escaping would revert to Nortraship. It was also announced at this meeting that George Binney would shortly be returning to Sweden to undertake preliminary planning and to take charge of the operation.

In April 1941, facing the prospect of a legal skirmish preceding the main battle of running another cargo through the blockade, Binney flew from Scotland to Sweden. For the moment the Foreign Office had made their peace with him: he was carrying the diplomatic bag.

PART II

OPERATION PERFORMANCE
'Twice is not once over again'

WHEN Binney returned to Sweden in April 1941, he found his reception there equally enthusiastic. The members of the Jernkontoret, the industrialists, the shipowners, and his own colleagues and friends, overwhelmed him with congratulations. And the moment of his arrival could not have been more opportune, coinciding as it did with the newspaper announcement of his knighthood in the Birthday Honours List. There followed an amusing pantomime at the Legation with Victor Mallet. Despite all the evidence, Mallet was not prepared to recognise the truth until he had been personally informed by signal from the Foreign Office: until that time, he affected not to know what all the fuss was about. 'There must be some mistake. I recommended you for a CBE.' Nothing, however, was good enough now for Binney, and Mallet offered him a sumptuous new office in the Legation. Binney declined: the basement had been good enough for him before and he preferred its comparative anonymity.

Binney's objectives this time were clearly defined. They were:

> 1. To secure substantial tonnages of semi-finished war materials for British manufacturers—materials which were either unprocurable in the United States or which, by reason of slow delivery, were causes or potential causes of production bottlenecks in the UK.
>
> 2. To secure machine tools for the expansion of the ball-bearing industry for increased tank and aircraft production.
>
> 3. To secure for the Dominions, and for Russia, machinery and equipment ordered prior to the blockade of the Skagerrak and lying warehoused in Sweden for lack of transport facilities.
>
> 4. To secure for the Ministry of War Transport and the Norwegian Government as much shipping tonnage as possible.

So far as the ships were concerned, Binney was relying on ten sizeable Norwegian vessels that he knew to be laid-up in Sweden. These were: five tankers, four cargo vessels, and a whale-oil factory ship; all were reasonably suitable for his purpose. Of the tankers, the largest and fastest was the B.P. Newton, 10,324 tons, and the smallest and slowest the Lind, 461 tons. Waring had already restarted work on the other three—the Rigmor, the Buccaneer, and the Storsten, all of 5,000 tons or more. Of much the same tonnage were the two larger cargo ships, the Dicto and the Lionel; the other two, the old Gudvang and the more modern Charente, were coal-burners of less than 1,500 tons. Oldest of the lot and the biggest at 12,000 tons was the whaler Skytteren, originally built in 1901 by Harland and Wolff in Belfast for the Argentine meat run. These, Binney hoped, would comprise the fleet with which he would aim a second time to run the blockade.

Of first importance, however, were the cargoes, and orders for most of these had still to be negotiated. There was no doubt now of the goodwill of the Swedish people; but would Government approval be forthcoming? The initial German reaction to Rubble had been to put a stop to the Gothenburg traffic, but for reasons of self-interest they had relented, since a thriving Swedish industry remained important to them. But they warned the Swedes against co-operating in any such operation in the future. Nevertheless, when Mitcheson called a meeting of the Anglo-Swedish Joint Standing Commission under the War Trade Agreement on 16th May 1941, and Binney told Marcus Wallenberg, Chairman of the Swedish half of this Commission, about the plans for a second operation (to be code-named Operation 'Performance'), the Swedish Government acquiesced. German threats had not altered their view that there was nothing unlawful in a belligerent power purchasing Swedish materials in Sweden and loading them in Swedish ports on merchant vessels duly chartered for that purpose; and this position they seemed prepared to maintain. Later that month they granted export licences for all the materials ordered.

Fred Fuglesang was already busy recruiting crews, many of them Norwegian seamen who had slipped across the frontier with the sole object of getting to Britain to join the Norwegian forces. And some three thousand other Norwegians who were not seamen at all were languishing in Swedish camps, and they were ready to serve in any capacity to get a place on one of the ships. Thus Binney was nothing like so dependent as before on the British crews at Hälsingmo. This was just as well as when he visited the camp he found the demoralising effect of long internment even more apparent than before. And whereas the Norwegians generally were of a keener patriotic purpose than many of those recruited for Rubble, the British at Hälsingmo consisted of those who had rejected Binney last time. Many of them regretted having done so and were anxious to remedy their error; but for some of them the motivation for volunteering was boredom with their existing lot. Binney judged that there would be troublemakers among them, and he warned them that there were plenty of Norwegian volunteers this time and that any man who gave trouble would be sent straight back to Hälsingmo.

The three British captains who had opted out last time—Nicholas, from South Shields, who had been their spokesman, Donald, who had been Escudier's captain, and Nicholson, the stolid Welshman whose opposition had been the most vocal—were all keen to redeem themselves, while two ships' officers with master's tickets, John Nicol and James Kirke, also offered their services. The precise relationship they would hold to the Norwegian captains was as yet undefined; but Binney appointed Nicholas, as the senior British captain, to the Dicto, the ship in which he intended to sail himself, and he earmarked ships for Donald and Nicol. Nicholson he kept waiting a while. 'He had worked against me before,' was Binney's attitude, 'and I was in no hurry to give him the opportunity to do so again.'

There was one other source that Binney intended to draw on. In the early stages of the Russo-Finnish war in 1939, the British Government had encouraged volunteers for an International Brigade to be attached to the Finnish Army. Some 500 single men were recruited, at a rate of a shilling a day, but owing to transport delays they did not reach Finland until 13th March 1940, the date of the armistice between Russia and Finland. At the request of the Finnish Government, they remained in Finland as a military unit until the summer of 1941, when the Finns again joined issue with Russia, this time alongside Germany. The British volunteers were then evacuated to Sweden. From his experience in Rubble, Binney anticipated that Nazi Quisling agents would be active again and that sabotage would be attempted; and he even feared that in some circumstances the ships might be sailed not to a British but to a German or German-occupied port. He wanted a number of reliable British subjects capable of acting as guards on the ships, men who, in emergency, could be relied upon to enforce the captain's will. And he had a second but equally important role for them in the operation itself. He did not intend that the ships should be so completely at the mercy of air attack as in Rubble; some armament, however primitive, must be provided as a deterrent. It would be the task of the sixteen Finland volunteers whom Binney recruited, together with selected Norwegian Army escapees, to help protect the ships from low-level attack while on passage.

Already one of these men had impressed his personality on Binney and Waring, and this was the man whose advice they sought when it came to selecting the men. His name was Brian Reynolds—Sylvanus Brian John Reynolds, to give him his full name—and he was to be associated with the running of the Skagerrak blockade from this point until the end of the war, eventually taking over the leadership from Binney. 'This man walked into the office one day out of the blue,' writes Anne Waring. 'He was the most hearteningly British person one could hope to have seen in that city of spies, deceit and treachery.' A Yorkshireman, he was a mixture of sportsman, countryman and adventurer. Holding an executive position before the war at the stables of J. V. Rank, he had a colourful background. His motto was 'anything for an unquiet life', and his build and thinning red hair soon earned him the title of 'The Lion'. Unable to get into the Services on the outbreak of war, he had volunteered to go to Finland. When his battalion was disbanded he made three attempts to escape by sea from Petsamo, ending up in a Finnish gaol; but eventually he was dumped over the border into Sweden. Anne Waring found him 'the best-natured man I have ever met', and records that he willingly did the work of a general dogsbody at the Legation until Binney and Waring realised his worth. Binney needed a deputy and second-in-command for the operation, Waring, the obvious choice, was much too valuable ashore, and the choice fell on Reynolds. Binney rewarded him by giving him overall responsibility for two of the trickiest jobs of the whole operation—seeing to the installation of the limpet mines by means of which the ships might be sunk in emergency, and arming each ship with Lewis machine-guns. He was also responsible for selecting and training the men who would man the guns. Since it was illegal for foreigners to be in possession of either arms or explosives, the whole process had to be clandestine, in collaboration with junior members of the Legation in Stockholm, who smuggled the goods into and across Sweden, and with the Consulate in Gothenburg, where Peter Coleridge acted the part of distributor. Eventually Major Andrew Croft, assistant military attaché at the Legation, went down to Gothenburg to plant the mines in the holds of all the ships. In controlling this highly secret process at the receiving end, Reynolds showed just the qualities of resource and discretion that were needed.

During that spring and early summer, discussions between the legal adviser to the Ministry of War Transport, W. L. McNair, and Hysing Olsen of Nortraship, produced a legal ploy which was designed to forestall the anticipated attempt by the Germans to entangle the ships in litigation and thus delay their sailing. It was expected that the question the Swedish courts would be asked to decide was whether the decree of the Royal Norwegian Government remained valid in Sweden, or whether the Norwegian shipowners, in Oslo, Bergen and elsewhere, had the better claim. Here was ample scope for protracted litigation. The antidote suggested was for the Royal Norwegian

Government to lease or convey the vessels to the British Government under a demise charter-party on bare-boat terms. The right to possession would then be conferred on the British Government, and once in charge of British masters the ships would enjoy immunity from any action that could be brought against them in Swedish courts. The scheme was equally acceptable to the Norwegians, since it would eliminate the possibility of action over the rightful ownership developing around the disputed decree of 18th May 1940, or around the authority of the Norwegian Government in exile. The demise-charter-party deal was concluded on 1st July 1941, but for the moment it was kept as an ace-in-the-hole. Meanwhile the necessary British captains to augment the five Binney had recruited at Hälsingmo were being sought, and a call went out in Allied shipping circles for volunteers for 'a voyage of particular hazard'. There were eleven ships for which masters were needed, although one of them was not on Binney's operational list but was merely chartered to keep her out of German hands. Later that month Binney flew home to select the men he wanted. Because of shipping losses there were plenty of captains without ships, and Binney was able to give preference to men with experience of the Skagerrak. His final list included four captains from the Ellerman's Wilson Line, based on Hull in peacetime and thoroughly familiar with the Gothenburg run. These were the ten operational ships and their appointed captains, British and Norwegian:

SHIP	TYPE	TONNAGE	WHERE BUILT	YEAR	CAPTAINS	SPEED IN KNOTS
B.P. Newton	Tanker	10,324	Malmö	1940	J. W. Calvert E. R. Blindheim	14
Rigmor	Tanker	6,305	Gothenburg	1931	W. Gilling P. K. Monsen	11
Buccaneer	Tanker	6,222	Rotterdam	1927	G. D. Smail B. Reksten	12
Storsten	Tanker	5,343	Glasgow	1926	J. Reeve R. Bull-Nielsen	10½
Lind	Tanker	461	Slikkerveer (Holland)	1938	J. R. Nicol H. A. Trovik	8
Lionel	Cargo	5,653	Odense	1926	F. W. Kershaw H. Schnitler	10½
Dicto	Cargo	5,263	Gothenburg	1939	D. J. Nicholas	14
Skytteren	Factory Whaler	12,355	Belfast	1901	W. Wilson H. Kristiansen	10
Gudvang	Cargo (Steamship)	1,470	Fredrikstad	1912	H. Nicholson H. C. Seeberg	9½
Charente	Cargo (Steamship)	1,282	Porsgrunn (Norway)	1935	J. W. Donald K. M. Nordby	11

The eleventh vessel, the Rapid II, was allotted to Captain Kirke.

Throughout that summer the Swedish Foreign Office, under continual pressure from the Germans, lost no opportunity to express to the British the great anxiety felt by the Swedish Government at the prospect of further blockade-running operations. The men principally involved on the Swedish side were Christian Günther, the Foreign Minister, and Erik Boheman, Secretary-General at the Swedish Foreign Office. Günther, a former career diplomat, was by no means pro-German, but the British classified him as defeatist and felt that he was committed to steering a course which would avoid any sort of collision with Germany. Boheman, a tall, handsome, capable and witty diplomat with a talent for mimicry, was an Anglophile who exercised a considerable influence on Swedish foreign policy. Although cautious and calculating, he was not timid, and he showed himself capable of resisting German demands. On the German side, the Minister in Stockholm, Prince Wied, was elderly, and certainly not a Nazi; but as well as being dominated by a pro-Hitler wife he was under direct orders from Ribbentrop. In addition, whenever the time came for pressure to be applied, a man named Karl Schnurre, sometimes described as 'Hitler's special negotiator in Sweden', was called in. Schurre, first assistant to Karl Ritter, the man in charge of Germany's economic foreign policy under Foreign Minister Ribbentrop (and also the Ministry's representative at Hitler's Headquarters), was to come increasingly into the picture as time went on.

On 24th July the German Government received a report that about ten Norwegian ships planned to escape in the immediate future. The burden of providing patrol vessels to prevent such a valuable tonnage of shipping from reaching England fell on the forces of the Flag Officer Commanding Baltic, whose task was rendered doubly difficult by the transfer of one of his flotillas to the central Baltic following the attack on Russia. Meanwhile the Germans were reluctant to rely on submitting their case for ownership of the ships to the Swedish courts in case they lost it, and on 28th July they fell back on the specific threat that the newly contracted Gothenburg agreement for 'safe conduct' traffic would be immediately cancelled if a single Norwegian ship actually left Sweden. Boheman objected that the Swedes would have to reckon with British retaliation if ships whose papers were in order were prevented from leaving port; but the Germans simply repeated their threat.

The objective of Swedish diplomacy, in accordance with their wait-and-see policy, became to find some means to delay the ships more or less indefinitely, thus avoiding a clash of wills in which they could not escape involvement. When they found the British obstinately unresponsive and the Germans increasingly menacing, they told Prince Wied that they shared his wish that the ships stay in port, but that to accomplish this the Germans must take legal action. An arrest order, Günther told them, could be issued within twenty-four hours. Still the Germans, fortified by an appreciation from their naval staff that an immediate breakout could be discounted, hung back, and towards the end of August Günther gave them an assurance that the Swedish Navy had the vessels under continual surveillance and that although he believed that three ships were preparing to leave, a surprise escape was simply not possible. Again Günther urged them to use the time available to them to transfer the ships into German control in a legal manner.

Having recruited the British masters, Binney had to arrange for their passage to Sweden by air; and here, by issuing entry permits in ones and twos instead of *en bloc*, the Swedes pursued their delaying tactics. Norwegian sensibilities over the impending replacement of Norwegian masters were satisfied by an arrangement under which each ship had two captains. The British captain, to satisfy the terms of the demise charter, was to be the man in charge while in port and before leaving Swedish territorial waters, while the Norwegian master would take over for the rest of the voyage. Other matters that occupied Binney while he was in London were the naval and air escorts in the North Sea; the enemy forces likely to be employed against the breakout; fresh German mine-laying activities in the Skagerrak and the North Sea; and arrangements for weather broadcasts and the detachment of a naval meteorological expert to Gothenburg. In all Binney was in London for two months, and during his visit he was commanded to present himself at Buckingham Palace for a private investiture. The newspapers, frustrated by the security embargo that had suppressed all news of Rubble, dubbed Binney 'The Mystery Knight'.

*   *   *

On his return to Sweden early in September Binney found that only one or two of the British masters had arrived ahead of him. Fred Fuglesang was completing the work of sifting and signing on Norwegian crew members, Peter Coleridge was acting similarly for the men from Hälsingmo, and Brian Reynolds was busy accumulating guns and explosives and organising and fortifying bridges and wheelhouses against air attack. 'If the Swedish police had been watching us carefully,' admitted Bill Waring, 'they might have seen us carrying heavy suitcases to the ships. But we were careful to keep the weight reasonable.' Fortunately no one was ever stopped or searched. The guns and explosives were hidden on board and the gunners were trained in the saloon of the Dicto. Binney also installed tubes for the firing of rockets, to give the *Luftwaffe* the impression that the ships were more heavily armed than they were.

In this period, three additional members were added to the Gothenburg team. Ivar Blücker, dismissed as expected from his job, joined Binney as marine superintendent and ships' husband, and his unrivalled maritime and harbour experience proved invaluable. On the engineering side, Binney signed on an expert named Lindeberg, whose brief was to take overall responsibility for the care of all ships' engines. And on the meteorological side, confirmation reached Binney that a Lieutenant K. A. Clark, RNVR, would be joining him in October, to take on the task of deciphering and plotting the six daily transmissions that had been laid on by the Admiralty for the especial benefit of Performance. Meanwhile the loading of cargoes was begun; and this, together with the steady influx of British and Norwegian seamen, set tongues wagging throughout Gothenburg, suffusing the dockside with an atmosphere of excitement that was heightened by the knowledge, passed on to the British by Boheman, that the whole question of legal ownership was about to be brought to a head.

On 6th September the British learnt that a representative of the owners of the tanker Rigmor had arrived in Gothenburg with a fresh crew whose orders were to seize the ship by force. The Germans urged the Swedes to assist them in this action, but Günther held firm to the view that the Swedish police could not act without legal authority. Several of the British masters had still not arrived, and on 7th September Binney appointed British subjects as temporary masters so that the terms of the demise charter could be fulfilled. He also ordered the transfer of the Rigmor from the fjord where she was sheltering to Gothenburg waters, preferring the jurisdiction of the Gothenburg courts. Meanwhile Mallet deemed it advisable to inform Boheman that the eleven ships had been under a demise charter to His Britannic Majesty's Government since 1st July 1941, and to remind him that under the established principles of international law they thus enjoyed complete immunity. Boheman's reaction was that this was a matter for the courts, but Mallet urged that the Swedish courts were not competent to try such a case. Taken aback by the revelation of the demise charter, Boheman now frankly admitted that the Swedish Government did not want any blockade-running attempt to be made that year. The situation might be easier, he thought, in a few months' time, when Britain would be stronger and the Germans might be fatally weakened by their campaign in Russia.

Towards the middle of September the German Government began to receive further reports of an imminent breakout, and regular air reconnaissance flights along the Swedish coast, backed up by surface patrols in the Skagerrak, were started. These patrols soon proved their value: on the evening of 14th September a reconnaissance plane spotted the tanker Rigmor steering south inside territorial waters for Gothenburg, and an auxiliary patrol vessel confirmed the sighting next day. One and a half to two flotillas were employed on the surface task, and they were considerably reinforced as the dark periods lengthened.

On 16th September Schnurre arrived in Stockholm from Berlin with a special message for the Swedish Government from Karl Ritter: if the Swedes did not stop Binney's convoy from sailing, they might expect the direst consequences. 'The German Government,' Schurre told Günther, 'could not tolerate that the Swedish Government allow British ships to be loaded by the British with war material in Swedish ports and assist the British in exporting them to England.' The Swedes must hand over all the Norwegian ships to Germany; failure to do so would result in extreme measures, with the complete cessation of all seaborne traffic as the least of the consequences. It was at this stormy meeting that Schnurre learned from Günther 'the surprising and so far unknown information that the Norwegian ships were chartered to England by the Norwegian Shipping Office so that now England had the right of disposal'. The secret had been well kept. Schnurre, although as taken aback as Boheman had been by this disclosure, tried at first to brush it aside, renewing his demands; but Günther repeated that the Swedish Government had no legal right to interfere unless the Swedish courts could be convinced on the question of title. Any claim from the owners to take over the ships, he said, must be proved in court. But although holding to this view, Günther reminded Schnurre that an arrest of the ships could be obtained by the Norwegian owners within a few days, and that the legal process might take as long as six months to resolve. The date of this meeting was 17th September 1941.

Having bullied the Swedes into what they probably regarded as a virtual promise of six months' delay if the case were taken to court, the Germans set the legal campaign in motion. Under the Swedish Execution Act, anyone who claimed to have a better right to property in the possession of somebody else could apply to the Court of First Instance, in this case the local chief magistrate (known as the over-executor), for an embargo to be placed on the property in question;

and on 19th September the Oslo firm of Waages Tankrederi applied through their agent Johan Stenersen, a known collaborator, for *Kvarstad*, a Swedish word meaning sequestration or distraint, or 'staying behind', to prevent the Rigmor from leaving port pending the establishment of their right to the vessel in the Swedish courts. In support of their request for *Kvarstad*, they would be bringing an action to dispossess the captain and secure damages from him for wrongful possession. They would also be bringing an action for damages against the British Government. The over-executor, A. Cervin, granted an interim arrest on the same day.

The revelation about the demise charter brought another bitter attack on the Swedes from the German Government. Clearly, said Ritter, Günther must have known about it all along, yet he had acted deceitfully and allowed this measure to be put into force behind the Germans' back. It could only mean that the Swedes were actively supporting the British plot to get the ships over to England. Schnurre, passing this indictment on, stressed again the drastic consequences for Sweden if a single ship were allowed to escape. Meanwhile, to intensify the pressure, Schnurre summoned the German shipping representative in Oslo to Stockholm and ordered him to get the other Norwegian shipowners to follow Stenersen's example. The owners were duly summoned through the Reichkommissariat to the office of the Shipping Commissar in Oslo and their powers of attorney demanded. Two of the owners refused to sign and were arrested; but under duress the necessary authorities were obtained and the Germans were able to start proceedings against all ten ships.

In long and heated discussions with Schnurre on 20th and 21st September Günther rejected the German allegations of duplicity and insisted that his Government must stand by the decision of the courts. If the papers of the ships were in order, they could not be prevented from leaving Sweden. Sweden had done everything, said Günther, to meet German wishes on military and war economy matters, allowing half a million men and hundreds of thousands of tons of material to pass through Sweden or Swedish territorial waters, to and from Norway and from Norway to Finland. The Swedes knew well enough that they could only preserve a free and independent Sweden on the basis of friendship with Germany. But they would not be drawn into the struggle between Germany and Britain, and their attitude over the ships would have to be kept fully consistent with the conception of neutrality. Schnurre raised the stakes at this point by promising that if Sweden did not give way on this matter, 'German naval forces would not hesitate even to enter Gothenburg to take the law into their own hands regardless of the consequences'. Günther replied that they could not yield to threats; but this firm forecast of a naval 'cut-out' operation on Altmark lines was to make a deep impression on subsequent Swedish policy.

On 22nd September Mallet, in a cable to the Foreign Office, stressed the risk of involving Sweden in war with Germany and urged that the breakout attempt be delayed. Were the supplies so vital, he asked, as to make them worth the risk of opening a new theatre of war and losing Sweden as an observation and intelligence centre? The Foreign Office attitude was that if the Germans wanted to invade Sweden they would do so, breakout or no breakout; and even the Swedes believed that German preoccupations in Russia rendered them safe that autumn. If the Germans succeeded in holding their winter front, however, they might, thought the Swedes, attack them in the spring.

Mallet, on the receiving end of all Günther's and Boheman's pleas and complaints, had still not reconciled himself to Binney's presence in Sweden. Sweden's neutrality, he firmly believed, was an asset the Allies could not afford to endanger. 'The Minister disapproved of all George's activities and gave him little or no help,' writes Andrew Croft. 'George, with his tiny staff, had to mount his operation as best he could, assisted where necessary or practicable by the Service attachés or the press attaché. Under such circumstances, to do anything constructive in Sweden towards the British war effort was frustrating and never easy.'

British policy on the question of litigation was to submit to process, albeit under protest, on the understanding, first, that they were free to raise the plea of immunity, and second, that the Swedish Government would take all steps to respect that immunity; and on 22nd September a declaration from the master of the Rigmor, together with a statement on immunity, was presented to the over-executor. The result was that two days later the over-executor rescinded his previous decision and raised the embargo. The plaintiffs then filed a petition for re-arrest before the Appeal Court (Göta Hovrätt), as they were perfectly entitled to do, urging that immunity did not apply.

While the Appeal Court ruling was awaited, application for the interim arrest of the other nine ships was presented in Gothenburg on the 25th; but on the same day the over-executor rejected it, presumably on the basis of his ruling on the Rigmor. The plaintiffs again lodged an appeal with the Upper Court; but in this case the circumstances were different, since the nine ships had never been placed under arrest. Under Swedish law it was not permissible for the Court of Appeal to grant a re-trial when a claim for interim arrest had been refused by the Lower Court.

In 1938 a commission for the reform of Swedish law procedure had recommended that this loophole be closed, but for three years matters had been left as they stood. Thus because of a technicality the nine ships remained legally free. However, an interim arrest of the tenth, the Rigmor, was granted by the Appeal Court on 30th September pending final judgment.

Since applications for ships' clearance had to be made seven days in advance, the Swedes were again able to assure the Germans that there was no immediate prospect of any ships leaving; meanwhile if the British plea of immunity failed over the Rigmor, the arrest of the other ships could be immediately applied for. But this did not satisfy Ribbentrop, who had information from the Abwehr (German Military Intelligence, operating in Sweden under German military attaché Hans Georg Wagner) that one or more of the ships might attempt a breakout at any time. If a single ship left Gothenburg, Ribbentrop warned the Swedes, it would be regarded as a hostile act.

This, for the Swedes, was the second time the stakes had been raised. An unfriendly act might be condoned. A hostile act might not be.

The Abwehr's information was not ill-founded: Binney was proposing to take the Dicto out alone while she remained free from arrest. She had nearly 6,000 tons of cargo on board, which was approximately one-third of the total commitment for Performance, and with German naval attention focused for the moment on the Gulf of Finland and in the Baltic, a single ship with a speed of fourteen knots might get through. Despite the promptings of Björn Prytz, who was urging the Foreign Office in London to postpone all projected sailings, Anthony Eden, the British Foreign Secretary, agreed on 20th October that Binney's proposal had advantages. The proposal was approved by the Defence Committee, and on 22nd October the Chiefs of Staff concurred. Binney at once notified the Swedish authorities that the Dicto was loaded and ready to leave, which with normal clearance delays meant that the earliest sailing date would be the 29th. Binney was not intending to sail in her himself as he felt that whichever way the attempt went he would be needed in Gothenburg.

The Swedes were now placed in exactly the dilemma they had been trying to avoid; and when it came to the point they were not prepared to face German reproaches that they had facilitated the British escape plan. Bearing in mind the armed intervention that Schnurre had threatened, the Foreign Ministry informed Mallet that after clearing Gothenburg the ships would not be allowed to remain in

Swedish waters (as they had in Rubble), there to await an opportunity to escape. To enforce this ruling, ships would be escorted from the harbour direct to the three-mile limit. Meanwhile the German Legation Counsellor, similarly summoned to the Foreign Ministry, was warned that the time of year had now come when due to darkness and fog an attempt at escape by the Norwegian ships might be counted on. According to German documents, the Counsellor was then told in confidence that the Swedish Government had issued orders which would prevent the use of Swedish territorial waters as 'escape havens'. From all this the Germans rightly concluded that clearance of at least one of the ships had already been applied for, and Flag Officer Baltic himself put to sea in his flagship Meteor, accompanied by the light escort ship Rugard, and patrolled the Swedish coastline north of Gothenburg.

Meanwhile the Appeal Court passed its judgment on the Rigmor: the *ad interim* arrest was to stand, and the case was to be referred back to the over-executor's court for trial. This, however, left the other nine ships still free. Despite delaying tactics employed by the Swedes—the hold-up of the entry permits, the slow-timing of work, and the withholding of rail and port facilities—the loading of two more tankers, the Buccaneer and Storsten, was virtually complete; but the recruitment of crews had been suspended until the result of the legal battle was known.

New applications for the arrest of all the ships other than the Rigmor were made on 25th October, but two days later these applications were again refused by the over-executor on immunity grounds. Since there remained no appeal against this decision, the Dicto, the only ship that was actually ready to go, was free to do so.

With the climax of the struggle about to be reached, the Swedish Government stepped in. Late on 27th October a short *ad hoc* Bill was submitted to the Commitee of the Riksdag in secret session whose effect was that, if an interim arrest was refused in the Lower Court, applicants could go at once to the Appeal Court and ask for an immediate arrest even though the Lower Court had not given its decision on the main issue on which the case was to be tried. The Government justified this alteration in the law by arguing that it was the only certain way of allowing the case to be tried impartially. It was not impartial if the objects of litigation could be removed from the jurisdiction of the courts before legal proceedings ran their full course. The Riksdag took the exceptional step of passing this Bill through all its stages in one day, and the law came into effect on 30th October.

Next day the plaintiffs again applied for the arrest of the nine ships, and once more the over-executor refused; but now the plaintiffs were able to apply to the Appeal Court. Having already given the necessary seven days' notice, however, Binney sought a permit from the naval authorities in Gothenburg for the Dicto to leave; but the officers charged with the duty of issuing permits made themselves scarce. When at length he located them at four o'clock that afternoon, they replied that they must refer the matter to the Swedish Admiralty in Stockholm. The Customs officials at Gothenburg regretted that they could not give clearance meanwhile. At 18.20 permission came through; but by that time the Customs Office had closed.

When the office reopened at nine o'clock next morning, 1st November, Binney again applied for clearance. The officer on duty said he must have confirmation from his head office in Stockholm, which did not open until ten. At 10.30, on being applied to again, the Gothenburg Customs refused clearance on the grounds that they had been advised that the ship had been arrested that morning by the Appeal Court. Whether in fact the arrest order had been made at that time is a matter of some dispute; but late that afternoon an arrest order was slapped on the masts of all ten ships.

On 6th November the over-executor, giving judgment, confirmed the Royal Norwegian Government's legal requisition of the vessels on 18th May 1940 and their nominee's right to dispose of them as they wished. His courage in promulgating this decision, despite the pressures he was subjected to, is worth noting. But it was an academic victory. Under the revised law, an appeal was immediately lodged, and the known constitution of the Court of Appeal gave the defendants little hope. Next day, as expected, the re-arrest of the ships was ordered, the necessary monetary guarantees being made available under pressure by Swedish banks. Orders to prevent the ships from escaping were meanwhile issued to the Swedish Navy.

The Swedish Government's legitimate fear of the Germans had tempted them into what the British saw as a dishonest act, and they protested strongly that the most elementary principles of justice had been flouted, in that the rules of the game had been altered during play. They did not believe that the Swedes would be seriously incommoded by the loss of the Gothenburg traffic, nor that Sweden was in any danger of attack while the Germans were fully engaged in Russia, nor that a German attack on the Performance ships in Swedish waters would be at all likely to involve Sweden in war. On the other hand the cargoes were of great importance to Britain's armaments programme, quite outweighing the political dangers.

Rounding on their representative in Stockholm, the Foreign Office accused Mallet of not being half forceful enough. Mallet had annoyed his masters by accepting the Swedish excuse of 'giving the merchant vessels adequate protection in Swedish waters', and by assessing the hold-ups as no more than 'tiresome'. Most irritating of all, he had favoured 'allowing legislation to run its course'. The Foreign Office were not so ready to acquiesce in Swedish excuses, and they refused to accept that the Swedish Government could not influence Swedish courts. They pointed out that by their recent legislation the Government had in fact altered court procedure during the course of an action before those very courts. They could have exempted such proceedings, but they did not. Thus it was clear that the legislation was passed with the object of altering the rights of the British Government, and the Swedish statement that they could not influence the decision of the courts was a threadbare pretence.

Since both the Germans and the Swedes had got exactly what they wanted, these protests fell on deaf ears, and the objectives of British diplomacy were reduced by early December to getting the decision of the Appeal Court on the plea of immunity, and to preventing the operation, when it could be attempted, from being hopelessly prejudiced by Swedish naval restrictions. Binney wanted to be able to lie-up in territorial waters as before; and he regarded the proposed escort as useful only to advertise the ships' departure to the Germans. But the Swedes, still nervous of Schnurre's threats, would not be moved on either of these counts.

On 15th December came the verdict of the Appeal Court. They unanimously rejected the British plea and decided by a majority of 4–1 that the Oslo owners had a greater right to the ships than the Royal Norwegian Government. This judgment allowed an appeal to the Supreme Court on or before 14th January, and an appeal was immediately lodged; but as the British were now the appellants, the Swedes were able to require them to serve writs on the Norwegian shipowners, some of whom were still in gaol, and this delayed proceedings by a further five weeks. To add the final Gilbertian touch, service of the writs was undertaken on behalf of the British by the Swedish Consul-General in Oslo.

*   *   *

It was now clear from the attitude and conduct of the Swedish authorities that the ships were to be held in port by fair means or foul until the nights became too short to make the operation practicable. After discussion with the British captains, Binney therefore submitted a cut-and-run plan to London which by its very nature was extremely hazardous. Gothenburg harbour being over ten miles from the sea, and the channel through the Rivö and Vinga fjords being intricate and guarded with forts, the first phase of the voyage presented entirely new problems. To make matters worse, in order to hinder an escape plan the ships had been ordered by the port authorities to tie up with their bows facing towards the land, and in the narrow confines of the harbour it would be difficult to manoeuvre them into the stream without tugs. Binney intended to start at dusk and at a week-end, when garrisons and harbour police might be under-manned; but the fog he would need would almost certainly result in the grounding of some of the ships. As for the Swedish Navy, he knew they had instructions to stop him, and the only recourse he could think of was to fly the White Ensign as a *ruse de guerre* in the hope that the Swedes might think twice before firing on it. It was a plan of desperation; and since the British Government had agreed to submit to process, such an act would create an awkward situation for the diplomats, so once again Binney found himself at loggerheads with Mallet.

On the last day of 1941, in a report to the Legation, Binney reminded them that the nights were growing shorter and his crews restive; but he added that in his opinion the operation remained a practicable proposition at least until the end of March. Mallet for his part thought characteristically that it would be ill-advised to anticipate the decision of the Supreme Court, or to act in defiance of it if it went against Britain; but on 24th January Prime Minister Churchill decided that Britain could not afford to wait any longer and that the ships must sail at the first opportunity. Since the cargoes were of such a key nature, and since the Swedes could do little else either to help or to hinder the Allied cause, no one in the Cabinet doubted that this was the right decision. Towards the end of January the Foreign Office and other interested parties gave Binney complete discretion on the timing of the attempt, whether the ships were under arrest or not. Virtually the whole of the 19,000 tons of materials ordered by Britain and the Dominions had been loaded, plus a further 5,500 tons which the Russians had been unable to ship through the Gulf of Finland and which had lain idle in Swedish warehouses for many months. The principal cargo carriers were the Dicto and the B.P. Newton, over 5,000 tons each, followed by the Lionel (which carried the bulk of the Russian cargo) and the Buccaneer, both over 4,000 tons. But all the ships were carrying important cargoes.

Under Swedish law no vessel could remain under arrest for more than ninety days unless in the meanwhile an action had been brought for damages in support of the arrest; and this period, as Binney well knew, was due to expire on 5th February. The Germans, however, had not overlooked this provision, and they made frantic but unsuccessful efforts to serve writs on Christopher Warner, head of the Northern Department of the Foreign Office in London, and on Victor Mallet in Stockholm. Meanwhile the Foreign Office were assembling the arguments they intended to use to justify the sailing of the ships while the case was still *sub judice*. As long as there had seemed a possibility that the Swedish courts would treat the issue of immunity with proper seriousness and urgency, they had been ready to await their verdict. Only when the courts decided that service of notices of appeal must be made personally on shipowners in Norway, coming at the end of a succession of other procedural delays, making it obvious that a decision could not be reached within a reasonable time, had the British Government reluctantly decided to compel the immunity plea to be treated with proper respect by ordering the ships to sail. At the same time Mallet was instructed to deliver a protest warning the Swedes that the British Government could not stand by and see their plea treated as it had been. Britain was in a life and death struggle and the cargoes were of vital importance to her war effort. The operation could only be undertaken in the depth of winter. The complacent attitude of the Swedes to the German delaying tactics left the British with only one course open to them.

This protest infuriated Boheman. 'I have never seen him so angry,' wrote Mallet. The British had no conception of Sweden's appalling political difficulties. The moment the ships left, the Gothenburg traffic would be stopped and Sweden would be in a worse position to defend herself than ever. If war came to Sweden, added Boheman bitterly, they could expect no help from His Britannic Majesty's Government, 'who had invariably been unable to save small nations from aggression'. He demanded to know why, if the cargoes were needed so badly, ships couldn't be sent over with Royal Navy protection to collect them. No—Britain was afraid of the risk; but she was prepared to expose Sweden to a far graver risk. The question of immunity was in any case a highly complex one, and Boheman hotly refuted the charge that there had been undue delay. The German Government, he said, were furious that the case had been left to the courts, and believed for their part that the whole strategy was a ruse to deliver the ships eventually to the British.

At the end of January the Swedish lawyers acting for Britain advised Binney that with the writs still unserved the ships would be free to sail any time after 5th February, although they would be expected to await the judgment of the Supreme Court. Binney now had to face the decision that had been left to his discretion; and he decided that such a desperate undertaking, as he conceived it to be, should only be attempted as a last resort. Only if time ran out, or the final judgment went against Britain, would he quote the ninety-day rule and go. But as it happened, towards the end of January a spell of intensely cold weather froze Gothenburg harbour solid, the fjords giving access to the sea became impassable without the help of ice-breakers, and this continued right through February and into March. 'There has never been so much ice in history in Gothenburg harbour as during the last two months,' Mallet told Warner, 'and in no circumstances could the ships have gone out without the assistance of Swedish ice-breakers.' Thus all temptation to cut and run was removed.

Farther afield the British were suffering the nadir of their fortunes in the Far East and elsewhere, and these catastrophes did not go unnoticed in Sweden. When the most distinguished Swedish lawyer acting for Britain, Axel Forssman, died after a short illness, it seemed to Binney that everything was conspiring against him.

There was trouble, too, aboard the ships, partly because of the long exposure to suborning and espionage. Although the ships were guarded by armed Swedish police, the crews were free to come and go, and this caused endless security problems. The idle and aimless life in the camp at Hälsingmo had not improved morale or discipline among the British, and although the Norwegians had proved themselves by escaping from Norway and volunteering to serve their country, they had money to spend and time on their hands, and inevitably a few collaborators were infiltrated amongst them. Three ships, the whaler Skytteren, the cargo ship Lionel, and the tanker Rigmor, were damaged by acts of sabotage, and it became necessary to appoint Norwegians of known integrity and loyalty to undertake Intelligence duties on each ship. These men reported regularly to one of the vice-consuls in Gothenburg, David Somerville, who had spent most of his life in Norway, and the disaffected were singled out and discarded.

Binney was under pressure to carry as supernumeraries several hundred more of the Norwegians who were awaiting passage to England; but under the terms of the charter-party, which specified that the ships were solely 'for the use of His Britanic Majesty's Government', the transport of these men had to be undertaken with caution, and Binney eventually limited the numbers to seventy. There were also about twenty authorised stowaways. The ordinary crew-members were signed on Norwegian as well as British engagement papers so that in the event of capture they would be entitled to the same treatment as the other Allied seamen, while the supernumeraries were engaged under the Norwegian mobilisation law of 9th April 1940 and were paid a nominal wage, entitling them to be treated as normal prisoners of war. Every member of the expedition was issued with a Swedish rubber life-saving suit.

The biggest anxiety so far as the ships were concerned was fuel-oil. Had the ships been allowed to sail in November or December there would have been enough and to spare, but as week followed week, and as the weather grew colder and colder, most of the fuel reserve was consumed for heating and light. Skytteren, for example, used four to five tons of oil per day when lying alongside, and the harbour authorities would not allow the ships to take electric power from the shore. One of the methods used to reduce the consumption of oil was to put one of the two coal-burners alongside one of the diesels so that the coal-burner supplied the steam and power for both. Thus Gudvang served Skytteren, and Charente served Buccaneer. But despite these and other economy measures, by mid-March Binney was seriously considering ways of scooping up the sludge in Skytteren's tanks and cleaning it in order to give her enough fuel for the voyage. In this ice-bound period the ships would have become completely immobilised had not Mitcheson, through his contacts as commercial counsellor at the Legation, provided a strictly unauthorised injection of 500 tons at a critical time.

*   *   *

On 17th March, six months to the day after the hint dropped by Günther to Schnurre of the likely duration of litigation—an extraordinary coincidence if nothing more—the Supreme Court published its judgment. It entirely confirmed the British in their plea of immunity. 'It follows,' concluded the judgment, 'that arrest is now lifted.' The ships were free to go.

Just in case the British should act on this ruling immediately, however, the Swedes gave the Germans prior warning and Flag Officer Baltic was informed by Berlin the day before. Karl Ritter reacted at once by stressing that if the Swedes allowed the ships to escape it would be regarded as an unfriendly act; but this was not so menacing a tone as that adopted six months earlier, when 'hostile act' and 'drastic consequences' had been the phrases used. Günther, satisfied with the success of his policy, reminded Prince Wied that it was only the intervention of the Swedish Government which had made it possible for the ships to be arrested at all, leading to the best possible result for Germany, namely the immobilisation of the ships throughout the period when conditions had been best for escape.

The Germans had kept a reduced watch along the Swedish coast as long as icing conditions allowed; but as the ships in Gothenburg harbour became frozen in, the watch had not been maintained in such strength, and several patrol vessels had been loaned to Flag Officer North Sea. Thus the release of the *Kvarstad* ships found Flag Officer Baltic with a much reduced fleet available for patrols. The vessels he had loaned to Flag Officer North Sea were immediately recalled, but for a few days, at least, the line would be thinly held.

The area of stationary high pressure that had settled over northern Scandinavia in early January, however, bringing with it the longest and severest winter for over half a century, remained unchanged, and the cold clear days continued. Binney had forecast that the operation would remain practicable at least until the end of March; but there was precious little margin left. And while he waited, and the Germans repositioned their forces, the success of the operation, and the wisdom of mounting it, were being assailed on all sides. Admiral Harald Akermark, commanding the Västkustens Marindistrikt, ordered that the ships must give four hours' notice of departure and sail under naval escort; his warships would need that notice to get into position along the coastline. Their arrival there, of course, could not fail to alert the German patrols. The *Kvarstad* ships would not be allowed to use any route other than the Vinga route or the passage at Stora Oset; and even more restrictive, they would not be permitted to stop or anchor in Swedish waters except for the embarking and disembarking of pilots and naval officials.

It had always been a sore point with the Germans that in allowing the Rubble ships to lie up in Brofjord the Swedes had facilitated their escape; and there was no doubt that this privilege had been fundamental to Rubble's success. The threat of a cut-out operation had inhibited the Swedes from granting such a concession this time; but Binney still looked for some worthwhile compromise. On 18th March he wrote to William Kjellberg to ask him to secure permission from the Swedish authorities to use an anchorage which offered a reasonable chance of leaving coastal waters quickly and without being observed. 'I recognise,' wrote Binney, 'that owing to the ice conditions and owing to the possibility of the Germans attempting to attack our ships within Swedish territorial waters the problem of finding a suitable anchorage is not easy. I suggest that you secure permission for us to lie in the Dana Fjord and Vinga Sundet which give easy access to the sea in thick weather.' Binney was trying to make the best of the naval escort by using it to protect the passage of the ships as far as Vinga, where he would drop the pilots and naval officials and then slip into Dana Fjord, two miles east of the Vinga Light, making the final breakout from there. Henry Denham followed this up by planting the excuse to the Swedish Foreign Office that the ships might in any case be forced to anchor if they met thick weather; but the reply was that this would not be allowed. Meanwhile the Swedes tipped off the Germans that the ships would not leave individually but in convoy under Swedish naval escort. Binney had thought about sending the ships off in twos and threes, but the first ship to emerge might alert the German patrols, its destruction would discourage the others, and they had more chance of dissipating the German defensive effort, he felt, if they sailed in strength.

Binney still remained hopeful. Following a thaw there was invariably a period of fog and thick weather, and this might compensate for the shorter hours of darkness. But even more than in Rubble, thick weather at the outset was going to be mandatory. On 23rd March Lieutenant Clark announced the approach of a depression which looked like moving up from the Atlantic, and the 'Alert' was signalled to London. Boat drills were held on the decks, lifeboats were swung out on their davits, mechanical and other equipment was checked, and radios were tested as far as the orders that forbade transmission allowed. On the same day, final instructions were received from Admiral Akermark; and although they remained unpleasantly restrictive, and although entering inner territorial waters, and stopping or anchoring in outer territorial waters, was still expressly forbidden, ships could follow outer territorial waters and even return to them provided they kept under way.

Next day back came the cold clear weather. And now Boheman, sensing that the British had made up their minds, had one more go at Mallet, who cabled the Foreign Office with a final reminder of Sweden's importance as an anti-Nazi and pro-Allied country ready to defend herself if attacked. This, and her value as a centre of information, said Mallet, had led Britain to a policy of allowing her to import goods to sustain her industry. If Britain went ahead with Performance, the Gothenburg traffic would certainly be stopped. Was the operation really so vital? At the same time Boheman, stressing that the Swedes had good reason to believe that the Germans might at some stage attack them, appealed direct to the United States to use their influence to stop the operation.

The British Chiefs of Staff had already expressed the view that a German attack on Sweden at that time was improbable, and that prolonged resistance to such an attack if it came was in any case unlikely, while the closure of the Gothenburg traffic would not affect the issue either way. On 25th March the Foreign Office, after briefing Lord Halifax, now British Ambassador in Washington, on the background, informed the United States of the operation. The ships, they told Halifax, carried cargoes the early arrival of which was of immense importance to the war effort both in Britain and in the United States. The Germans had done everything possible to prevent the operation from taking place. The Swedish Government had been anxious all along to delay the operation until the weather and the shorter nights made it impracticable. His Majesty's Government had decided, after consideration by the Chiefs of Staff, that the value of the cargoes to the war effort outweighed the possible consequences of any reprisal measure the Germans might take.

Sumner Welles, American Under-Secretary of State, made two points to Halifax: first, whatever the importance of the cargoes, the amounts carried were limited, and the possible consequences therefore seemed disproportionate; second, if the Gothenburg traffic were closed, the Swedish armed forces would be immobilised, with consequent damage to morale, while the prospect of Sweden playing a useful role in the war at a later stage would be destroyed. Halifax told Welles he had no doubt that these considerations had been fully weighed and that the action would not have been decided upon unless the British Government were satisfied that the scale was clearly tipped on the other side. This did not wholly assuage American anxiety; but on 27th March the Under-Secretary of State phoned Halifax and said his Government had decided to adopt the role of Pontius Pilate. They were accordingly telling the Swedish Government that the matter was one principally concerning the United Kingdom Government and that they could not take it upon themselves to dissuade that Government from the course on which it was set.

*   *   *

After their release from arrest the Performance ships had been allowed to berth towards the outer limits of Gothenburg harbour, some four miles from the centre of the city, where they were less under observation except from the Swedish naval base at Nya Varvet, which lay directly opposite. Soon afterwards, however, an armed German collier, the Ingrid Trabe, entered the harbour and was allowed to moor opposite the Skytteren and the B.P. Newton—the two biggest ships. The Swedes now learned that this ship's purpose was to follow the Performance vessels out, monitoring their position and radioing the German patrols that were standing by in Norwegian and Danish waters. This, the Swedes decided, was not consistent with their conception of neutrality and might lead to just the sort of incident they were determined to prevent. They therefore ordered the Ingrid Trabe to move out. The German naval attaché, indoctrinated almost daily by Berlin with different notions of what constituted Swedish neutrality, protested strongly; but the Swedes were insistent. At the same time they informed the British that they would be putting naval ratings on board all the Norwegian ships immediately prior to their departure, and that they would remain on board for the first half-hour or so of the voyage. This drew British protests in turn; but when Boheman explained that similar measures were being taken with all German ships lying in Gothenburg, to ensure that they didn't use their radios and didn't create an incident, the British were mollified.

General surveillance of the Norwegian ships by Nazi agents had been organised throughout by the Abwehr under Hans Georg Wagner, and this surveillance now became of prime importance. Three men were involved, all ex-members of the sss (Swedish Socialist Movement). The first, John Eichborn, aged 61, had originally worked alone, carrying out his surveillance on foot; but later he teamed up with a friend who had been a film photographer, and by renting a flat that commanded an excellent view of the harbour they reduced the dangers of being apprehended and charged under Swedish Penal Law. The 'third man' of the team was a Gothenburg Customs official; and on 25th March this man learnt that the ships' documents had been deposited and that the ships might sail at any moment. Eichborn immediately passed this information through a contact to Wagner, and the three men increased their vigilance.

Throughout this period Binney continued to seek concessions from the Swedes that might increase his chances of achieving surprise; but nearly every battle went against him, the Swedes insisting on the full implementation of the procedures they had laid down. The advance depositing of documents, for instance, which had alerted the pro-Nazi Customs official, had been waived for Rubble. The only concession Binney was granted—and this was Kjellberg's doing—was to be allowed to leave at sundown. The port was normally closed from dusk to dawn.

On Monday 30th March Binney held a captains' conference in the British Consulate to give the British captains their sailing instructions; from this conference the Norwegian captains were excluded. As with the Rubble operation, the Norwegian captains as a body were living ashore with their families, and they spent very little time on their ships. Told some weeks beforehand that they might be required to sail at any time, that under no circumstances were they to reveal any information to their families, and that from now on they would be required to sleep on board, they toed the line for a few days, but with the harbour iced-up they not unnaturally reverted to their old habits. These men had all accepted the division of responsibility with their British counterparts; but in port they were more of a liability than an asset to Binney, and no doubt they realised this and resented it, especially as the morale of the crews was still being largely sustained by the Norwegians. But Binney feared that one or two of the captains might be unable to resist the temptation to get in touch with their families, and he therefore felt obliged to exclude them. They were given all essential information, but the actual sailing instructions were to be retained by the British captains until after the ships had left Gothenburg.

The plan for the operation was that courses to steer through the Skagerrak were to be left to the discretion of individual captains, the first mandatory point to be reached—Point 'A', at 57.30 North, 07.00 East—being thirty miles south of The Naze. Course would then be shaped west-south-west through a believed gap in the new German minefields, taking in four more mandatory positions before reaching the surface rendezvous of 56.00 North, 03.00 East. This point was roughly equidistant from the Firth of Forth, where the escort was to sail from, and Lindesnes (The Naze). By this time the ships would be steering more or less due west for the Firth of Forth, having encompassed more than 400 miles of their 600-mile journey. Because of heavy naval commitments elsewhere, among them a Murmansk convoy, the escort was restricted this time to six destroyers, three from the hard-pressed forces of C-in-C Rosyth and three from the Home Fleet.

Binney told the British captains that the weather was shaping favourably and that he hoped to sail the following evening. He warned them, as he had warned them before, that the most dangerous part of the voyage would be the first hour or two after leaving the Swedish coast. He read them Akermark's orders, but reminded them that evasion remained the essence of the plan. Provided it was foggy when they reached the Vinga lighthouse, three of the ships, B.P. Newton, Charente and Buccaneer, keeping some distance apart, were to steer south for forty minutes inside territorial waters as if bound for Malmö before heading out to sea on their proper escape course. The other seven ships were all to turn north, three of them, Dicto, Rigmor and Storsten, covering twenty miles to a point abeam of Marstrand, and the other four, Skytteren, Lionel, Lind and Gudvang, continuing a further fifteen miles until abreast of Hallö Island, before leaving territorial waters for the open sea. Sailing times from Gothenburg would be staggered so that each ship left individually. In this way the ships would achieve a degree of dispersal that in favourable weather might achieve its object. Everything was to be ready for sailing the following evening, and there was to be no further communication with the shore.

The Swedish West Coast

PERFORMANCE

At a Chiefs of Staff meeting in London on Tuesday 31st March, attended by the three Service chiefs, Brooke, Pound and Portal, and Churchill's chief staff officer Ismay, Pound told the meeting that he had mentioned the operation to Churchill the previous evening and they had discussed the chances of success. Pound had recommended that the operation be allowed to proceed, and Churchill had agreed. Final discretion, however, was still left with Binney, and he was instructed to that effect.

Binney called a meeting aboard the flagship Dicto at four o'clock that afternoon, 31st March. It was the ultimate day of his appreciation of what was likely to be practicable, and he fervently hoped the weather would compensate for the shorter hours of darkness. Present at the meeting, in addition to the ten British captains—the Norwegians were again excluded—were Brian Reynolds as Binney's deputy, Bill Waring, and Lieutenant Clark. Clark explained the meteorological prospects and indicated the approximate position of the fog area and its trend. He estimated that thick weather was likely to set in within a span of six hours either side of four o'clock the following morning. As far as could be judged from the information available, prospects for an extensive fog area were good; but further data were expected to come in at seven o'clock that evening. It would not be dark until eight o'clock.

Binney reminded the captains that there was no question of leaving the coast until the fog materialised; but he warned them that if they put to sea that night they could not expect aircraft support at dawn as they would still be well short of Point 'A'. Unanimously the captains elected to leave Gothenburg at eight o'clock that evening and proceed along the Swedish coast inside territorial waters until the fog arrived. They faced the certainty of a full moon, but that would be obscured if the weather developed as anticipated. Each captain pronounced himself fully satisfied with his equipment and crew and with his arrangements for scuttling and defence. Finally Binney emphasised that from Vinga lighthouse each captain must use his individual discretion in conjunction with his Norwegian counterpart, within the framework of the general plan. They were in no sense part of a convoy, but must act as independent units striving by individual evasion tactics to reach a British port.

While the captains returned to their ships, Binney went ashore to originate the departure signal that would call out the naval and air escorts. But at 21.30, when he returned to the Dicto, a shock was awaiting him. Clark had plotted the latest meteorological observations and they showed that a clearance or cold front was moving rapidly in over the British Isles from the west. He was grappling with the problem of estimating how long the bad weather would last in the light of the approach of this front. His first reaction was to advise the captains to sail as soon as possible; but on reflection he felt unable to shoulder such a responsibility. With the whole weather canvas fraying at the edges, he felt he must leave it to Binney.

'When will the next report be available?' asked Binney.

'Between eleven o'clock and midnight.'

Binney decided to sail as arranged and make for the coast. There, if he deemed it advisable, he would cancel the attempt by radio.

*   *   *

In the fortnight since the warning had reached the Flag Officer Baltic from Berlin, he had had time to recover and reposition enough patrol vessels to form an adequate blockade line. Without the reserves that would enable him to relieve standing patrols, he could not hope to hold the line indefinitely; but the assumption was that the attempt, if it was to be made at all, must be made soon. Thus on the night planned for the breakout, the line was held in depth.

First and foremost was a concentration of armed auxiliary patrol vessels, mostly converted Danish trawlers, based at Aalborg and Frederikshavn on the Danish coast and positioned at sea off the Skaw. These auxiliaries, eleven in number, belonged partly to the 16th Patrol Vessel Flotilla and partly to a training flotilla, and they were poised to pounce on the ships as soon as they emerged from the narrow Gothenburg channel. Any ships that broke through this first line of defence would meet further opposition after rounding the Skaw, where a naval escort vessel was lying in wait.

Those ships which were lucky enough to dodge these first and second lines of defence might continue westwards unmolested for some hours. But the *Luftwaffe* would be out in strength in the Skagerrak from its bases in southern Norway; and the exit from the Skagerrak was blocked by four more auxiliaries, two patrolling to the north of Hantsholm, on the Danish side, and two off the barrage gap near Kristiansand South. In addition, two more escort vessels, Schiff 7 and Schiff 47, were *en route* west from the Skaw area to provide reinforcement and relief.

Even this was not the last of the blockade line. Three fast torpedo-boats, of the 3rd Flotilla, and three S-boats, of the 6th Flotilla, were lying at three hours' notice in Stavanger, ready to chase and destroy any ship that got through, and three U-boats were in position off the south-west coast of Norway, west of the Skagerrak.

British Intelligence sources were estimating that some forty surface vessels and sixty aircraft might be employed against Binney's blockade-runners, and their estimates were not greatly exaggerated. Nevertheless the Germans still feared that the ships might slip through their fingers in bad weather, and they pressed the Swedes to give them warning when clearance was requested. This the Swedes refused.

*   *   *

By the time the first ship, the Charente, was due to leave the harbour, the twilight had gone, the night was clear, and the moon threw a ghostly gleam across the harbour entrance, so that the ships loomed like wraiths out of the shadows. Binney had planned that the ships should sail at five-minute intervals, those ships which were moored nearest the city leaving last in the hope of postponing detection of the general exodus. But there was still some ice in and around the quays, and although Charente got away on time, most of the other ships experienced difficulty in weighing their anchors and manoeuvring through the ice into the stream. Thus the last ship to leave, the B.P. Newton, left her mooring not at 20.35 but at 23.15. Since the night was still clear, however, the delay was of little account. Indeed it may well have been fortuitous, since Eichborn and his associates, for all their diurnal vigilance, missed the surprise night departure altogether.

On board the escaping ships, spirits were high at the prospect of action. This was the day they had all looked forward to for many months, and their misgivings were swamped by an irrational sense of optimism, bolstered by a special Order of the Day (p. 108) that Binney distributed to all the ships. Yet few had any illusions about what lay ahead. The alternatives seemed clear cut: death from drowning on the one hand, a triumphant break-through to freedom on the other. They rated their chances as no better than even.

One by one the ships followed Charente down the narrow fjord, until the lights of Gothenburg became twinkling and indistinct, and the scattered islands at the mouth of the fjord heaved like great porpoises out of the gloom. In the centre of the procession, where communication with the other ships would be easiest, was George Binney in the Dicto. Accompanying him as far as Vinga was his old friend Ivar Blücker, whose mission was to transmit back to Bill Waring the news of the ships' final departure.

The Dicto reached Vinga just before 23.30. The ship that had left immediately before her, the Storsten, was anchored nearby repairing a mechanical defect, but in obedience to sailing instructions Captain Nicholas did not stop to offer assistance, simply slowing down to drop the pilot, the Swedish naval ratings, and Captain Blücker. The last

To the Masters, Officers, Crews
and other volunteers aboard:—

   M/T "BUCCANEER"   M/T "LIND"   M/T "RIGMOR"
   S/S "CHARENTE"   M/S "LIONEL"   S/S "SKYTTEREN"
   M/S "DICTO"   M/T "B.P. NEWTON" M/T "STORSTEN"
   S/S "GUDVANG"

                         from Sir George Binney.

O R D E R   O F   T H E   D A Y.

     Today at long last we are going to England determined, come
what may, to render a staunch account of our voyage, as befits
Norwegian and British seamen. Indeed we run a risk, but what of
it? If we succeed, these splendid ships will serve the allied
cause and with their cargoes we shall aid the task of war supplies.

     To sink our ships and cargoes rather than to see them
captured by the enemy is of course our Duty, and on your behalf I
have taken such measures as you would wish.

     Should we encounter misfortune at sea, remember that in
our homes and among our countrymen it will be said with simple
truth that we have done our best for the honour and freedom of
Norway and Britain; but I, for one, have never held with this
blockade and look once more to our success, believing that before two
days have passed your laughter will resound within a British port.

     So let us Merchant Seamen — 400 strong — shape a westerly
course in good heart counting it an excellent privilege that we
have been chosen by Providence to man these ships in the immortal
cause of Freedom. God speed our ships upon this venture.

  Long live King George.   Long live King Haakon.

                  M/S "DICTO"

                  Gothenburg, ...

link with Sweden was severed, and the Dicto headed westwards within the three-mile limit.

Captains Reeve and Bull-Nielsen, on the Storsten, were meanwhile getting an early indication of what to expect from the Swedish Navy. As soon as they dropped anchor, a Swedish warship appeared and lowered a boat, and five men came on board. 'You have no permission to anchor in Swedish waters,' Reeve was reminded. 'If you don't proceed to sea forthwith you'll be brought back to Gothenburg and interned for the rest of the war.' Reeve did all he could to play for time, the defect was cleared, and Storsten resumed her course; but the threat of internment was something new.

Once clear of the coast all the ships turned northwards, parallel with the shore; the instructions to three of them to steer south for forty minutes had depended on the existence of fog. With her greater speed Dicto soon began to overtake the other three ships which had left before her—the Charente, the Buccaneer, and the Lionel. These ships were accompanied by a Swedish warship, but the Dicto somehow escaped a close escort. Each of them, Binney noticed, was darkened from keel to masthead and was maintaining a separation of at least a mile. The night was still clear and the moon still high, though heavy clouds were scudding across the sky. From the second of the three ships, the Buccaneer, the contours of the Charente and the Lionel were easily visible.

To Binney it seemed that things were going reasonably well. Then, off Marstrand, the Dicto began to run into heavy drift ice which forced her seawards. Binney's intention had been to cling to the coast for this part of the voyage, where they would be less conspicuous and where the dead water to starboard would protect them from attack from that side; but now, as Captain Nicholas pushed out to the edge of the three-mile limit and beyond, the Dicto was silhouetted against the ice.

The lights of a cluster of fishing boats glimmered to seaward, and there was still no sign of the promised fog. Yet Clark pointed out that bad weather seemed imminent. The cirrostratus had thickened and lowered to ten-tenths altostratus, and the glass was still falling. Would it be better, mused Binney, to start heading at once for the bad weather that was known to be forming at the western end of the Skagerrak, rather than go on wasting precious time hugging the coast? At 02.00, off the Hallö Islands, he was discussing his options with Nicholas and Clark when he heard a shot from the port quarter. Hurrying to the wing of the bridge, the three men peered into the darkness astern and faintly discerned the smudged outline of a large trawler, darkened like themselves, and obviously armed. She fired again, and this time they saw the gun flashes. Seconds later, gouts of silver water rose harmlessly around them as the shells fell wide.

'Action Stations!'

Captain Nicholas altered course 90 degrees to starboard to take the Dicto back into the coastal ice. The trawler, still with her lights out, followed them inshore. But here the ice was two feet thick, and soon the trawler sheered off, continuing to shadow them from beyond the ice fringe. Almost simultaneously, Binney saw two more gun flashes out to sea and heard the reverberation of the explosions. But no other ship was apparently being attacked, and he assumed that the Germans were either alerting each other or firing the shots as a deterrent.

Interception, as it seemed to Binney, was going to be even swifter and more summary than he had feared. All they could do on the Dicto was grind on northwards through the ice as it splintered and scraped against the hull. Soon the carpenter reported that the ship was taking water and that some of the cargo had been damaged in No. 1 hold; but with the trawler still lurking to seaward, they could do nothing but reduce speed and hope for worsening weather.

For the first few hours after midnight the ten ships went on cruising at half-speed off the coast, some working their way steadily northwards, others steering north and south alternately, guided by the lighthouses on the prominences of Paternoster and Måsekär. But the glass was still falling, the wind had gone round north of east, and at 04.15 it started to snow. Binney was optimistic, but Clark was doubtful if the snow extended beyond the coastal belt. It certainly wasn't heavy or substantial enough, decided Binney, to justify facing the Skagerrak patrols in daylight. The next Admiralty forecast was due between seven and eight o'clock, and he resolved to lie doggo in the lee of the islands to the north of the Hallö Light, beyond Lysekil, and wait for the forecast.

Several of the captains, lacking the meteorological advice available to Binney, took a more sanguine view of the snowstorms, and soon after six o'clock, with visibility down to half a mile in fog patches, six of them, urged on by their crews, took the plunge quite independently and headed out into international waters to a chorus of cheers from the men. But their joy was short-lived. Rigmor, the second largest of the tankers, followed by Lind, the smallest, at a distance of two miles, ran within ten minutes into a clear patch, and there straight ahead was a German patrol boat. Fears expressed beforehand that the division of responsibility between British and Norwegian might impede decisive action proved unfounded as Captains Gilling and Monsen of the Rigmor moved with one accord to turn round and race back into territorial waters at full speed. There was a similar identity of view on the Lind.

At 06.30, just before regaining territorial waters, the Rigmor met the Skytteren. 'We've been attacked by a German ship,' called Captain Gilling by megaphone, 'and we're returning to Swedish waters. You should do the same.'

Captain Wilson, of the Skytteren, knew at once that he was in serious trouble. 'The ship's not steering, sir,' the second officer had reported five minutes earlier, 'the wheel's gone dead. No pressure in the telemotor.' And then had come the explanation, from the chief engineer, an old Tynesider named Thompson. 'Some bloody quisling's gone and shoved a hammer through a telemotor pipe.' Fixing a new pipe would not take long—but could it be done in time?

A few miles to the south, the tankers Storsten and Buccaneer, together with the Lionel, had been ordered out of territorial waters by their Swedish escort. They had got six miles clear of the limit when two of them, the Buccaneer and the Lionel, found themselves bearing down on another armed German trawler, from the bridge of which a signal lamp was flashing the imperious command 'K', meaning stop speed immediately. Captains Reeve and Bull-Nielsen, on the bridge of the Storsten, saw nothing of either of these patrol boats, however, and they seized their chance and broke through.

The captains of Buccaneer and Lionel—Smail and Reksten, and Kershaw and Schnitler—were also of one mind : they put course directly about and tried to regain Swedish waters. The trawler began firing at first on the Lionel. Then, seeing that the Lionel was making the better speed, it transferred its interest to the Buccaneer, enabling the Lionel to escape. As Kershaw withdrew he signalled a warning to the tanker B.P. Newton, which was now heading seawards at full speed. The tanker, too, had found that territorial waters were not the sure haven expected: two Swedish destroyers had fired rockets to the westward as she passed between them to indicate the direction she was to take, and soon afterwards she was hailed by two Swedish patrol vessels. 'Newton ahoy! Proceed to sea !' shouted the captain of one of them. 'I have orders to force you out of territorial waters.' This was translated for Captain Calvert by Captain Blindheim; but the two men decided to ignore the order. Five minutes later, however, when it started to snow, they decided to take their chance. The time was then 06.51. Now, ignoring the signals of the Lionel, they continued boldly on their course.

On the Buccaneer, the British master, Captain G. D. Smail, was one of the four Ellerman's Wilson Line masters flown out from

Britain. His immediate decision, when he saw there was no escape from the German patrol vessel, was to blow up his ship. He signalled stop engines to the engine room, then gave the order to take to the boats. But the Germans anticipated this and in an effort to prevent it started firing across the boat deck, first with machine-guns and then with cannon; by hindering the work of launching the boats they hoped to capture the ship intact. But Smail's sailing orders were clear: he must prevent his ship from falling into enemy hands at all costs. The explosive contacts were duly made and several violent detonations followed, blowing the skylights over the engine room aloft and choking the ship with storms of smoke and dust.

Despite all this havoc no one was hurt. And the Germans, seeing that the scuttling could not be prevented, ceased firing and allowed the evacuation to proceed without further disturbance. They could not therefore be blamed for the accidents which followed. During the lowering of the motor-boat the fore tackle sped through and the boat was left hanging by the aft tackle. The third mate, Roar Hom Olsen, who was in this boat, had his rubber life-jacket torn to shreds and was badly hurt. After a struggle the boat was righted and the evacuation went on. But when Captain Smail, the last man to leave the ship, was about to step into one of the lifeboats, he missed his hold on the davits, probably because of his cumbersome rubber suit and mittens, and fell backwards into the sea. As he fell his head struck the gunwale of the lifeboat, and although he was quickly hauled aboard he had broken his neck and he died soon afterwards, the first fatal casualty on Operation Performance.

On the Skytteren, Captain Wilson had given the order for slow ahead and was trying to swing round to landward on hand steering. But he found he could no longer manoeuvre his ship. Meanwhile the German guard ship was closing in rapidly astern, transmitting a continuous stream of stop signals by morse lamp, just as it had done to Rigmor and Lind. Believing that he must be near the protection of Swedish waters, if not already within it, Captain Wilson held his course as best he could. At this the trawler came up abreast of him and fired a warning shot which passed under the bridge and straight through the boatswain's cabin.

With no hope of escape, Captain Wilson turned as if to ram the trawler, which veered sharply to port. He rang down 'Finished with engines', then called out to chief engineer Thompson: 'Get all your crowd up. We're abandoning ship.'

'Stop! Do not use your radio. Am sending a boarding party.' As the trawler's Aldis lamp went on blinking its message, Captain Wilson moved to the scuttling switches. With the enemy vessel in close

Captain Henry Denham, R N

Captain Ivar Blücker

Alva Henriksson

William Kjellberg

Victor Mallet with Christian Günther, 12 May, 1945

Erik Boheman   Bill Waring

attendance there was no time for any further alerting of the crew. He made contact with the charges, and for the second time within a few minutes a series of violent explosions reverberated along the Swedish coastline.

The hull of the old Skytteren lifted visibly, then lurched drunkenly, finally heeling over in a marked list to port. As men slid helplessly across the decks it seemed as though she must capsize. Then the weight of water rushing into the hull began to stabilise her, and she righted herself a little. One of the Finland volunteers, Bill Hateley, searching the engine and boiler rooms for casualties, pulled one of the stokers clear of the rising tide of oil and water only to find that he was already dead. Several other men had been frightfully burned, but stoker Johannessen was the only fatal casualty.

It was impossible to keep to the rehearsed lifeboat plan, and only four boats could be lowered to the water. Some men jumped in as the boats descended, others leapt straight into the sea. No one had time to rescue personal possessions or clothes, some had their rubber suits on, some did not.

Of the four lifeboats, the one with Captain Wilson in it was taken in tow at once by the German trawler. A second lifeboat lay off to starboard to pick up stragglers and wounded; but the occupants of the other two boats began to row purposefully towards the ice edge. For several of them, refugees from Norway who were wanted by the Gestapo, escape from the fate of being taken prisoner was more than ordinarily important. When the men in the rescue lifeboat had picked everyone up it was too late for them to escape, but the oarsmen at once rowed northwards to distract the Germans from going after the other two. After fifteen minutes this boat was also taken in tow by the trawler; but by that time the other two boats were out of sight.

The Germans had not been unaware of what was afoot, and with two lifeboats in tow they steered at full speed towards the Swedish coast. The two escaping lifeboats had meanwhile reached the ice edge, but they found the ice too thick to force their way through. Nevertheless they were now well inside territorial waters and technically safe. But the Germans ignored their protests and forced them under the threat of using their guns to throw painters aboard the trawler. Then, with all four lifeboats in tow, the trawler headed back towards the Skytteren, which was burning fiercely some distance out.

Long before they reached the Skytteren, however, the men in the lifeboats saw a thick trail of smoke to the north. It was the Swedish guard ship Göta Lejon, and it was steaming towards them at full speed. Its crew must have seen the incident in territorial waters and be hastening to correct the infringement. The Germans responded by ordering the men of the Skytteren to come aboard, a demand that was again backed by threats. The men dawdled as much as they dared, but by the time the Göta Lejon arrived, the lifeboats were empty and everyone was assembled on the foredeck of the trawler.

What happened in the next few minutes the men of the Skytteren were never able to discover. There was some signalling between the two ships, but it did not result in the expected liberation. Eventually the Göta Lejon backed away, and to the chagrin of the prisoners the trawler was allowed to proceed. The last they saw of the sinking whaler as they sailed towards Frederikshavn and captivity was her grey hull growing more and more indistinct except for the occasional vomit of flame that illuminated her in the haze.

Thus by seven o'clock on the morning of Wednesday 1st April— April Fool's Day—two ships, the Buccaneer and the Skytteren, had been scuttled, two others, the B.P. Newton and the Storsten, had got clear of the Swedish coast, and a fifth, the Dicto, was waiting off the Hallö Islands for the morning forecast. Of the remaining five, Rigmor, Lind and Lionel had made an escape attempt and been turned back, while the two steamships, Charente and Gudvang, had not so far left territorial waters. Two other things were clear: the Germans were present in strength; and the Swedish Navy's interpretation of its instructions, presumably aimed at avoiding incidents in Swedish waters, was having the effect of flushing the ships on to the German guns. This was amply confirmed when Rigmor, Lind and Lionel, on returning to Swedish waters, were bombarded with lamp signals and loud-hailers from Swedish destroyers and guard ships ordering them out again. This action was not only contrary to International Law but at variance with the instructions Admiral Akermark himself had issued before the operation. Captain Kershaw, of the Lionel, imitating Nelson, hoisted his answering pennant to half-mast, signifying 'I do not understand your message'; but all three ships were repeatedly ordered to put to sea. It may not have been merely ironic that the destroyers involved were the Psilander and Puke, ships whose crews could perhaps be relied upon not to show undue bias towards the British.

*   *   *

By lying-up as far north as Hallö, Binney had inadvertently divorced himself from the centre of the action, and this proved to be a mistake. Although all the other captains had a rough idea of the progress of the operation so far, Binney, the commodore, had no knowledge of the events of the past two hours. And the forecast that he was waiting for proved disappointingly vague when it came. Eventually Clark, brooding over his synoptic charts, came to the conclusion that the fog in the Skagerrak was likely to clear long before the ships could slip through. This, Binney felt, was a situation that must spell disaster, and he felt bound to warn his captains. At 08.11, with great reluctance, he broke wireless silence to signal a coded message to all ships. Even now he did not feel justified in giving them orders; each captain was left free to act on his own discretion. But his message was meant to deter. 'Weather now unfavourable and likely to remain so for some days.'

To this signal Binney received no answer, and he did not expect to; it was a broadcast message to all ships. But by an extraordinary mischance, the message went out on the wrong wavelength. The Marconi engineer who had checked the sets, a Dane, was thoroughly trustworthy, as was Binney's radio operator, a rating from HMS Hunter named Brown. Brown checked his aerial current during transmission and was satisfied that the message had gone out. The ships were only a few miles apart, and Binney had no reason to doubt that they had received it. But the emergency port regulations at Gothenburg had prevented the operators from testing or even fully assembling their equipment before sailing; and in the darkness that morning the aerials on the Dicto had been re-erected the wrong way round, reversing the connections. Thus the long-wave aerial was connected to the short-wave transmitter, and vice versa. Whatever wavelength the message went out on, it was not received on any of the ships.

All this time the Psilander and Puke were flying the signal flag LNL (Put to Sea), and becoming increasingly aggressive in their endeavours to get their orders obeyed. The Lind, which was on the fringe of Swedish waters, had warning shots fired at her by one of the smaller patrol ships, after which she was ordered to 'stop speed immediately', an order which Captain Nicol complied with. The patrol boat steered straight at him and forced him out to sea, at the same time hailing him with shouts of 'Go to sea', 'Head west', and, most upsetting of all, 'If you re-enter Swedish waters you will lose your right to sail.' Captain Nicol steered a south-westerly course under protest, keeping near the territorial fringe, but another armed patrol boat then lay across his course, forcing him out still farther. Visibility had risen by this time to ten miles, the Lind was three or four miles outside territorial waters near the Paternoster Light, and her situation was precarious.

Sixty-year-old Fred Kershaw, of the Lionel, was another Ellerman's Wilson Line captain and he knew his Skagerrak; he had already reached the same conclusion as Binney. Nevertheless he was reluctant to abandon the attempt altogether, and after being further harassed by destroyers and patrol boats he asked permission, through his Nortraship representative Captain Schnitler, to use Swedish waters for a short time to await developments. This was no more than Admiral Akermark's instructions had appeared to allow. 'Go westwards,' answered the Swedes. 'You can't stay in Swedish waters.' Kershaw then asked if he was free to return to Gothenburg. 'Yes,' was the reply, 'but if you do you will never come out again.' The authority for this complete *volte-face* in Swedish policy, already communicated to the Storsten, was not quoted.

Kershaw decided that they would have to cross that bridge when they came to it, and at 08.45 he finally abandoned the breakout attempt and set course for Vinga and Gothenburg. The other four ships, Rigmor, Lind, Charente and Gudvang, had all manoeuvred within hailing distance during the parley, and by 09.00 the four captains had agreed among themselves to follow Kershaw's example.

Thoroughly crestfallen, the crews of these ships now faced an ignominious return to Gothenburg. 'How can we go back there?' asked a young Norwegian named Björn Egge, one of only five Norwegians on the Charente. 'How shall we face the Swedish girls? We'll be the laughing stock of the town.' But fifty minutes later the ships began to lose sight of each other in random patches of fog, and excitement returned. Kershaw, with his knowledge of the conditions, was the only captain who was not tempted. Still unaware of the Dicto's signal, the other four captains, under pressure from their crews, altered course westwards.

Once outside territorial waters the intention had been that the Norwegian captains should take over, but this procedure was not followed on the two coal-burners. On the Charente, with its largely British crew, Captain James Donald retained control, while on the Gudvang it was the Welshman Nicholson, that erstwhile opponent whom Binney had come to respect, who sounded out the crew— thirteen Norwegians and twelve British—and took the decision to sail. But on all the ships the decision was spontaneous and unanimous and was greeted with cheers. Rigmor and Lind, which had already attempted one breakout more or less together, started off again in company, but because of Rigmor's superior speed they soon lost sight of each other. The steamships Charente and Gudvang, invisible to the others in the fog patches, made their decisions alone, the last to head westwards being Captain Donald in the Charente.

For the rest of the morning all four ships made good progress through the fog, breaking through the German screen without further incident and getting occasional glimpses of each other as the weather turned to intermittent showers of rain and snow and visibility in the clear patches rose to four or five miles. After passing the Skaw about twenty miles out they headed at maximum speed for Point 'A'; and soon after midday the old Gudvang was glimpsed from both Rigmor and Lind, steaming at an astonishing twelve knots, her vertical funnel amidships betraying her vintage. Harry Nicholson had never set out to endear himself to anyone; but Binney would have been proud of him now.

The trim, neat lines of the Charente, the second and more modern of the coal-burners, were not seen from the other ships. But in fact this vessel, under another man who had rejected Binney when he first visited Hälsingmo and had since regretted it, James Donald, was still making lively progress through the Skagerrak. An hour later, however, the fog lifted, and at about 13.30 two dots were discerned on the horizon. They proved to be German armed trawlers. One of the trawlers fired a shot across the Charente's bows, while the other, which was flying the 'Stop' signal, closed rapidly. With two boats barring the way, Charente had little chance; but to gain time Donald pretended not to understand the German signals and asked for them to be repeated. Another shot across the bows and Donald stopped engines and gave the order to lower the boats.

The closer of the two trawlers was now observed to be launching a boat, manned by an officer and some ratings. As they rowed across towards the Charente, Donald pulled the switches that would detonate the charges. Nothing happened.

The explosive on the Charente had been placed in Nos. 1 and 4 holds, and Donald was fully conversant with the connections. What could have gone wrong? The German boarding party were drawing alongside, and the officer was about to join him on the bridge. Aghast at the prospect of the capture of his ship, the one outcome of all others against which he knew he must guard, he tugged once again at the levers. This time the ship blew up.

To Björn Egge, who was standing on top of the monkey island, struggling to release the Lewis gun that was mounted there and dump it overboard before the Germans saw it, it seemed that far too much explosive had been planted, that the entire bottom had been blown out and the ship must sink at once. Then, searching for one of the other Norwegians who seemed to be missing, Kaspar Ekland, he found him asleep in his bunk. One or two of the crew had been hurt in the explosions, but no one was seriously injured.

The Germans, cheated of their prize, and with their boarding party exposed to the same dangers as the Allied crew, raised the cry 'Save the Germans first'. Two of the Charente's lifeboats had been wrecked, but the entire crew of thirty-one got off the ship by one means or another and packed into the third. The exception was Captain Donald, whom Egge suspected of intending to go down with his ship, or at least of waiting until everyone, Allied and German, had been saved. The deck of the Charente was almost flush with the water when Egge dragged him over the side.

Within the next few minutes everyone was taken safely aboard the trawler, which then set course for Frederikshavn.

Three ships, Buccaneer, Skytteren and Charente, had now been scuttled and 186 prisoners taken. Dicto and Lionel, which carried more than half the total cargo between them, had abandoned the attempt. Storsten, B. P. Newton, Rigmor, Lind and Gudvang were still somewhere in the Skagerrak, spread out in that order; but there were many hours to go before dark. Of these five ships the most important was the B.P. Newton; built at Malmö in 1940, she was not only the biggest, the newest and the fastest of the four remaining tankers, she was carrying 5,000 tons of ball-bearings and special steels, by far the most important cargo after the Dicto. Next in size and importance was the Rigmor, which carried a small but valuable load of 600 tons, mostly ball-bearing material for the manufacture of aero engines.

Next came the Storsten. Built on the Clyde in the 'twenties, the Storsten was a typical tanker of its period—funnel and superstructure aft, long low silhouette broken by the bridge amidships. Of the forty-nine men on board, James Reeve was the only Britisher; he had been described by Binney as the 'most redoubtable' of all his British captains, and he was also the oldest at 63. But once outside territorial waters, command had passed to the Norwegian Ragnar Bull-Nielsen, an intelligent, quick-thinking sailor who had worried Binney at first by his quiet individualism and his habit of going his own way. Two of the crew, first officer Finn Bie and deckhand Sten Olsen, had their wives on board. Bie's wife was expecting a baby. Driven out of territorial waters early that morning by the ice-breaker Göta Lejon, the Storsten had had very little contact with the other ships since then. She continued on a north-westerly course at her full speed of about eleven knots until, at about ten o'clock, two sizeable vessels were distinguished through the murk. At first these ships were thought to be Rigmor and Lind. Then the men of the Stortsen realised they were being fired on; unwittingly they had come up with the two west-bound escort vessels Schiff 7 and Schiff 47. But the German fire was inaccurate, and within a minute or so the fog closed in around them and the tanker, altering course now to the south-west, was lucky enough to escape.

For the rest of the morning the Storsten made steady progress, until by one o'clock Bull-Nielsen put her thirty-two miles south-east of Kristiansand. The fog, although shallow in depth, kept the German reconnaissance planes grounded all morning, and the mood on the Storsten remained one of optimism, which the cooks sustained by serving an appetising lunch. Soon after two o'clock, however, a twin-engined bomber, identified as a Dornier (but from German records undoubtedly a Ju 88), spotted them through the haze, and the Lewis gunners had hardly opened up when the ship was rent by a deafening explosion. It seemed that either the plane had laid a mine dead ahead and the Storsten had run on to it, or the pilot had dropped a torpedo. Yet neither missile had been seen. Visibility from the deck of the tanker was still so poor that no one could be sure what had happened. But it was the fore part of the ship that had been hit, which supported the mine theory. (The Storsten had in fact run on to a floating mine.) The hull had been torn open on the starboard side, the fore-deck, riven and splintered, was twisted over to port, and the starboard life-boat had been torn away, leaving only the buckled remnants of the davits. The helmsman was thrown from the top of the bridge to the boat deck, and the carpenter was injured when a part of the concrete bridge protection collapsed. Both captains were on the bridge, where they were soon joined by the mate. Reeve was running from one wing of the bridge to the other, firing at the attacking plane with a .5 Colt.

Already the Storsten lay deep down at the bow, and with her propeller and rudder almost clear of the water, normal steering became impossible. The reserve steering gear was connected but this did not help.

The enemy bomber had not finished with them yet. Attacking from broadside on, flying at about a hundred feet, and aiming between the aerial masts, it trailed a line with a hook on the end which carried away the aerials just as Tor Jorfald, the telegraphist, was transmitting an sos. Fierce and accurate return fire from the Norwegian gunners, during which they could see their tracer pouring into the target, did not deter the German crew from dropping two bombs with deadly accuracy, a heavy one which fell in the water only twenty yards away and a smaller one which did not explode but which slithered along the deck and was neatly sidestepped by the bos'n before it rolled overboard.

At this traumatic moment the Storsten's luck finally ran out. A German patrol vessel appeared out of the mist to the south and at once opened fire. It fell to Bull-Nielsen, with Reeve's approval, to make the decision to abandon ship, and three boats were lowered—

the port lifeboat, the motor-boat, and a gig. While the telegraphist tried in vain to get an acknowledgment of his sos, and with the gunners still manning the guns, the three boats were brought hastily round to the starboard or Norwegian side, on the blind side of the trawler. Hurriedly but in good order the men took to the boats, Captain Reeve staying just long enough to blow the explosive charges. The last man to leave the ship was the telegraphist. Bull-Nielsen, in the motor-boat, took the other two boats in tow and kept the Storsten between him and the trawler. The Ju 88, damaged in the action, left the scene, and by good seamanship the tanker's boats got away unnoticed by the trawler and disappeared into the fog.

With Bull-Nielsen in the motor-boat were his second officer, Einar Tönnesen, and fifteen others. Most of the remaining thirty-two, including the two women, were in the port lifeboat, where the man in charge was Finn Bie. Reeve and a few others brought up the rear in the gig. There was a small tank of water in each of the larger boats, but very little food. Yet with wind and sea moderate, an alternative to the prospect of returning to Norway to face imprisonment occurred to the more adventurous. Why not try to reach the rendezvous with the British naval forces? Was it really such a preposterous idea? With the motor-boat to start them on their way, the suggestion awoke an enthusiastic response. After a discussion it was agreed that they should make the attempt, and course was set.

*   *   *

At about the time of the mining of the Storsten, B.P. Newton was being attacked by a small armed trawler from the port beam, but the firing was ineffective, and with her superior speed the tanker was soon out of range. Now, at 14.00, two more vessels were sighted, this time on the Norwegian side. The tanker was then thirty-five miles off Kristiansand. The trawlers approached to within four cables and ordered the tanker to stop. Captains Blindheim and Calvert ignored the order, but they sent an sos — 'We are being attacked by surface craft' — and gave their position, sixty miles east of Point 'A', more as a warning to the vessels behind them than with any hope of assistance. The trawlers, moving in astern, opened up with shell and machine-gun fire, and as inky splashes nine or ten feet high erupted round the tanker, both captains decided that with capture imminent their duty was to scuttle the ship while they could, and they rang down the order 'Stop engines'. That would have been the end of B.P. Newton; but the second officer, Gunnar Album, a strong personality who talked little but was quick to act, ran forward and rammed the engine-room telegraph to full ahead. All this was watched with enthusiastic approval by the helmsman, Arne Sörbye. Although the bridge was holed by machine-gun fire as the tanker gathered speed, none of the fifteen or twenty shells that were fired found their mark and the tanker drew steadily away.

On the Rigmor, which had now dropped a long way astern of the Newton, the sos was picked up and the position noted. It was also picked up on the Swedish coast, where George Binney, listening out in the wireless cabin of the Dicto, heard the message in a mood of despair. At midday Captain Nicholas had signalled for a pilot to take them back to Vinga, and Binney had plied the pilot with questions about the other ships. The pilot could tell him no more than that he had heard the sound of gunfire from seaward several times that morning. From this Binney naturally suspected the worst; and now it seemed he was about to lose B.P. Newton. Of the other ships he had heard not a word.

B.P. Newton, as it happened, was safe—for the moment. But the trawlers had called up the *Luftwaffe*, and at 16.10 that afternoon another Ju 88 appeared from the Norwegian side. Using cloud cover to mask its attack, it dived down and sprayed the tanker's deck with cannon and machine-gun fire. Because of her importance the tanker had been allotted three Lewis guns, and the gunners, trained and led by Brian Reynolds, gave the Ju 88 crew a nasty shock: no one had told them that the Norwegian merchantmen might be armed. A second sos was transmitted, but the enemy plane sheered off without dropping its bombs, and Reynolds and his gunners eventually drove it away altogether. They knew, though, that they must expect further attacks before dark.

Despite poor visibility which hampered the bombers throughout the afternoon, three more attacks did indeed follow in quick succession, the second bomber slanting in from astern, absorbing everything that the gunners could throw at it, and scoring a near miss to one side, so that the crew felt the vessel lift out of the water. The bomber staggered away leaving an ominous trail of black smoke; but expressions on the tanker tautened as the ship failed to answer her helm. Chief Engineer Lorentz Lund, however, put on a front of calm unconcern. 'Take it easy, we'll find out what's wrong.' He soon established that there was no physical damage, merely that the fuses on the electric steering had blown.

B.P. Newton was not the only one of the four remaining breakout vessels to attract the attention of the *Luftwaffe* that afternoon. Soon after half-past four an aircraft was sighted through the mist on the port quarter of the Lind, flying low over the sea and heading west. The pilot seemed to be flying erratically, as though he were having trouble with his controls. John Nicol was on the monkey island, manning the Lewis gun, the Norwegian Hans Trovik was on the bridge. But Nicol, to his disappointment, did not have to use his gun. As the plane turned towards them it wobbled awkwardly, then disappeared into a rain squall. Immediately afterwards the men on the Lind saw a flash of flame, and the plane did not emerge from the cloud. This was almost certainly the bomber that had scored a near-miss on B.P. Newton. German records show one Ju 88 missing, the pilot having claimed a hit on a tanker before sending an SOS.

Five miles astern of the Lind was the Gudvang, still being pressed by Captain Nicholson to its maximum speed. Only once, at about five o'clock, did the crew get a glimpse of the Lind, and then she was lost to sight within seconds as the weather thickened.

By six o'clock that evening the fog had eased and visibility, except in rain squalls, was improving, just as Clark had predicted. All four of the escaping vessels were still afloat, but there were still nearly two hours of daylight to go. The Rigmor had drawn well clear of the Lind and the Gudvang; and it was the turn of the Rigmor to face air attack. Soon after 18.00 a German bomber, approaching from port to starboard at low level, flew straight over the top of the Rigmor and dropped two incendiary bombs. The gunners did all they could to put the Germans off their aim, but they were under heavy fire themselves, and the attack was nicely judged. The second bomb was a near-miss to starboard; but the first bomb hit the trunk on the third centre tank fair and square, ripping it open and splitting the surrounding deck, besides doing other minor damage. Fortunately this tank was being used as a ballast tank and was full of water. The German crew made several more machine-gun attacks, but the Lewis gunners, getting the feel of their guns, soon earned the enemy's respect. The bomber circled the Rigmor until dusk, then headed for Norway.

So far the Gudvang, pursuing a course some miles to the north of the other vessels, but slowly overtaking the Lind, had escaped the attentions of the *Luftwaffe*. In another few minutes it would be dark. But the German patrol boats, acting now on sighting reports from the *Luftwaffe*, were still combing the Skagerrak for the three tankers, and soon after eight o'clock it was the old cargo steamer Gudvang's misfortune to run into them. The trawlers had been spotted on the port bow in good time, and Captain Nicholson had altered course to starboard to avoid them. But the separation was no more than three or four miles, and once sighted the old Gudvang, her funnel perpendicular against the last reflected glow of the sunset, had no hope of escape. Another few minutes and she might have made off into the darkness; but although Nicholson ignored the persistent signals of the patrol boats to stop, he prepared for the scuttling that he knew was inevitable.

With their signals still unanswered, the trawlers began sending up star shells to help their gunners to aim. Meanwhile the engines of the Gudvang were stopped for the last time, and Nicholson summoned the crew on deck. He ordered the starboard lifeboat, on the blind side of the trawlers, to be launched, hoping that some at least of the crew might get away unseen; but as he did so a volley of shells straddled the ship. The aft hatch was hit, the hatch coaming was flung into the air, and the motor-boat, which was stowed on top of the hatch, was blown to fragments.

Events now moved so rapidly that the majority of the crew hardly knew what was happening. In the semi-darkness the atmosphere of confusion, aggravated by the shrill howl of a jammed steam whistle, bordered on panic. One man who retained his customary stolid, cold-blooded demeanour was Harry Nicholson. As the distance between his ship and the trawlers closed he decided to test his scuttling switches, just to make sure they worked. He pulled half the levers, and an explosion of sledgehammer violence rocked the ship. The Gudvang took a perilous list to starboard, and the crew, thinking the ship had been torpedoed, made a rush for the starboard lifeboat. This boat eventually reached the water in an overloaded state. Nicholson immediately blew the port charges to straighten up the ship, and there was a second shattering explosion, spreadeagling the men who were struggling with the port lifeboat; but they now found it possible to launch it. After picking up Captain Nicholson, they rowed clear of the wreck and set off for the Norwegian coast in the wake of the starboard boat. But in spite of the darkness the trawlers overtook both boats and ordered the men on board. After first setting course for Kristiansand, the trawlers were diverted to Frederikshavn, bringing the number of prisoners on the way to that port to 211.

In the last two hours or so of daylight the crews of B.P. Newton, Rigmor and Lind, which were all now in the region of Point 'A', either approaching it or beyond it, began to look hopefully for air protection. And there were in fact two RAF Beaufighters combing the area, though their search was hampered by rain. It had originally been estimated that, with a sailing time of 20.00 hours on 31st March, the first ship would just about be emerging from the jaws of the Skagerrak at first light on 1st April, and two Coastal Command Blenheim crews from Dyce had been briefed to arrive overhead at 05.30 that morning. During the night, however, the Admiralty received information via Blücker and Denham that the sailing had been delayed, enabling them to postpone the take-offs for some hours. Nevertheless the actual times of sailing were still not known for certain, and seven separate sorties (four pairs of Blenheims of 404 Squadron, and three pairs of Beaufighters of 248 Squadron, all operating from Dyce), had reconnoitred throughout the afternoon and found nothing. It was not until the eighth and last sortie of the day that a sighting was made, at 18.27 that evening; and although it showed that the RAF crews were prepared to penetrate far beyond Point 'A', it brought depressing news. Both Beaufighter crews had sighted the tanker Storsten. She was listing to starboard with decks awash, a damaged and empty raft lay alongside, and there was no sign of life on board. (Unknown to the RAF crews, the Germans had tried to take the tanker in tow but had finally left it to sink.)

Soon after leaving the Storsten the first Beaufighter crew sighted what they described as 'three large boats', which they estimated as containing about a hundred men. This was almost a 100 per cent exaggeration; but much to the joy of the occupants, the pilot came down low, and they waved excitedly. The RAF men could even recognise the Norwegian flags that were held aloft for their benefit, and they also noticed that two of the boats were being towed by the third. But they do not seem to have recorded the direction the boats were taking.

The other Beaufighter crew, on their way east, sighted the B.P. Newton, but they could not identify her. A patrolling Ju 88 was then intercepted and chased into cloud. Four minutes later, when the Beaufighter returned to the ship, the Ju 88 was sighted again, but this time it quickly assumed a good firing position on the Beaufighter's tail and it was the British crew who had to run for cover. When they eventually broke cloud they hit a snow and sleet squall, and a further search failed to reveal either tanker or aircraft.

Left to herself after nightfall, the Newton reached the outer fringes of the Skagerrak, where she was exposed to a Force 6 westerly. The moon was still bright and only intermittently obscured by cloud, but with her crew fully alerted and wearing their rubber suits, the tanker nosed her way through the suspected gap in the minefields. Astern of her, still well inside the Skagerrak, the Rigmor ploughed on into a darkness that was rendered impenetrable by mist and rain. Only on the Lind were enemy patrol boats sighted, and four times before midnight the keen-eyed Welshman Nicol was forced to take avoiding action, altering course at right angles and not resuming his course until the patrols were out of sight. He and Trovik made further sightings after midnight, and although they judged them to be fishing boats they took no chances, altering course until they were clear.

Of the other Performance vessels still afloat, Lionel reached Gothenburg without further interference in the early hours of Thursday 2nd April; but the Dicto was subjected to a final indignity. Anchored inside territorial waters the previous evening on the written instructions of the Swedish pilot she had taken aboard, she was accosted by a Swedish destroyer. 'Follow after me to Gothenburg,' ordered the destroyer captain by loud-hailer. 'If you do not follow I am going to use my guns.'

* * *

Storsten's boats, still strung together, and powered by the motor-boat, were running into trouble as the headwind blew with increased force. The sea ran so high that even continuous baling failed to keep the boats dry, and as more and more water was shipped the soaked occupants shivered with cold and exposure. Long before midnight the engine of the motor-boat failed, and the plight of the would-be escapers looked desperate. In the early grey dawn, however, the wind changed to a strong easterly, and although the gig had to be discarded, making the lifeboat uncomfortably crowded, it was the lifeboat that now hoisted sail, took the motor-boat in tow, and ran before the wind. Despite the volume of water that splashed over the gunwales, the spirits of the occupants rose as speed increased to three or even four knots, and to warm themselves up they started to sing.

The tally on that Thursday morning was five ships sunk, two returned to port, and three approaching the final stages of successful escape. If these three ships could survive the next few hours, all the losses might yet be justified. B.P. Newton had reached the middle of the North Sea and the crew were scanning the horizon for the naval escort. Rigmor, a hundred miles astern, was a long way short of surface help but well within reach of air cover. Most vulnerable seemed to be the Lind, which had passed through Point 'A' at the mouth of the Skagerrak at 02.00 but was still uncomfortably close to land.

Of the naval escort, three old destroyers, Wallace, Valorous and Vanity, veterans of the 1914-18 war, had sailed from Methil in the Firth of Forth at 21.25 the previous evening, and the remaining three, Faulknor, Eskimo and Escapade, had sailed from Rosyth two hours later, the whole under the command of Captain A. K. Scott Moncrieff in Faulknor. Wallace's force was thus well in the van, and at 06.40 that morning, to the accompaniment of a crescendo of cheering, the three destroyers were sighted from B.P. Newton. Fifteen minutes later the first Beaufighter appeared overhead. Valorous was detached to escort the tanker to Methil, and the Beaufighter, too, accompanied it. The other two destroyers continued eastwards.

Two hours later, on the Rigmor, an attack alarm was raised at 08.45 when two unidentified aircraft were sighted to starboard; but fear turned to jubilation as they were recognised as RAF Beaufighters, the third pair to take off from Dyce that morning. Surely the Rigmor, too, must now be safe. The Lind, progressing at an agonising eight knots through weather that grew more crystalline every minute, seemed unbearably vulnerable; but mid-morning came and neither air nor surface craft, friend or enemy, was seen.

The fourth sortie from Dyce was flown by two Blenheims of 404 Squadron which sighted the three Home Fleet destroyers at 09.20 as they joined up with Wallace and Vanity. All five destroyers now formed into a single force and sped eastwards, but they had no news as yet of Rigmor and Lind; for either ship to radio its position would only attract the enemy. Fifty minutes later the Blenheims came up with the Rigmor, heading due west at twelve knots, and while one of the Blenheims stayed to escort the Rigmor, the other flew back to signal its position visually to the destroyers.

Flying low past the Rigmor and reading its name on bows and stern, the Blenheim crew kept it company for the next two hours. There was only one incident in that time; at 11.30 a German reconnaissance plane was sighted by the Blenheim crew and chased off to the north-east, where it escaped into cloud. But the position, course and speed of the Rigmor would now be known to the enemy. At 12.07, with no relieving sortie in sight, but nearing their prudent limit of endurance, the Blenheim crew were forced to set course for base. Rigmor was now less than 180 miles from the Scottish coast; but although the weather was still perfect on the Norwegian side, low cloud and rain were spreading west across the Scottish coastal airfields and out into the North Sea, hampering the Coastal Command squadrons. Thus the Rigmor, with the destroyer escort still fifty miles away, and the *Luftwaffe* alerted, was left for the moment without air cover.

The Lind spent the morning feeling her way through the gap in the minefields. The weather was still the same—a clear blue sky, almost devoid of cloud, and bright sunshine. The North Sea was a duckpond, and a rating, expectorating over the rail, followed the ring of spittle for a quarter of a minute. It was out of that spring sunshine, just before noon, that an enemy plane approached the Lind in leisurely fashion from the starboard quarter. It began by dropping red and white flares, as though it had all the time in the world. Then it crossed in front and passed down the port side, dropping more flares. On the Lind it was identified as a Heinkel 111.

With Captain Trovik on the bridge, Captain Nicol went aft to man the single Lewis gun, which was mounted on top of the galley. The Heinkel passed astern of them, came round on to the starboard beam, then turned in to attack. Nicol, puzzled until now by the flares and the manoeuvring, suddenly realised what the Heinkel pilot was up to. He was carrying torpedoes. 'Tell Captain Trovik not to let him get us broadside on,' he yelled. Within seconds, as the helm was brought over and the Lind steered bows-on for the Heinkel, then zigzagged, Nicol knew he could rely on the Norwegian.

The Heinkel pilot rocked his machine left and right to confuse the man at the helm, but the skill of the Norwegian captain, the small size of the Lind, its manoeuvrability, and the pugnacity of Nicol, continually frustrated him. Delighted by Trovik's masterly navigation, the little Welshman danced excitedly round his gun, cigarette-end hanging from his lips, his expression changing from amused admiration to belligerent spite as Trovik manoeuvred expertly and the Heinkel came within range of his fire. Again and again the Heinkel pilot started his torpedo run, first from abeam, then from the starboard bow, then from the port bow, even from the starboard and port quarters, and each time he found himself lined up on a parallel course. The action had lasted nearly half an hour and was still inconclusive when, at exactly noon, a second aircraft arrived, bringing the threat of attack from more than one angle—something that even Trovik might find impossible to counter. The two planes circled at a respectful distance—from the Lind, and, noticeably, from each other. Then came the staccato racket of machine-gun fire as the new arrival, to the astonishment and delight of the men on the Lind, set about the Heinkel. It was a Beaufighter, one of two from the fifth sortie of the day from Dyce. Its companion had sighted nothing, but this one chased the Heinkel into a rare bank of cloud to the south-east before losing contact. Returning to the Lind, it circled protectively for a time. But the Beaufighters, like the Blenheims, were operating near the limit of range, giving them little margin for search and escort, and after twenty minutes the pilot turned reluctantly for home.

No sooner was the Beaufighter out of sight than the Heinkel reappeared from the wings as though right on cue and made an immediate surprise attack. Hurrying in on the port side of the Lind at low level, the pilot dropped both his torpedoes at 500 yards, and this time there was nothing Trovik could do to avoid them. Too low and too close to break away without exposing the Heinkel's belly, the pilot held his course at fifty feet, giving Nicol a point-blank shot. Even if the Lind herself was doomed, Nicol determined to take the

Heinkel with him. He blasted away at it throughout its run and repeatedly hit it, and it was not until the Heinkel had passed overhead that there was a short burst from the rear gunner as the pilot climbed unsteadily away.

The German pilot may well have been deceived by the perfect proportions of the Lind into thinking he was attacking a much bigger vessel, otherwise he might have come in closer. His aim and his timing were good, and both torpedoes were running unerringly towards their target. But the little tanker had one more trick up its sleeve—its shallow draft. Both torpedoes passed safely underneath the keel—one about thirty feet from the bows and the other about twenty feet from the stern, and the ship sailed triumphantly on.

Resuming their westerly course, the men of the Lind looked anxiously for the renewal of their air escort, certain that the Germans would soon come back. But by this time, both Germans and British were busy elsewhere.

The Blenheim of 404 Squadron that had left the Rigmor at 12.07 had still not been replaced. At 12.30, five minutes after the unsuccessful torpedoing of the Lind, an unidentified aircraft was sighted from the Rigmor. For a time it circled, and the men of the Rigmor were uncertain whether it was friend or foe until they recognised the black crosses. At first the gunners kept it at bay. Then, attacking from the starboard side, it machine-gunned the decks as it dived before dropping two bombs and pulling up over the top. Both bombs overshot slightly and fell in the water on the port side, doing only superficial damage. An SOS was sent, and the destroyers received it, but the co-ordinates transcribed were corrupt. Meanwhile two more aircraft, unmistakably German bombers, began circling, and this time the Rigmor's gunners, almost out of ammunition now, had to hold their fire. Attacking in quick succession, the two bombers machine-gunned the decks, then dropped their bombs. Two scored hits or near misses on the starboard side, blowing a great gash in Rigmor's hull, and two more fell close to the stern. As the ship took a heavy list to starboard, the engineers reported that the near-misses astern had broken a shaft.

All three bombers then followed up with machine-gun attacks, taking advantage of the helpless gunners to plaster the bridge and radio cabin. Captain Gilling went down with wounds in both legs, but no one else was hit. At 13.15 a second SOS was sent, this time giving an accurate position, but with the tanker unnavigable and defenceless and listing heavily, Captain Monsen gave the order to abandon ship. Meanwhile the SOS was plotted correctly by the surface escort and Scott Moncrieff ordered speed to be increased to twenty-four knots.

There was a short lull now as the crew of the Rigmor took to the boats. Then, almost simultaneously, but from different directions, two new forces appeared over the horizon. From the east, watched by the men in the boats, came two German seaplanes, each clutching torpedoes; and from the west, visible from the air but unseen as yet from sea-level, came the five destroyers led by the Faulknor.

As Scott Moncrieff ordered an increase to twenty-eight knots, the two seaplanes began a long scuttering run across the water towards the crippled Rigmor. If the destroyers could get there first and break up the attack, a reboarding operation still looked possible. But this the crews of the seaplanes were determined to pre-empt. Racing in to beat the destroyers to it, they had the tanker at their mercy. The tracks of the torpedoes passed right by the boats, and one of the torpedoes struck the Rigmor amidships. Yet for the moment she seemed to soak up this further blow, and she still showed no signs of sinking.

Circling the wreck, the five German planes, three bombers and two seaplanes, came down one by one for a closer look. Then, running in towards the lifeboats in menacing fashion, they gave the men of the Rigmor some unpleasant moments; but not one of them fired on the boats.

The first indication the survivors of the Rigmor had that help was near came when puffs of smoke started to explode around the circling planes. In line abreast, with their rivets rattling, the destroyers were a magnificent sight for the men in the lifeboats. But the time was now 14.10, and the damage, it seemed, had been done.

The seas were much heavier now, and the destroyer Eskimo had to make a lee for the lifeboats and drop her scrambling nets to get the men safely on board. But Rigmor was still afloat, and Captain Monsen, for one, was not giving up without a fight. The air attack had faded, and the tanker and her small but valuable cargo might yet be brought to Britain. Couldn't the destroyer take her in tow? After consulting Scott Moncrieff, the commander of the Eskimo agreed to try, and the Rigmor crew, limp with the exhaustion and relief of rescue, were rallied by a shout from Monsen. 'Come on boys, we're going back to board her!' With volunteers from the destroyer crew to stiffen their ranks they clambered back into the lifeboats and rowed back to the tanker, intending to board her on her listing side. But this was also the weather side, making boarding impossible, and they soon had to give up and return to the Eskimo.

All the men were back on the destroyer except the man at the tiller of one of the boats when the Eskimo suddenly cut the lines and raced from the scene; she herself was under torpedo attack. The man thus abandoned, second officer Wessel Berg, was one of the many Norwegians who had escaped to Sweden with the ambition of getting to Britain. He didn't give much for his chances now. Half an hour later, when the torpedo attack was over, the Eskimo came back and picked him up.

This attack, although unsuccessful, finally convinced the Navy that salvage of the Rigmor would be too dangerous, and at 17.00 orders were received from C-in-C Rosyth to sink her, a task that was promptly executed by the Faulknor. Thus after completing three-quarters of her voyage, surviving all kinds of obstacles and hazards in doing so, and expending all her ammunition, the Rigmor was finally and tragically sunk by the forces that had come to protect her. The destroyers then withdrew westwards.

Air activity, and occasional fierce engagements, continued over the North Sea all that afternoon; but the Lind, still far short of the surface rendezvous and apparently left to her fate, saw nothing of this until dusk, when two large enemy bombers were sighted by Captain Trovik, heading towards him from the east. But in the failing light the grey hull of the miniature Lind was almost invisible from any distance, and long before the bombers had come within range they turned away south.

*   *   *

To the north of the Lind, in the Storsten's boats, the wind blew westwards all day, and with the lifeboat still towing the motor-boat, exciting progress was made. The mouth of the Skagerrak was left behind and the crossing of the North Sea begun. But that evening, as B.P. Newton passed abeam of May Island in the Firth of Forth and the Lind crept nearer and nearer to the surface rendezvous, the wind off the Norwegian coast grew so violent that towing had to be given up, and the boats lay-to for the night. Next morning, Good Friday, 3rd April, sails were again set in the lifeboat and the towing continued, but the wind had changed direction and it proved impossible to steer a westerly course. Progress to the south-west was made until ten o'clock, when the wind grew so strong that towing was given up altogether and the sails taken in.

The two boats were then drawn together, and the occupants conferred. They estimated their position as approximately thirty miles south-west of Flekkefjord, and although this meant that 270 miles separated them from the nearest point on the Scottish coast, the men in the motor-boat were in no mood to give up. 'We intend to row westwards for the UK,' shouted Bull-Nielsen. Bie translated this for Reeve, who reacted sharply. 'You have thirty souls in this over-loaded boat,' he reminded Bie. 'Consider that.' He was excluding himself and Bie from consideration. The lifeboat was certified for twenty persons only. But when Bie asked him for advice he closed up. 'You are in command and have to take the decision.'

Bie made up his mind that Reeve was right; it was hopeless to con-tinue westwards. The occupants of the lifeboat were exhausted, and two of them, who had been allowed to transfer earlier from the motor-boat, were hysterical. As visibility improved he could see Denmark on one side of the Skagerrak and the Norwegian mountains on the other, and he called across to the motor-boat. 'We'll try to reach Norway unseen.'

Only one man in the lifeboat—pumpman Arne Borge—objected; he was not prepared to risk capture by the Germans. Stowaway Gustav Nordstron, from the motor-boat, agreed to change places with him.

At eleven o'clock, in brilliant sunshine, the two boats parted com-pany, the seventeen men in the motor-boat, without mast or sail and with their engine still unserviceable, rowing seawards while the thirty men and two women in the lifeboat headed for land. Both parties were still full of hope—for those heading westwards, hope that they would soon be spotted by British planes and that their ordeal would be short; and for those heading landwards, hope of succour in their homeland, the avoidance of capture, and a second escape over the border towards freedom.

On that Good Friday, while seventeen Norwegians faced the North Sea in an open boat, seventeen Britishers of the Dicto, back in the safety of Gothenburg harbour, rejected Binney's appeal for volun-teers for a second attempt at a breakout. Demoralised by their years at Hälsingmo, and in some cases let down by their officers, they elected shamefacedly to return to the camp. By comparison, of the all-Norwegian crew of the Lionel, a slower and therefore a more vulner-able ship, only four men defected. The best of the British crews had of course gone with Rubble; but the contrast exemplified Binney's regard for the Norwegians as the backbone of Performance.

While B.P. Newton was being cheered into Leith, the Lind was reaching and passing the surface rendezvous, and Captain Trovik was beginning to feel that his was a forgotten ship. Fortunately she seems to have been forgotten by the Germans as well, very probably because the Heinkel torpedo pilot reported her sunk.

In fact, Hudsons from Wick and Kinloss and Beaufighters from Dyce were out searching for the Lind all that morning; but the weather had now broken completely in the west, and the crews were finding her as elusive a target as the enemy had done. It was not until just before one o'clock that a Hudson from Kinloss sighted a small and as yet unidentified tanker. 'As aircraft approached,' reported the Hudson pilot, 'vessel was flying no flag, but as aircraft circled and was recognised, the Norwegian flag was run up on the flag-post astern. Crew climbed rigging and waved handkerchiefs. A large white flag, bearing the letters "GB", was run up on the foremast.' From that time on, air escort was continuous, and as darkness fell on the third day of her voyage the Lind was at last joined by a destroyer escort. She reached Methil Roads the following afternoon, Saturday 4th April, after eighty hours at sea.

The mate of the Storsten, Finn Bie, in charge of Storsten's lifeboat, had planned to reach Jossingfjord on Friday night and get his party ashore in small groups in different places in the darkness of early Saturday morning, finally sinking the lifeboat. But lack of food and water, the debilitating hand of seasickness, and a night that was so cold that ice formed on the oars, left only three or four men fit to row. (Among those suffering from frostbite was Captain Reeve.) Coaxed and cajoled by Bie at the point of a pistol, the men rallied, and they brought the boat within a few miles of the shore on that Good Friday evening; but then, as it was still daylight, Bie slowed them down, resting them for a final effort to overcome the coastal currents as darkness fell. 'We thought we were just outside Jossingfjord,' wrote Bie afterwards. 'We advanced quickly inwards until midnight when we saw high ground fairly close on both sides dead ahead. A searchlight was seen inshore—probably from a patrol vessel. We stopped and lay quiet for about an hour. Then we proceeded inwards. A strong wind was now blowing up from the fjord which made rowing almost impossible. The mast was stepped and sails set. By this time the boat was half waterlogged, and spirits were low as the men bailed, rowed and vomited in turn. I went on begging and threatening, and one by one the hands rowed till they collapsed from exhaustion, when others took their place.' Outstanding, according to Bie, was the boatswain, Hans Fjelly, who was marvellous in encouraging them all.

'The boat didn't come into the fjord, but reached land at last on the east side of the mouth of Rekefjord near Sogndal. This happened at dawn on 4th April. Just before landing we met two small fishing vessels, but they disappeared without answering our questions.' Then they saw three men silhouetted on the top of the cliff, running towards a known German battery, and they knew they had been seen and reported.

Bull-Nielsen and the men in the motor-boat were having better luck, or so it seemed. By dawn on that Saturday morning they were eighty miles clear of the Norwegian coast; and at 08.10 they were overjoyed at the sight of a Lockheed Hudson, crewed by members of the Royal Danish Naval Air Service who were on a training flight from Leuchars. Captain Stork, the pilot, reporting the sighting by radio, described it as a motor-lifeboat containing nine or ten people, gave its position as 57.45 North, 04.26 East—approximately ninety miles off The Naze—and added that it was heading north-west on a course of 330 degrees. This remarkable piece of good fortune for the men in the lifeboat was dissipated somewhat when, after circling for twenty minutes, the Hudson crew left the scene to continue their training patrol.

At 09.40—more than an hour later—the controlling group, No. 18 Group at Pitreavie Castle, near Edinburgh, very sensibly ordered the Hudson crew to return to the lifeboat and escort it until they were released from that duty. It was another forty-five minutes before the Hudson crew regained the position they had themselves computed; but the motor-boat could hardly have travelled far in the two hours or so that had elapsed. Nevertheless a square search failed to reveal it, and at 11.10, three hours after the original sighting, and five hours after taking off from Leuchars, Captain Stork was forced to set course for base.

At Group Headquarters the Hudson sighting had been promptly acted on, and a Sunderland flying-boat from Invergordon had been ordered to go to the position given, its crew briefed to locate and attempt to rescue the occupants of the motor-lifeboat if the sea conditions allowed. Routed via Dyce, where it was to be joined by an escort of four Beaufighters, it was to return to base if it lost its escort in bad visibility or for any other reason. Invergordon was not an operational station, but the pilot appointed to fly the Sunderland was the Chief Flying Instructor, Squadron Leader G. G. Stead, and he took an experienced crew.

The Sunderland met its escort at 12.36 and set off into worsening weather. Within half an hour it had lost three of its escort in cloud, and when it reached the search area, visibility was down to one mile and the cloud base to 400 feet. Ten minutes later the last of the Beaufighters lost contact, and with conditions clearly impossible the search was called off.

Next day the Scottish coast was virtually blotted out by continuous rain, the cloud base was low and frequently right down on the surface, and visibility over the sea was extremely poor. This may account for the fact that no further search of any kind appears to have been ordered or made.

On the Norwegian coast the German occupation forces, warned by local collaborators, soon rounded up most of the survivors of the lifeboat, some of whom were already in a pitiful state. Mary Bie was taken to the local hospital, where she had her baby; but her husband was one of nine men who, avoiding the roads and striking out into the mountains, somehow evaded the cordon. Reaching a river crossing where the Germans were guarding the bridge, they took shelter at a nearby house, where they were given food, clothing and money, and where they slept in the family's own beds; and when a car stopped outside the house, and two Germans came in to ask questions, they listened to their host's answers from the dubious security of a closet. 'The Germans found nothing but eight eggs,' says Bie, 'which they took.' From that point on they were helped by relays of the Norwegian Resistance until they finally crossed again into Sweden, where within a month they were flown to Britain to join the Norwegian forces. Not all of them survived the war; but Bie rejoined his wife in Trondheim in 1945.

What of the seventeen men in Storsten's motor-boat? Captain Stork had reported seeing only nine or ten, but it seems likely that they had all survived up to this point: the first Beaufighter crew to spot the three Storsten boats off Kristiansand had been no more accurate in their estimate. Yet from the weakened condition of the party who landed in the lifeboat, some deaths from exposure may already have occurred. That the survivors did not reach Scotland can occasion no surprise; that nothing more was done for them evokes anguish.

The greatest single catastrophe of Performance, and the one insoluble mystery, was the loss of this boat. The riddle of what happened to it was deepened four months later when a lifeboat drifted ashore on the west coast of Denmark. It did not belong to the Storsten; but in it were found some personal effects of second engineer Erling Bakke, one of the men known to have been in the motor-boat. The lifeboat had originally belonged to a Norwegian ship which had been requisitioned by the Germans in April 1941 for use as a hospital ship; but this particular lifeboat had been missing at that time. Assuming that Storsten's motor-boat must have been swamped in the storms of that Easter week-end, had Bakke managed to stay afloat and scramble aboard the mystery lifeboat as it drifted fortuitously by? Or had the entire crew of the motor-boat been rescued by another ship, only to suffer a second shipwreck, to be lost this time without trace, or almost so? Because of this tantalising scrap of evidence, a question mark must forever hang over the fate of the motor-boat's crew.

*   *   *

Despite the punctilious rescue work of the crews manning the German patrol boats, there was a tragedy of even greater proportions to come; but it was not fully realised until the end of the war. For nearly a year the Norwegians captured during Performance were interned with their British colleagues at a camp for merchant seamen near Bremen; and although the whole group were imprisoned at first in an isolation barracks, where conditions were bad, they were released into the main camp after three months and were accorded normal prisoner-of-war status, to which the terms of their engagement entitled them. But in February 1943 most of the Norwegians were moved to Rendsberg, in Schleswig-Holstein near Kiel, where their clothes were confiscated and prison garb substituted. Here they found themselves in the hands not of the German Navy but the German Police; and here interrogation by the Gestapo began. Their crime in essence was their refusal to accept the Nazi 'liberation' of Norway, demonstrated by their emigration from Norway into Sweden. Despite all the formalities that had been so carefully completed before the breakout, their legal status was ignored and they were treated as though they were German citizens and sentenced under the notorious *Nacht und Nebel* (night and fog) Nazi decree. This meant that they were condemned without trial to annihilation as individuals while still alive. After sentence most of them, numbering about 150, were transferred to an old German civil prison at Sonnenburg, east of the Oder, where conditions were appalling, and where a slave labour routine of fourteen hours' work a day and very little to eat soon made apparent that a protracted stay must mean death from brutality and malnutrition. Had they not been toughened as well as emaciated by their imprisonment so far, and had they not developed a comradeship during Performance which continued to sustain them in captivity, few could have survived. As it was, forty-three of their number died before the war ended, thirty-one in the terrible conditions of deprivation and disease at Sonnenburg. To this tragedy must be added the post-war debilities, mental and physical, from which nearly all the survivors have suffered as a late sequel to their experience as political prisoners.

All these men were volunteers who, although doubtless infected by Binney's optimism, had gone into the operation fully appreciating its dangers; not one of them would have disputed that. But it would be surprising if some bitterness had not been harboured against the British for involving them in an operation of such hazard while being unable to protect them from the enemy's spite after they were captured. And the focus of this bitterness was bound to centre around George Binney. His critics, it seemed, had been right, and the Norwegian Government in London were the first to demand an enquiry. This dissatisfaction was crystallised into three salient points:

1. That it was too late in the season to undertake the operation with a reasonable chance of success.
2. That the Norwegian captains were not consulted on the final arrangements.
3. That the support of the British Navy and Air Force was superficial, and that unnecessary losses had consequently been incurred.

There were many other minor criticisms. The Rigmor should never have been lost. Even B.P. Newton, it was said, would have been scuttled but for the quick action of the Norwegian first officer, while the Lind had only escaped because of her small size and shallow draft. The Germans had known every move in advance and had had six months to assemble their forces; they were far better prepared than the British, who had relied on improvisation and chance. The success of Rubble had gone to Binney's head, distorting the lessons that should have been learned. 'Zweimal ist nicht einmal nochmal,' quoted the Norwegians: twice is not once over again. Binney's knighthood had cost the Norwegians many ships and many lives. It had been the Charge of the Light Brigade over again.

Something of this backlash was bound to reach Binney, and he must have found it painful. But he had not been acting alone. The operation had been declared essential by all the Ministries involved, approved by the Chiefs of Staff Committee, pressed for by Churchill, and given his final blessing. But if a scapegoat was going to be demanded it was bound to be Binney. Failure of the most expertly planned expeditions always brings calumnies on the organisers, as Binney knew well enough, and he was quite prepared to face up to his critics. Less welcome was the charge—eagerly seized upon by Nazi propagandists—of cowardice: after forcing unwilling Norwegian crews on to their own ships at pistol point, went the story, and making them sail for Britain, Binney had saved his skin by skulking in a backwater while the other ships sailed to destruction. Many loyal Norwegians, indeed, shook their heads over the recall signal and doubted that it had ever been sent. It was not for some time that a full investigation ordered by the Admiralty was able to show what had happened; and since the results of this investigation were never made public, the doubts persisted.

Even Swedish sympathisers could not understand why the operation had been left in the hands of a steel control official rather than a naval expert, and why adequate naval and air support could not have been given. They surmised that the British had egged on the Norwegian seamen and then let them down, as earlier they had let down other allies. Certainly the surface escort was weak; and to compound this weakness the air operations were severely hampered at times by the weather. But fifty-nine Coastal Command aircraft flew a total of over 350 hours on escort duties, and many of the bitterest air combats took place out of sight of the ships themselves. Nevertheless the overall losses could not be disguised, and, in neutral Sweden, confidence in Britain's ability to conduct warlike operations was shaken.

The exaggerated claims of the Germans, however, who began by describing the breakout as a 'complete failure', with all ships sunk except one, and that severely damaged, worked in Binney's favour, so that when it was known in London that two ships and three crews had reached Britain, that two more ships were safe in Gothenburg, that not a single ship had been captured, and that nearly all the missing crews and supernumeraries had survived to be taken prisoner, the Ministry of Information felt able to classify the attempt as 'partially successful'. Of the total tonnage 34 per cent had been lost through enemy action, but the second most important ship, carrying 27 per cent of the total cargo by value and 20 per cent by weight, had got through, and of the remainder, 45 per cent by both value and weight was safe in Dicto and Lionel. The greatest deprivation on the cargo side was the heavy machines for making ball-bearings that were still aboard the Dicto. On 4th April Eden noted: 'Not as bad as I feared'; and when Binney, who had remained aboard the Dicto, suggested trying again with the two remaining ships if an opportunity presented itself, the Foreign Secretary pronounced himself ready to sanction this subject to operational considerations.

Postscript to Performance

Binney had never expected more than 50 per cent success with Operation Performance; but he was convinced that much more would have been achieved but for the hostility of the Swedish Navy, and as soon as he returned to Gothenburg he called on Admiral Akermark to demand an explanation. In ordering the ships out of Swedish territorial waters when they had not stopped or anchored, in firing warning shots, and in forecasting that a return to Gothenburg would debar the ships from coming out again, the Swedes had clearly exceeded their instructions as communicated in writing to Binney eight days before the breakout. Akermark was noncommittal, but he claimed to have protested to Admiral Tamm, Head of the

Swedish Navy, that the regulations were too severe and to have been overruled. His defence of the Swedish patrols was that they had been preventing the ships from entering inner territorial waters, which was certainly prohibited by Binney's instructions, though German vessels were normally allowed to lie there; but Binney retorted that none of his ships had had any reason to go into these waters, nor had they attempted to do so. Even if that had been their intention, he added, with heavy sarcasm, they could not have done so at the points where the incidents took place without travelling some distance overland.

Angry as Binney was with the Swedes, and not without reason, he was not any angrier than they were soon to become with him. By smuggling arms and ammunition aboard he had committed the sin of exporting arms to a belligerent country, a serious breach of Swedish neutrality. The Germans had alleged from the first that the ships had fired back at their aircraft; now, following the examination of the prisoners they had taken, they were able to reconstruct the breakout attempt in considerable detail. The venture, they said, had been under the leadership of Sir George Binney, and his closest collaborators had been Messrs Waring and Coleridge. All the ships had been armed. Machine-guns and ammunition had been smuggled aboard in accordance with Binney's instructions. It was Vice-Consul Coleridge, they alleged, who had conveyed them to the ships, in mail sacks in a *corps diplomatique* car. Thus not only had Sweden's neutrality been violated, but the protection of diplomatic immunity had been deceitfully invoked to effect that violation. Since the Swedes had emphatically declared to the Germans that the Norwegian ships would not be allowed to use Swedish territorial waters to wait for a favourable opportunity to escape, the German Government questioned why two of them had been allowed to return to territorial waters and assumed they would not be allowed out again. Would the Swedes now arrest Binney for having violated Swedish Customs and explosives restrictions and take him to court?

It might have been possible to deny these allegations altogether had not a report appeared on the front page of the *Daily Express* on 7th April, under the headline 'The Men of Hell Passage', which quoted a first-hand account of how one of the escaping ships had fought off first one plane and then another. 'We gave him a surprise when we opened up at him with our two Lewis guns—the only guns we had— and gave him a lot of lead. We had only a thousand rounds for each gun, and we had to be careful, but for two hours we kept that Jerry at bay . . . Later another German plane attacked us with machine-guns. We fought him off for half an hour, and he flew away. Twenty minutes later he came back with three heavy bombers. We were nearly out of ammunition by now.' The speaker had clearly been on the Rigmor. Somehow this report, and a BBC broadcast on similar lines, got past the censor, who could not have realised the implications, and the cat was out of the bag. At the Foreign Office, and at the British Legation in Stockholm, faces were uniformly red. Boheman had twice stressed to Mallet that the ships could not be equipped with arms of any kind in Sweden, and Mallet, carefully kept in ignorance by Binney, had emphatically denied that any such arming was contemplated; now, following the newspaper report, Mallet was summoned to Boheman's presence and asked to explain. He replied that he had absolutely no knowledge of any of the ships being armed.

It had been the objective of the Swedes to place the whole controversy about the ships on a legal rather than a political level, so that, in the event of complications, they could plead non-alignment. Now both Germans and British were accusing them of bad faith. For their part they complained to Mallet that their confidence had been abused and that they had been put in the position of admitting to the Germans that they were either knaves or fools. The Swedish Chancellor of Justice ordered an investigation, and Binney was called before Boheman and the Director of Political Affairs, Steffan Söderblom, on 12th April in company with Mallet. Binney decided that in the circumstances he had no option but to own up, especially since the Swedes were threatening to search Dicto and Lionel, discharging their cargoes in doing so for examination, which would have meant forfeiting any chance of sailing in the near future. He told Boheman he had felt it necessary for the safety of the crews to procure and to place aboard the ships a total of twenty Lewis guns with a thousand rounds for each gun. No one at the Legation, he asserted, had had any knowledge of this. Binney took it that Boheman would not expect him to give details of how the guns were obtained, but he hinted at the presence of war material left behind from the Norwegian and Finnish campaigns. According to the Swedes, while he was making this confession Binney 'endeavoured to look totally calm, whereas the British Minister looked extremely depressed and embarrassed'. Mallet, who confirmed in his memoirs (so far unpublished) that he knew nothing of Binney's arming of the ships, must surely have extracted a confession from Binney before this meeting; but Binney complimented him afterwards on 'his restrained gestures of surprise, pain and despair at my confession of guilt'.

All this amused Boheman no end. He was pleased at Binney's frankness, and ready to treat the proffered explanation of how the guns were obtained as an acceptable cover for the improper uses of the diplomatic bag which he had no doubt had taken place. For his part he had disliked the hastily effected law amendment which had caused the delay in the first place, and he felt no animosity towards Binney and eschewed recriminations. But diplomacy must take its course. 'I had the impression that Binney regarded the whole matter as a glorious adventure. Personally I could by no means look at it that way.' He made it clear, at this and subsequent meetings with Mallet, that the Swedes would be asking for Binney's recall. As for Dicto and Lionel, these, suggested Boheman, should be laid-up in Gothenburg, where Norwegian and British rights to the ships and their cargoes would be respected; he did not imagine that the Swedish Government would allow any further attempts at escape. This policy was taken a step further on 16th April when Björn Prytz delivered a protest note to the Foreign Office in London and told Eden of his Government's desire that Binney be recalled and the boats laid-up. Eden apologised for the embarrassment that had been inflicted on the Swedes and promised that Binney would be called home for consultation; but he rejected a similar demand for the removal of Waring and Coleridge. The British Government, added Eden, did not want to dispense altogether with their breakout plans for the ships, but there would be no attempt during the coming months. Unknown to the British, Günther had already informed Prince Wied in a personal letter that Dicto and Lionel would not be permitted to leave port again. Indeed there is evidence that, if it came to it, the Swedish Navy had orders to sink them rather than allow them to do so.

Binney flew home on 18th April, and on the 24th proceedings were started against the masters of Dicto and Lionel for smuggling arms without export licences, to a background of calumnies in the pro-German press, and particularly in the evening newspaper *Aftonbladet*, against Binney in person and the British in general. Parts of guns, it was said, had been concealed on the persons of British officials whose diplomatic immunity rendered control difficult. These were underhand methods, involving the exploitation of privileges. 'The British say "Play the game",' said one newspaper. 'This game was not clean.' 'Such action,' was another comment, 'accords ill with the gentlemanly qualities attributed to the British.' Other newspapers, and especially the *Göteborgs Handels-och Sjöfartstidning*, owned by Professor Torgny Segerstedt, a passionate Liberal and a proved friend of Britain, put the matter in a different perspective. More than 350 Norwegians had taken part in the attempt, and it had been quite clear to all of them what risk they were taking. There had been no coercion: of their own free will they had defied death and capture to get to Britain and fight for their country. These men were not foolhardy; they had risked their lives for their ideals of liberty and democracy. It was clear which side the moral strength was on. As for breaches of neutrality, that was not a game that had been begun by the British.

The defence offered on behalf of Captains Nicholas and Kershaw was that they had been acting on the orders of their Government. It had been necessary to arm the ships to protect the lives of the crews and to ensure that the vessels could continue in the event of air attack. The weapons had not been taken on board until the ships had been improperly prevented from leaving Gothenburg in the dark season, and they were not used then until after international waters had been reached. The two masters, although found guilty, were not sentenced to imprisonment, and the fines levied on them—£70 and £50— were little more than nominal, demonstrating that the attitudes of a section of the Swedish press were not typical.

Two other investigations were going on behind the scenes; the first was an appraisal of Binney's complaints against the Swedish Navy, which was undertaken by Henry Denham; the second was the Foreign Office enquiry, demanded by the Norwegians, into the general conduct of the operation. Against the Swedish Navy, Binney had advanced four main complaints:

1. That by putting to sea some hours before the Performance ships, they had advertised their departure to the Germans.

2. That when five of the ships were proceeding through outer territorial waters, as they were entitled to do, warning shots were fired at them by a Swedish patrol boat and they were ordered to put to sea, and told that if they returned to Gothenburg they would never get out again.

3. That the Dicto having anchored at the request of a Swedish pilot near Hallö was arrested by a Swedish destroyer on the penalty of being fired on.

4. That the Norwegian ships were wrongly denied the use of inner territorial waters, although the Germans consistently used them.

Denham narrowed Binney's complaints down to two points, which he put directly to the Swedish naval staff: the advertising of the departure, and the orders to put to sea. The Swedes replied that the departure must have been generally known, since all the preparations had been visible to German agents ashore (in fact, as related, they had missed it, and they did not discover it until next morning; but the argument was a reasonable one). As for the orders to put to sea, they produced the evidence of their ships' logs to support their contention that the Norwegian ships had in fact entered or attempted to enter inner waters. (All the captains, British and Norwegian, would certainly have disputed this; but if this were the case, why wasn't the release of the Skytteren prisoners insisted on?) The Swedes contended that they had allowed 'a considerable part of the Swedish west coast to be used for a base for breaking through the German guard lines'; and there was some truth in this. But this concession, they admitted, had been restricted in order to minimise the risk of the Germans being provoked into taking offensive action in Swedish waters, first by a limit of time, in that the ships must not stop or anchor in the neutrality channel, and second by a limit of place, in that they were not allowed to enter inner waters.

Denham concluded that Sweden's sole wish had been to prevent, at almost any cost, incidents of an Altmark kind within her waters, and regulations had been gradually introduced to support that policy. From the British point of view, these regulations had been embarrassing and had seriously restricted the chances of making any reasonable plan to run the ships through the blockade. In addition, some of the Swedish crews had been over-zealous in forcing the ships out of Swedish waters and had clearly exceeded their duty. The men responsible, Denham was assured, had been reprimanded. But Denham did not believe that this over-zealousness had seriously influenced the subsequent course of the operation. From his study of the documents made available to him, he acquitted the Swedish Navy of treachery.

The Germans, as the Swedes were never tired of repeating, had professed themselves equally dissatisfied with Swedish measures regarding the breakout; but extracts from the German naval attaché's diary reflect a more contrite Swedish attitude. 'Profound regret' was expressed, according to the diary, and the Swedish Navy 'felt most distressed' if it could be thought that they had failed to uphold Swedish neutrality, especially since 'the Navy's behaviour throughout had favoured the interest of Germany predominantly'. There was no doubt that this was so. But following Denham's report, all complaints against the Swedes were dropped, and the Foreign Office, with the eventual clearance of Dicto and Lionel still very much in mind, sought to repair the political damage that had been done. Although the two ships were kept in commission, further operations, as Eden had promised, were abandoned for the summer.

It was not until August that the Foreign Office produced the results of their enquiry. So far as Performance's *raison d'être* was concerned, they confirmed that the cargoes had been sufficiently important to make it essential to sail the ships out in the spring, even though from the purely operational point of view it would have been better to wait for the winter. As for the plan of operation, they dealt briefly with a variety of criticisms.

1. The attempt had involved a higher risk than in 1941.

2. Binney had chosen the best and shortest route.

3. Expert meteorological information had been continuously available.

4. Binney had made the most thorough and detailed preparations right up to the departure from Gothenburg.

5. All possible efforts had been made to protect the ships from air attack.

6. Protection of the ships from sabotage had been difficult but on the whole successful. The single exception might have been the Skytteren, but this was unproved.

7. The operation had been deliberately delayed by the legal wrangle throughout the winter, and further delayed by ice conditions in the final fortnight.

8. At the request of the Norwegian Legation, as many Norwegian supernumeraries as was reasonable had been added to the crews.

9. Difficulties had been caused by the Gothenburg naval and Customs authorities.

10. Binney had made the perfectly reasonable decision not to allow the Norwegian captains at the final meeting in view of their disobedience of his orders to remain on board and to forbid any communication with the shore. They had been accorded their full rights once outside the territorial limit.

11. The weather had developed unfavourably, a long fog being necessary to offset the shorter hours of darkness.

12. The Swedish authorities had not permitted the ships to use anchorages that would have allowed full advantage to be taken of such fog as there was.

13. Descriptions of the various voyages reflected misfortune rather than poor leadership or faulty organisation.

14. The failure of the surface forces to make contact with more than three of the ships was because the others didn't get far enough to come within range of help. Considerable effort in appalling conditions was made to save Rigmor.

15. Air operations by Coastal Command had been badly hampered, and German air operations considerably aided, by the weather conditions. But air action had been on a much larger scale than those on the escaping vessels imagined.

16. The order from the destroyer to Dicto to follow her into Gothenburg or be sunk ought to dispel any feeling that Binney deliberately turned tail when the going got sticky.

The only criticisms begged, perhaps, by these summaries were the failure of the recall signal, which was later dealt with by the Admiralty, and the vexed question, repeatedly asked by the Swedes and others, of why, if the supplies were of such consequence to Britain's war industry, stronger naval forces were not risked to extend the surface escort into the jaws of the Skagerrak and beyond. Did the paucity and timidity of the naval dispositions reflect an exaggerated estimate by some Government Ministries of the importance of the cargoes and the ships that carried them? Reference back to the modest surface forces allocated to Rubble, whose importance has been demonstrated, and then forward again to the maritime catastrophes of 1941/42, and especially to the escape six weeks earlier of the Scharnhorst and Gneisenau from Brest through the Channel, would seem to provide an acceptable answer. The British Navy were simply not equipped at this time to risk conclusions with the *Luftwaffe*.

If Binney ever saw the Foreign Office report it must have given him considerable satisfaction, since it cleared him of all the charges that had been levelled against him. He held firmly to the view that the Swedish Government, by their delaying tactics, and by the orders they had caused to be issued by the Navy, had wrecked the operation; but in retrospect he conceded that if the Swedes genuinely believed that a successful operation would endanger their security, they had had a right to act as they did. The Swedes, he believed, had made an initial blunder in countenancing the expedition in the first place: when export permits were applied for, they should have refused them. But they wanted the best of both worlds—the continuity of trade with Britain and the West, and the maintenance of a peaceful co-existence with Occupied Europe. They thus pursued a policy of wait and see, hoping that by the time the ships were ready to sail, the war would have reached a decisive stage, making up their minds for them. Despite Germany's attack on Russia in June 1941, and the entry of the United States into the war in December—events which between them had changed the whole war picture since Rubble—the Allied disasters that followed had convinced the Swedes that they could not yet afford to incur the extremes of Nazi wrath.

Rubble had brought Binney honours and plaudits that had astonished and delighted him. Performance had been the other side of the coin. Yet the Foreign Office, the Ministry of Economic Warfare, the Ministry of Supply and the Ministry of War Transport all stood by

The *Charente*, and (inset) Björn Egge

The *Rigmor*, and (inset) F. Wessel Berg

'Ginger' Stokes

Harry Whitfield

Four of the five 'Little Ship' captains

'Jacko' Jackson

George Holdsworth

him. The need for special machinery and ball-bearings—not so much in quantity now as in quality—remained, as did all the other factors which had made it desirable to preserve the Anglo-Swedish War Trade Agreement as a reality. Binney might for the moment be *persona non grata* in Sweden. But by the end of that summer he was already replanning the escape of Dicto and Lionel.

PART III

OPERATION BRIDFORD
The Grey Ladies

In the latter part of 1942 the British Government continued to impress on the Swedes the urgency of developing a supply line for the further import of special steels. It was, they said, 'vital to the general war effort of the United Nations', and would have 'widespread effects on our whole war production'. There is no reason to believe that these resounding phrases were in any way an exaggeration. But any plans for the breakout of the Norwegian ships from Swedish waters had to be approved by the Norwegian Government in London; and although the Admiralty, and particularly Rear-Admiral E. J. P. Brind, Assistant Chief of Naval Staff (Home), and Captain J. A. S. Eccles, Director Operations Department (Home), believed that the best chance of a breakout for Dicto and Lionel was to dash out of Gothenburg in thick weather, without necessarily waiting for an escort, the Norwegians flatly refused to countenance any escape plan that left the ships unprotected. The Royal Navy remained equally unwilling to expose their warships to attacks in the Skagerrak by the *Luftwaffe*, and because of the political row after Performance there was no possibility of providing the ships with anti-aircraft guns; not, anyway, while they were in Gothenburg, or any other Swedish port. Binney now suggested an alternative: the despatch of a number of motor gunboats to the Swedish coast, with the object partly of acting as escort and partly of carrying Oerlikon and Lewis guns and Merchant Navy gunners for transfer to Dicto and Lionel at an agreed rendezvous. A scheme was worked out in collaboration with the Admiralty, and the Norwegians agreed. The operation was to be mounted in the dark period and was planned for December 1942. George Binney, basing himself in Britain, was to have overall control, with Brian Reynolds, released from the Commando unit he had joined that summer, as his assistant and Bill Waring in charge in Gothenburg. Three 'D' (diesel) class motor gunboats, under the command of Lieutenant-Commander Duff-Still, RNVR, were allocated from the Navy's Coastal Forces for this task, and consumption tests showed that they had enough fuel to reach the rendezvous, complete the transfer, and return to what was called their 'waiting position' in the middle of the North Sea, at a maximum continuous speed of twenty-three knots. On this basis, plans were concluded for the MGBs to sail from Britain to make a rendezvous at dawn off the Hallö Islands, just outside Swedish waters, where the transfer would be made. Ivar Blücker, flown out from Stockholm to Britain after Performance, was appointed chief navigation officer. The MGBs would then return to their waiting position and the ships would seize the first opportunity to break out into the Skagerrak. If all went well this would follow at dusk on the day of the transfer.

The three motor gunboats made ready to leave Rosyth in December as planned; but the Swedes had promised the Germans that Dicto and Lionel would not be allowed to leave Gothenburg again, and although they had no legal right to restrain them they continued to refuse them clearance. Meanwhile, lest the ships should attempt to leave without it, they placed chains and other obstacles in their way.

The Swedes were caught in a dilemma that was becoming all too familiar to them: whichever side they displeased would immediately stop the Gothenburg traffic. Since the Germans continued to back up this threat by hints of even more drastic consequences, they prevailed upon the Swedes to procrastinate throughout 1942. By the end of that year, supported by strong representations from the United States, the British had devised an equally effective form of blackmail. Not only did the Allies deliver an ultimatum on the closure of the Gothenburg traffic, but they also referred specifically to the moral right the Swedes would earn, by their co-operation now, to imports of oil and other basic materials that might be in short supply both during and after the war. This veiled threat of being treated as lepers on the post-war scene, to a Government that was beginning to believe in the possibility of an Allied victory, brought immediate results, and on 13th January 1943 the Swedes signified their readiness to give clearance for the ships to leave Gothenburg as from 00.01 on 17th January, and to lie-up subsequently in Hakefjord, a small fjord near Vinga (not the larger fjord of the same name farther north). But they were still looking back over one shoulder, and what they gave with one hand they took away with the other. Next day, 14th January, in an effort to make their conduct unexceptionable to the Germans, they advised them of their intention to release the ships.

Dicto and Lionel duly left Gothenburg on the 17th, and after compass adjustments in Rivöfjord they anchored in Hakefjord on the afternoon of the 18th. The Dicto had seventy tons of diesel fuel on board and the Lionel fifty-two, which would allow them to remain at anchor for about twenty days and still have enough for the passage to Britain. But it looked as though they might not have long to wait: Bill Waring, deputising for George Binney on Dicto, reported that conditions were ideal. It was warm and foggy, and there was no ice.

The Germans, however, reacted quickly and incisively. They suspended the Gothenburg traffic, they redoubled the strength and vigilance of their surface and air patrols in the Kattegat and Skagerrak, and they despatched three fleet destroyers to Kristiansand to deal with any ship that got through. 'The Germans are now patrolling the coast with armed trawlers and Norwegian whale-catchers,' reported one agent. 'These latter are capable of at least sixteen knots. The coast has not been patrolled in this manner since July 1942.' And when the presence of the destroyers at Kristiansand was confirmed by aerial reconnaissance, the grave threat to the success of Operation 'Cabaret', as the venture was code-named, was recognised.

To complicate matters the Swedes now ruled that the ships could not remain at Hakefjord after dawn on 19th January, which meant that they must leave straight away. They justified this ruling on the grounds that extensive naval arrangements were involved which could not be prolonged indefinitely. If the ships had not sailed by that time they must return to Gothenburg. Boheman even asked how it was, if the operation was as urgent as the British maintained, that the ships hadn't sailed already.

Binney visited the Admiralty on the morning of the 19th and reviewed the situation with Eccles. Since there were strong naval grounds for believing that the positioning of the three destroyers could be no more than a temporary measure, the decision was taken to postpone the operation until they left, and no objection was therefore raised to the return of the ships to Gothenburg. But the blame for the fiasco was put firmly on the Swedes, first for informing the Germans that the ban had been lifted, and second, and more importantly, for imposing the ban at all. If clearance had been given when it was first asked for, the Germans could not have mobilised the destroyer force which had become the chief obstacle to success.

Boheman's answer was that German patrol craft had been exercising off Gothenburg since the beginning of January, preparations for the breakout could not be hidden, and in informing the Germans the Swedes had merely been stating the obvious. His view was shared by Victor Mallet, who pronounced himself 'more and more mystified at the long delay'. The postponement, he said, only increased his doubts of the suitability of both Binney and Waring for the tasks they had been entrusted with. 'I have never been able to understand why an operation of this kind, which is basically a naval one, should, in so far as its organisation at this end is concerned, be placed in the hands of a man without professional naval experience,' he told the Foreign Office. 'As you doubtless know, Denham was not uncritical of Binney's judgment during the last operation, and on this occasion we are far from feeling reassured by the fact that an operation of such vital importance has been placed at this end in the hands of a man who, though a courageous and ingenious fellow, is by profession a chartered accountant.'

The Admiralty estimated that no less than twenty-four German vessels of war, ranging from fleet destroyers to armed trawlers and U-boats, were being kept from their normal duties to prevent a break-out; and so long as the destroyers remained at Kristiansand they believed the operation had little chance of success. Meanwhile the Norwegians in London renewed their opposition, irrespective of whether the destroyers moved or not. The weather, they believed, was too unpredictable at the point of leaving Swedish territorial waters, and the planned air cover inadequate at the point of leaving the Skagerrak. Nevertheless when news came through on 4th February that the German destroyers had left Kristiansand, Operation Cabaret was set in motion.

The weather forecast was favourable, and that evening the three MGBs, with George Binney on one of them, sailed from Aberdeen. But next day, when the flotilla was within seventy miles of the Skagerrak, Admiralty Intelligence received warning of an enemy naval force on passage southwards from northern Norway, escorted by destroyers and supported by air reconnaissance. (The heavy cruiser Hipper and the smaller Köln were being moved down to the Baltic.) To add to the discomfiture of the MGBs, an unpredicted southerly Force 9 gale sprang up which compelled them to reduce speed. The three boats were recalled, and they suffered extensive minor damage before reaching Berwick-upon-Tweed. Equally significant for the future, their Coastal Forces crews were not accustomed to long spells of bad weather at sea, and a combination of fatigue and sea-sickness brought the majority of them to the point of physical collapse.

A fortnight later the various Ministries concerned decided regretfully but unanimously that the operation must be cancelled. The nights were getting shorter, and the MGBs were in any case due for a major overhaul. Dicto and Lionel, however, were to be kept in commission. Although Cabaret had proved abortive, it had served a useful purpose in helping to absorb German naval and air energies, and if these energies were relaxed, the possibility of a breakout could always be reconsidered.

* * *

On 5th March the Controller of Bearings spoke of the impossibility of increasing production in Britain of certain special types of ball-bearings for at least twelve months. The most serious shortages were in the smaller sizes of airframe and engine bearings. A new factory, devoted to filling the gap, was being planned, but it would be a year before production began. The bearings required were only available in Sweden. Small quantities were being transported from Stockholm by air, mostly in the Lockheed courier service, but these were measured in kilos rather than tons. Even a small vessel of the size of a motor gunboat could carry in one trip the equivalent of about forty Lockheed flights from Stockholm. Herein lay the germ of a new type of operation.

On 13th March the Ministry of Aircraft Production spelt out in simple terms what a delivery of even as small an amount as 100 tons of ball-bearings could achieve. Assuming a sensible selection of types and sizes was made, 100 tons would be sufficient, they said, to cover 75 per cent of the airframe work on 1,200 Lancasters and 60 per cent of the airframe work on 1,600 Mosquitoes, the remainder of the bearings being available from stock. This led George Binney to put forward one of his most imaginative schemes, in which fast diesel-engined coastal craft were to be employed to run the Skagerrak blockade. Such craft, he argued, with their high speed and shallow draft, had an excellent chance of evading detection and could penetrate ordinary minefields with impunity. They would not be so vulnerable to air attack as petrol boats, and would not need to refuel in Sweden. The only doubt was whether they would be robust enough for a round trip of 1,000 miles in the conditions to be expected in the North Sea in winter. Summer operation was hardly thought to be possible.

Binney's proposal was taken up enthusiastically by the naval staff, who envisaged two possible methods of operation, one by Merchant Navy crews under the Red Ensign, the other by Royal Navy crews under the White Ensign. The Red Ensign seemed preferable as combatant crews were restricted to a stay of twenty-four hours in Swedish ports; but against this the only crews trained to operate motor gunboats were naval ones. So on balance the White Ensign was favoured. The proposition was put to the Swedes, with the promise that if an MGB operation were facilitated and if it proved successful, Dicto and Lionel would be laid-up. They reacted favourably at first, then remembered a Royal Decree (No. 222) of 12th April 1940 which specifically forbade all belligerent ships from visiting Swedish ports except in distress. There proved to be no way round this decree, and the only alternative was to postpone the operation until the autumn and train selected merchant seamen meanwhile. This was an ideal solution for the Swedes, who could get the Germans to re-open the Gothenburg traffic while Dicto and Lionel were laid-up, and import all the cargoes they needed before the start of the MGB operation in the autumn resulted, as it inevitably would, in the Germans closing the traffic again. For the British the delay was a further frustration, but it was hoped to get a selection of urgent supplies transported by air.

Lest the Swedes should misinterpret Britain's acceptance of the delay, the Foreign Office were at pains to emphasise that 'we did not exaggerate in the slightest the importance to the war production of the United Nations of the cargoes in Dicto and Lionel'. The failure to obtain these cargoes, they said, remained a serious blow.

Binney envisaged the employment of six fast motor gunboats each capable of carrying forty to fifty tons of ball-bearings. They should enter the Skagerrak at dusk under suitable conditions of weather and no-moon and arrive off the Swedish coast at dawn. After entering territorial waters they would make for Brofjord, where Dicto and Lionel would be positioned as depot ships, providing cargoes, maintenance and spares facilities, meteorological information, and communications. Again choosing the right conditions, they would sail westwards through the night at high speed and be well into the North Sea by daylight, where air cover would be provided.

Success would depend on evasion; although the MGBs would be faster than any patrol craft that might be employed against them, they could be caught by destroyers. This meant winter operation only, with its inevitable problems for craft which had not been designed to cross the North Sea in winter at high speeds carrying heavy loads. Their sailings would be restricted severely, probably to not more than one short period per month. They could only operate at speed in moderate seas, and their fire-power would be seriously affected by rough weather.

The Ministries concerned requested Special Operations Executive to mount the operation, and SOE deputed Binney to organise it for them; his task was to run 400 to 500 tons of supplies through the blockade in the next winter season. On 25th April the Admiralty allocated five motor gunboats for conversion, one of which was already in commission and the other four in various stages of completion at Messrs. Camper and Nicholson's yard at Gosport. The boats had originally been part of a flotilla of eight ordered by the Turkish Navy in 1938/39. They were rather larger than the majority of naval gunboats, being 117 feet long with a ten-foot beam. Plans for the conversion having been agreed, Camper and Nicholson were authorised to undertake the reconstruction of three of the boats at Gosport and Southampton while Messrs. Amos and Smith converted the other two at their works at Albert Dock, Hull.

To make space for sizeable cargo holds, the entire forward crew compartment was gutted out, while the officers' accommodation, wardroom and pantry were similarly transformed into an after-hold, making an overall cargo capacity of up to forty-five tons. A light-weight plywood deckhouse, whose overall dimensions were only 36′ x 14′ 6″, was constructed amidships to provide accommodation for the crew of eighteen to twenty, and this also housed the galley, the shower, and a wireless cabin, about 5′ x 4′, in which navigational, radio and radar instruments were installed. An armoured box bridge, open to the elements, was superimposed over the fore part of the deckhouse, reached either by ladder at the after end or through a hatch in the roof of the wireless cabin. Within the bridge, and flush with its height, a wooden hut was built, enclosing a small chart table at which there was just room to sit. A mast and a collapsible derrick were also fitted.

The boats were triple-screw, with a centre and two wing engines. The Turks had specified Davey Paxman Ricardo sixteen-cylinder diesels each developing 1,000 b.h.p., so the nominal propulsion was 3,000 h.p., with a theoretical top speed of twenty-eight knots. But in their modified form the boats were expected to have a top speed of twenty-three knots, a cruising speed of twenty, and a range of 1,200 miles at seventeen knots—a performance which was regarded as satis-factory for Operation 'Bridford' (the code-word allocated), provided sailings were confined to the winter period.

The boats were armed with two hand-operated twin Oerlikons with emplacements on the deck fore and aft, and on either wing of the bridge there were external platforms carrying twin Vickers ·303 machine-guns. A central battery of quadruple Vickers was mounted aft of the bridge box on the upper deck. Navigational aids included gyro and magnetic compass, echo-sounder, and ASV (air-to-surface vessel), a primitive but effective form of airborne radar which proved useful at sea level. Scuttling charges were installed as a precaution against capture. Gross registered tonnage after conversion was 149. The ships were painted an anonymous grey; but there were portraits of Churchill in the saloon and of Drake in the captain's cabin.

Binney turned to the obvious agency for operating and manning the boats—Ellerman's Wilson of Hull. Ellerman's called for volun-teers for a service entailing special risks, and this no doubt accounted for the calibre of the crews they recruited, 70 per cent of whom were Hull men. In the cramped conditions on board, each man would have to fit in like the pieces of a jig-saw, and the crews were chosen as much for their adaptability as for their skill. They were young men mostly, many of them no more than twenty, and they were given young captains—first mates holding masters' certificates being appointed to each ship to enjoy the thrill of their first command. Second mates were appointed mates, the chief and second engineers were specially recruited diesel experts, and each boat carried two wireless operators. The pay, by the standards of the time, was good. After preliminary vetting by the Marine Superintendent of the Wilson Line, likely candidates were sent to London to be interviewed by George Binney, and he it was who made the final choice.

By this time Binney had been officially appointed commodore of the flotilla, with Brian Reynolds, masquerading under a beard and the pseudonym of Bingham (because of his involvement in Performance), as his vice-commodore. It was not thought feasible for Binney to adopt a disguise, and anyway it was thought that the Swedes would accept him; but to protect him in the event of capture he was granted the rank of Commander, RNVR. Bill Waring remained Binney's representative in Stockholm, and Jack Aird was appointed to act as Waring's deputy in Gothenburg. The operation was controlled by a committee which included old friends in 'Jas' Eccles, Harry Sporborg and Mike Wheeler. Headquarters would be at Hull, but an alternative operational base was provided farther down the Humber in the comparative isolation of Immingham. Naval jurisdiction was to be exercised by Admiral Sir John Tovey, now C-in-C Nore. A special Naval Intelligence Department team under Commander (S) N. E. 'Ned' Denning, aided by regular aerial reconnaissance and a continual study of enemy signals traffic, would watch the German dispositions in the Skagerrak and advise Nore Command on when and how Binney and his little ships could best beat the blockade.

In naming the boats for registration, Binney wanted to recall significant events in Britain's maritime history; but from his original choice the only name available was Nonsuch, the ship which made the first voyage for the Hudson's Bay Company. This, however, was singularly appropriate. Four of the boats, including the Nonsuch, were to be delivered by the end of July, and Binney chose Hopewell, Gay Viking and Gay Corsair for the other three. The fifth boat was not due to be delivered until the end of August, but Binney was anxious to have its name ready. 'We have our tradition in Nonsuch,' he wrote, 'our aspirations in Hopewell, and our light-heartedness in Gay Viking and Gay Corsair. I have been groping to find a suitable name which would crystallise the steadfastness of our purpose. I think Master Standfast will do that.' With this excursion into *The Pilgrim's Progress*, the naming of the ships was complete.

THE BLOCKADE BUSTERS

One aspect of the operation that was probably unique was the appointment of the chief officers. Experience with Cabaret had disclosed the real danger of physical collapse in this type of small-ship operation; and the deck officers and crews, with their deep-sea training, might not easily accustom themselves to the strain and racket of winter voyages in motor gunboats in the North Sea. The operation would demand a degree of endurance and discipline which would almost certainly be outside the experience of even the most hardened merchant seamen. The appointment to each ship of a chief officer of rather wider background than might be found in the junior ranks of the Merchant Navy, senior to all on board except the master, sea-minded and physically proof against sea-sickness, was therefore suggested by SOE and agreed upon by all parties. Although acting as staff officers to the commodore, they would owe full allegiance to the master while on board ship and would stand watch in turn with master and mate. Their principal overt duty would be gunnery officer, and they would be held responsible for the efficient handling of all the fighting equipment, smoke apparatus, scuttling charges, and operational things of that kind. They would also undertake the duties of Security and Welfare Officer. But implicit in their appointment was a personal responsibility for the confidence and morale of the crews and the standard of fighting efficiency they attained.

First to be appointed of the five chief officers was Brian Reynolds, or Bingham; it was a job he could comfortably double with the role of vice-commodore. Lieutenant Roger Thornycroft, RNVR, a member of the boat-building family, was a personal choice of Binney's; an expert in small boats, he had been a contemporary of Binney's at Eton and a lifelong friend and squash adversary. Pensioned off by the Navy following an injury, he was thrilled at the chance to get back into action. Summing-up George Binney as a 'brave little fellow who knew damn-all about boats', he was nevertheless prepared to follow him. The third chief officer, Captain the Earl Fitzwilliam, of the Grenadier Guards, had served with Brian Reynolds in the Commandos; having recently succeeded to the title, he was given the cover name of Peter Lawrence to avoid being singled out in case of capture. Alwyn Reynolds Brown, loaned by the Naval Intelligence Branch, was a foreman boat-builder and repairer; he soon earned the reputation of knowing every sea shanty there was. The fifth man, Sub-Lieutenant J. Johnsen, was loaned by the Royal Norwegian Navy and would also act as an interpreter.

The men appointed as masters and mates were all regular officers of the Wilson Line. Of the masters, perhaps the most colourful were Robert Tanton and David 'Ginger' Stokes. Bob Tanton, who took over from another man at the last moment and missed all the early training, was a dapper little man with a twinkle in his eye. Stokes, red-haired and blue-eyed, and the only master who didn't hail from Hull (although like the others he lived there), was more rugged, with a town crier voice and a boisterous laugh to go with it. The others, H. W. 'Jacko' Jackson, tall, gaunt and sharp-featured, but amiable; and Harry Whitfield, short, dark and hook-nosed, with plodding, placid mien, were equally outstanding. Two other captains, Hewetson and Goodman, fell ill and had to be replaced.

*   *   *

While delivery of the boats was awaited, training of selected officers and crews was begun. At Hull, at Davey Paxman's works at Colchester, and at HMS Bee, the Coastal Forces base at Weymouth for the special training and working up of new MTB and MGB flotillas, every facility was made available. But the long months of delay that this training period meant in the delivery of the cargoes was not lightly accepted, and several alternative suggestions were put forward, among them one from Victor Mallet which was actually prompted by Erik Boheman. In view of the grave shortage of ball-bearings, and in view of the five new Dakotas (C47 transports) about to be allocated to the UK–Stockholm courier service, could not the service be turned into a military operation during the summer months? From 15th May to 15th August the service automatically closed down because of the long hours of daylight and the clear nights; but surely if the need was so desperate, risks should be taken as in any other wartime operation. These risks, suggested Mallet, would be no greater than those run by merchant seamen every day in the Atlantic.

When this suggestion reached A. V. Alexander at the Admiralty he passed it on to Oliver Lyttelton, Minister of Production, with a sting in the tail. 'I shall be most interested to hear what comes of this suggestion, particularly in view of the peculiar importance of the ball-bearings to the RAF aircraft programme.' This point was taken up by C. H. M. Waldock, Head of Military Intelligence. 'If the ball-bearings are as important to the RAF as has been represented to us, the risk would certainly seem justified.' The proposal should, felt Waldock, be examined most carefully in view of the hazards the MGBs and their crews were being asked to accept on the RAF's behalf.

As it happened, the courier service was run not by the RAF but by BOAC; and only one of the Dakotas was yet available. BOAC declined to risk it on any regular service during the short summer nights, but for several weeks that summer they ran an almost nightly service of Mosquitoes which brought in limited but urgent supplies for Britain and Russia. These loads, however, were still measured in kilos rather than in hundredweights or tons.

Early that summer Bill Waring flew back to Britain by Lockheed to confer with Binney; and in the middle of June he was ordered back to Stockholm to place urgent and substantial orders for ball-bearings. This was not so much to provide the loads for the motor gunboats as to block German purchases by pre-emptive buying. According to British Intelligence the Germans, following heavy Allied raids on their ball-bearing factories, were about to place large orders in Sweden, and Waring was to intervene as soon as possible. He was to be accompanied and supported by Ville Siberg, of SKF Luton, an old friend and helper of Binney and the blockade-runners.

The two men travelled to Leuchars in Scotland just before midsummer day, having been told that a Lockheed had been specially detailed to fly them to Sweden. As this was the lightest time of the year the crew were ordered not to fly without seven-tenths' cloud cover. But the weather proved obstinately clear, and while Waring and Siberg enjoyed frequent rounds of golf at nearby St. Andrews, five vital days went by. Here is Bill Waring's account of what followed.

On the fifth day I telephoned London and asked them if something could be done as I was afraid that with this delay the Germans would get in first. The Ministry of Economic Warfare counselled patience, and another day went by. Next day I again telephoned London without any noticeable result.

The following afternoon, 24th June, I was down at the swimming pool when an RAF car came speeding up and the driver said I was required on the airfield immediately. I went off right away in my swim shorts and found a number of rather worried-looking technicians standing around. They had received instructions from London that at all costs Siberg and I were to be flown to Sweden that night and that if no cloud cover developed we were each to be taken in the bomb-rack of a Mosquito, one man to a plane. This had never been attempted before and the technicians were nervous because of the close proximity of the petrol tanks, with the danger that fumes would be present in the bomb-rack. Other unknown factors were the temperature and the effect of the extremely cramped conditions.

The technicians expressed considerable doubts about the whole affair and asked whether I would take a trial flight and I said that as far as I was concerned I was going to take off once and once only. It was agreed that they would provide oxygen in the bomb-rack, as we would be flying at about 26,000 feet, and that a string leading up from the bomb-rack would be tied round the pilot's leg. If conditions became intolerable we were to pull the string and the pilot would return as rapidly as possible.

We were to be ready to leave our hotel at 19.30 that evening, and we must not drink any alcohol in the meantime.

I returned to the hotel and broke the news to Willie Siberg, and I'm afraid doctor's orders, too, were broken and we had a couple of stiff whiskies on the strength of it.

When we went out to the airfield that evening we found a large crowd assembled, including Viscount Knollys, then Chairman of BOAC. The machines of course were unarmed, with civilian markings.

Wrapped in a selection of flying suits, helmets and masks I staggered to the first machine and just managed to squeeze myself inside, after which the doors of the bomb-rack were closed. I was to take off a quarter of an hour before Willie, and if news was not received that the string had been pulled and the aircraft was returning, he would take off in the second machine.

In fact the flight was amazingly rapid, and we reached Sweden in about $3\frac{1}{2}$ hours. Conditions in the bomb-rack were quite reasonable although not altogether ideal for anyone with claustrophobia. The only drawback was that the bomb-doors had a tendency to creep and it was uncomfortable to contemplate even half-an-inch of nothing gradually widening.

We arrived in Sweden about 3 a.m. and the Minister sent a telegram saying 'Waring and Siberg arrived alive'.

They had been described on the freight manifest as 'one piece Waring, one piece Siberg', and each man was suitably grateful to arrive, as advertised, in one piece. Next day they began a successful campaign of commercial competition with the Germans, the sizes and types of their purchases often being those which the Germans were believed to be deficient of and bearing little relation to Britain's own needs. Once this task was behind him, Waring was able to concentrate his attention on making administrative arrangements for the gunboats, and with plenty of supplies now available, it was decided not to interfere with the loads on Dicto and Lionel.

It was obvious from the first that the co-operation of the Swedes would be essential, and on 12th August it was decided that all details of the plan except proposed sailing dates should be disclosed to them. Matters that Waring took up with Boheman were the use of Dicto and Lionel as a base from which the boats could be loaded while the crews rested, directives to Swedish Customs officials to cover the loading, blanket export licences (which were already in use for air transport), the issue of import and transfer licences for outward cargoes of fuel and spare parts, speedy and secret clearance when the ships were ready to go, and the embarkation of supernumeraries at the last moment, to allow the passage to Britain of selected Norwegians.

The use of Dicto and Lionel for loading and unloading was at once resisted by Boheman; such activities were forbidden by law at other than appointed Customs ports. And it soon transpired that he considered the whole scheme unsound and hazardous in the extreme. 'In my opinion,' he told Mallet, 'George Binney's plans have previously shown an optimism not always justified by the results.' He feared that the Germans would attack while the coasters were loading, and that a serious incident in Swedish waters would thus be provoked. He doubted the British view that the coasters would take some catching at night; and remembering past experience he thought the Germans would soon muster the necessary forces for preventive action. Nevertheless his regard for Binney shone through all his objections; the plan, he thought, had 'a certain boyish appeal'.

The obvious alternative to the use of Dicto and Lionel was the small fishing port, railhead and holiday resort of Lysekil, in Gulmarfjord. As it was a restricted area, no foreigners could reside there, and enemy agents would find it difficult to operate there. Cargoes could be sent up by rail, they could be handled on the town quay, storage space for up to 250 tons of ball-bearings could be leased, and there was easy access to Brofjord by car. If Dicto and Lionel were allowed to anchor in Brofjord, communications and maintenance work could continue as planned and the whole operation would be perfectly legal. At first the Swedes resisted; but under diplomatic pressure they agreed to all Waring's arrangements for transport, the erection of cranes, stevedoring and pilotage, the accommodation of crews for one night ashore, and the transfer of Dicto and Lionel from Gothenburg. These ships, agreed Boheman, could be moved up any time after 1st September, provided no attempt was made by either of them to break out before 1st October. With three ships due in Gothenburg in September from South America, the Swedes had to guard against the sudden closure of the Gothenburg traffic. Binney, as the Swedes rightly guessed, was still prepared to run Dicto out if an opportunity presented itself; but he did not intend to attempt it until the MGB operation had been given a thorough trial.

Subsequently the Swedes, alarmed that their traffic might be stopped before the cargoes got through, asked for a postponement of the operation until 1st December or anyway 1st November, but to this the British would not agree. Dicto, still under Captain Nicholas, and Lionel, under the Norwegian Captain Gotheson, duly arrived in Brofjord without incident on 7th September, and two days later the Swedes finally promised all possible assistance at Lysekil, instructing their officials there to be as helpful and elastic as possible. And to prevent the sort of incident they feared, they laid a boom across the neck of Brofjord and stationed a gunboat in the anchorage and an anti-aircraft battery ashore. The Germans, for their part, positioned a force of destroyers at Kristiansand as soon as Dicto and Lionel moved out of Gothenburg.

Two factors now caused a combination of doubt and delay. First were worries about security, since so many Swedes were in the know, and some of them were originating signals and memoranda that were not even marked confidential; and second was the development, revealed soon after the boats were delivered, of serious faults in the Paxman diesel engines and accessories. These engines were experimental, they had been rushed into service, and teething troubles were expected; but the problems that developed were of a fundamental nature.

In all other respects the crews settled down amazingly well. Gay Viking and Gay Corsair, having been sailed up from Gosport on completion, joined Hopewell and Nonsuch in Hull, and the crews then undertook what almost amounted to a circumnavigation, starting from Hull on 5th September and going 'northabout' via the Caledonian Canal to Holyhead, on the Isle of Anglesey, then returning 'southabout' to Hull. 'Man-handling the boats through the locks of that canal really helped to knit the crews together,' writes Eric Hodgson, first radio officer on Gay Corsair. Then 21, he was small and fresh-faced and looked little more than a schoolboy, despite several years of experience in Hull trawlers. 'During many subsequent years at sea I never met crews so completely compatible, especially in such cramped conditions.' These conditions were almost worse than they would be operationally as the fifth boat, Master Standfast, had not yet been delivered and her crew were spread over the other four. 'How we were picked in the first instance I don't know except that Sir George had expressed preference for Humberside men after his previous exploit. One or two minor misfits did inconspicuously disappear but the original crews were a pretty fine collection.' Those who pulled out were mostly the suggestible ones who listened to rumour. No one knew what their task was to be.

During nine days at Holyhead the crews concentrated on gunnery, flotilla manoeuvres, signalling, station-keeping, and air defence. They then faced a Force 10 gale in the Irish Sea as they ran down the west coast. On this stretch, from Holyhead to Portsmouth, they spent thirty-two hours at sea—four hours short of the anticipated length of an operational trip—in dreadful weather, and learnt for the first time what they had let themselves in for. 'The corkscrewing motion of triple-screw vessels,' writes Hodgson, 'combined with the pitch and pound, was unusual to most of us, and queasiness and actual sea-sickness were not uncommon, even to those who had "never been sea-sick in my life".' One of these was Tommy Mallory, an 18-year-old AB on Gay Corsair. 'Rounding Land's End,' he writes, 'was the only time I can remember being sea-sick.'

After calling for one night at each of the naval MGB bases along the south and east coast the boats returned to Immingham. Further exercises, including radar plotting and homing, were then carried out between Spurn Head and Flamborough Head, the ships going out almost daily to accustom dock personnel to frequent departures and arrivals. The actual operation of the radar was primitive in the extreme, the antenna at the masthead being rotated by means of a chain running down the mast, along the deck and into the radio cabin, where it was cranked on a bicycle pedal by hand. A minute or two of this in a rough sea was enough to emasculate anyone.

Subject to a reasonable weather forecast, it was intended that the ships should leave the Humber on the night of 23rd/24th September and sail in formation to the Swedish coast, taking an outward cargo of fuel-oil for Dicto and Lionel in drums. The combined fire-power of operating as a flotilla was preferred to attempting to run the blockade singly or in pairs. But shortly before the proposed departure, all five ships were out of action with main bearing trouble, and examination of the lubricating oil in four of the five vessels revealed traces of white metal, indicating serious engine defects. 'In the circumstances Sir George Binney considers this operation should be postponed,' wrote Flag Officer Humber to C-in-C Nore, 'an opinion with which I entirely concur.' Admiral Tovey proposed an enquiry, which was subsequently held at Immingham. 'Enquiry discloses serious omission in construction of engines,' Tovey told the Admiralty. The deferment of the operation until the ships could be re-engined, or until Paxman's had examined all the existing engines and made good the defects, was recommended. With diluted wartime labour and overstretched repair facilities, this almost certainly meant cancelling the operation altogether for that winter, which was quite unacceptable to Binney. 'In the circumstances,' he wrote afterwards, 'the volunteer crews were willing to subscribe to the doctrine that if we could not expect to use all the engines the whole of the time, we must make do by using some of the engines for most of the time.'

The additional risk, Binney felt, was not as great as might at first appear. The ships, he argued, were only in serious danger during the twelve-hour passage of the Skagerrak, which in any case they would traverse in darkness. If they suffered engine failure before reaching the Skagerrak, they would automatically return on their remaining engine or engines. An engine failure after passing Kristiansand would still give them time to reach the Swedish coast in darkness on two engines. On the return voyage, similar safety factors held good. C-in-C Nore and the Minister of War Transport both recorded their misgivings, but Binney was allowed to proceed.

All the indications were that the Germans were still preoccupied with preventing the breakout of Dicto and Lionel. Aerial reconnaissance showed that the principal gaps in the minefields covering the approaches to the Skagerrak had been filled in, and that the Germans were engaged in extending the minefields within the Skagerrak itself; this was all in favour of the shallow drafted motor coasters, since it restricted the areas in which they could be chased or intercepted by enemy warships other than E-boats. It was not expected that destroyers would be used for routine patrols, but they might be employed in guarding the minelayers and minesweepers at night between Kristiansand and Hantsholm, so they had to be reckoned with. If attacked by armed trawlers or E-boats the ships would attempt to fight their way through, but if they encountered heavier naval units they would make for the shallow waters off the Danish coast. Farther inside the Skaggerak, on a line connecting Arendal in southern Norway with Hirtshals near the Skaw, a force of armed patrol boats was known to be keeping watch for blockade runners, but it was hoped to evade these by aiming to reach territorial waters at about first light.

The greatest threat seemed to come from the air, either in the form of fighter attack in rough weather, when the coasters would be hard put to defend themselves, or in the form of surveillance; if the coasters were spotted at dusk on either the outward or return voyages, the destroyers would have time to intercept them. It was reassuring to know, from the Naval Intelligence Department team under Ned Denning, that there were no concentrations of aircraft lining the Skagerrak such as had been mobilised against Operation Performance.

Another continual preoccupation was the weather. An Admiralty meteorologist was appointed to compile weather reports and forecasts at Hull and Immingham, while a second naval man, Sub-Lieutenant Michael Choyce, was flown to Sweden, where he established a meteorological station aboard Dicto. The possibility of heavy gales and variable winds producing conditions totally unsuitable for motor coasters made accurate forecasting essential. With prevailing winds from the west it was easier to find weather which would assist the outward rather than the homeward voyage, but the probability of engine failure in the North Sea, enforcing a return to base, meant that a start could not be made from Immingham if there was a prospect of more than a Force 5 wind from any quarter.

Also flown out to Sweden to live and work on Dicto were three technicians for maintenance duties, one of them a Paxman expert. In the Humber, Lieutenant-Commander (E) E. C. Thomas, 'Tommy' Thomas, controlled his own naval maintenance staff, careering around Albert Dock on an Italian motor-cycle he was reputed to have 'liberated' in North Africa.

* * *

While all these preparations were going ahead in Britain, Bill Waring was setting up a temporary headquarters at the wooden-fronted Stadshotel in Lysekil. Here, in an atmosphere of musty commercial respectability, he finalised his arrangements for the arrival of the ships. For this first attempt he decided to load the ships only with those items which were either too heavy or too bulky to go by air and which, while having priority, did not have top priority. These latter he still preferred to send by air as opportunity arose. But the heavier items included machinery for the setting-up of the new ball-bearing factory, and this, for the long term, was the most important of all Swedish cargoes at that time.

Since Swedish regulations prevented Dicto and Lionel from using their radio transmitters, communications were to be passed exclusively through SOE channels between London and Gothenburg, where Anne Waring was to handle cypher messages and pass them on to her husband in Lysekil by telephone, again in cypher. Mrs. Sally Ladell, who had been working as a cypher clerk in the Legation in Stockholm, moved into the Stadshotel to deal with the cypher work. Others who were preparing to meet the little ships at Lysekil and assist in the handling of cargoes were William Kjellberg and Alva Henriksson of the Wilson Line agency, and of course Jack Aird.

Having missed the September no-moon period, Binney had to wait until late October before trying again. By 11th October he was confident that the engine troubles could be rectified without major alterations, and when all went reasonably well in further trials he planned to make the first attempt about 23rd–25th October. But the four-week delay inevitably placed an additional strain not only on the crews but also on security, and this was particularly dangerous in Sweden, where the activities of Waring and Aird could not be wholly camou-flaged. On 19th October the chairman of the Swedish Shipowners' Association, returning from a visit to Oslo, reported that he had been asked by a German shipowner whether he could confirm that the British intended to open a route for the transport of ball-bearings from Lysekil to the United Kingdom with fifty-knot gun-boats.

This sounded rather like a leakage from the Swedish Cabinet or Foreign Office, especially the estimate of the gunboats' speed, which for propaganda reasons Binney had consistently exaggerated. But on the whole he hoped that the Germans, still obsessed with Dicto and Lionel, would mistake this for a cover story intended to divert them from an escape attempt. He decided to continue as though nothing had happened, and orders were issued through C-in-C Nore on the morning of Monday 25th October 1943 for the ships to sail at 16.00 that afternoon. At 16.13 the order was cancelled due to an adverse weather forecast, but the operation was delayed for twenty-four hours only. With George Binney leading in the flagship Nonsuch, and with Harry Whitfield, having proved his skill at station-keeping during trials, bringing up the rear, the flotilla put to sea from Immingham at 16.45 on Tuesday 26th October and proceeded in cruising order down the Humber. Thus, in the gathering gloom of a late October afternoon, Operation Bridford was set in motion.

Half an hour after leaving the Humber boom the ships ran into thick fog, and with visibility reduced to less than half a cable they had difficulty in keeping station. Rounding the Bull Light Vessel off Spurn Point, they steered northwards via the inner route for Flam-borough Head. When that promontory curled encouragingly towards them out of the mist they began a wide turn to starboard on to 030 degrees to pass through the cleared channel that would take them through the coastal minefield.

Once through the minefield they increased speed to fifteen or sixteen knots and shaped a north-easterly course for the Skagerrak, five streamlined grey shapes with distinctive square transoms pushing out a broad bow-wave and a foaming wake. Rapidly the truth about their destination spread round each ship. 'It's Sweden!' 'No!' 'Didn't I tell you?' 'Might have been worse!' Already a comradeship had developed aboard each vessel that would never have been possible on a larger ship. Binney, chubby, approachable, and pipe-smoking, didn't look like the conventional leader, while his officers retained their aura without losing the egalitarian touch. These were the men who had recruited and trained them. 'But they didn't stand on the quay and wave us good-bye. They came with us.'

Already Whitfield, in Gay Viking, was having trouble with his starboard engine, which he soon had to bring to a stop. Brian Reynolds, his chief officer, informed Binney on the voice radio by coded signal and got an acknowledgment. Shortly afterwards the engineers cleared the trouble, the engine was restarted, and the earlier message was cancelled. But by this time Gay Viking had lost sight of the fourth ship in line and was only keeping station on the extreme limit of its wash. Whitfield's crew saw the signal being given to increase speed as the minefield was cleared, but soon afterwards they lost contact altogether. After flashing their Aldis lamp to try to attract attention, they signalled by voice radio that they had lost contact but were proceeding at 1,200 revolutions. This message was not received by Binney.

'What do we do now?' Whitfield asked Reynolds. With the engine situation apparently restored, and with the coastal mist dispersing and weather conditions generally favourable, Reynolds said he felt there was only one answer. 'We must carry on.' Very probably they would sight the flotilla at dawn next day, or failing that at the dusk position at the entrance to the Skagerrak. In any case he saw no reason why they shouldn't get through on their own.

Crossing the Dogger Bank during the night, the flotilla sighted a number of Danish fishing vessels, and they swung off course to avoid them. But one, a straggler showing no lights, suddenly loomed out of the darkness within a mile of them. As they turned away it switched on its lights, so they knew they had been seen.

On the Nonsuch, Binney was still unaware that Gay Viking had lost contact. He had heard her report an engine defect, then signal that the fault was cleared. When he found at dawn next day, 27th October, that Gay Viking was missing, he assumed she had had a relapse and returned to the Humber. No further signals were received from her.

By 08.45 that morning the flotilla of four ships, in diamond formation, was half-way across the North Sea and well ahead of schedule. With time in hand Binney decided to reduce speed to avoid too close an approach to the Skagerrak in daylight.

Soon afterwards they sighted a seaplane on their port quarter. Either this was extremely bad luck or security had indeed broken down and the Germans were out looking for them. Now their position, course and speed would be reported. To try to give the impression that the objective was towards the west coast of Denmark rather than the Skagerrak, Binney ordered a change of course 25 degrees to starboard. The seaplane began circling at a radius of about a mile.

After a few minutes the crew of the seaplane, evidently not satisfied, came in for a closer look, then withdrew and continued orbiting. But not for long. Shortly before nine o'clock they ran in across the bows of the Nonsuch at 1,000 feet and opened fire. All four ships opened up with their forward Oerlikons, and several hits were scored on the seaplane, which dived to low level and then made off. Almost immediately a twin-engined but unidentified machine passed over the formation at high speed.

Visibility was five to seven miles and the cloud base 1,500 feet, and a concerted attack on the flotilla looked probable. Since he was still within range of fighter protection, Binney radioed a 'Help' message to 18 Group, as previously arranged with RAF Coastal Command, and told them he was being shadowed. Soon afterwards, with the flotilla's position known to the enemy, he decided to head back towards the English coast at thirteen knots with the object of placing the boats temporarily out of reach of the *Luftwaffe*.

No fighter protection was forthcoming from 18 Group, and in fact Binney's signals were not received. But there was no more enemy interference either, and after two hours on a westerly course Binney turned the formation north for a further hour with the idea of approaching the Skagerrak from a different angle. Finally, at about 12.30, he ordered a turn towards the Skagerrak and called for full speed to reach a point fifty miles from the Danish coast by dusk.

As speed was increased, air locks developed in Nonsuch's fuel system. She was subject, too, to a fault that had become all too familiar during the training period—overheating of a gear-box, this time on the port engine. Then her radar batteries went flat, and Hopewell took over radar guard. Soon afterwards the port engine on Nonsuch seized up altogether. Thus handicapped the flagship was unable to make more than fifteen knots. Master Standfast, too, was experiencing minor engine troubles, and this also delayed the flotilla's progress.

At 14.00 Hopewell reported the presence of enemy aircraft circling the flotilla. They kept the four gunboats under continual surveillance for the rest of the afternoon. At 17.00, presumably running short of fuel, they left; but at 18.00 another seaplane swooped down out of cloud cover with its engines shut off. It was briefly engaged by the flotilla's guns before disappearing into the gathering dusk.

Forty-five minutes later it was almost completely dark; and with air attack no longer reckoned to be a danger, Binney signalled for the other three boats to close in on Nonsuch for a conference. The flotilla was still twenty miles short of the dusk position originally aimed for, and to reach the Swedish coast by first light they would have to travel at their maximum speed continuously throughout the night.

All Binney's experience with these boats had convinced him that they would cruise fairly reliably at sixteen to seventeen knots but that at maximum continuous speed defects quickly developed. Nonsuch could not possibly make the Swedish coast on two engines before daylight, and the engineers on Master Standfast also expressed doubts about proceeding at maximum speed for so long a spell. Ginger Stokes, on Hopewell, and Bob Tanton, on Gay Corsair, both wanted to go on; but Binney was doubtful of the wisdom of letting them do so. He had been especially anxious to get all five ships through on the initial voyage. He had accepted a reduction to four, and he might have countenanced three; but he hesitated to compromise the operation for the uncertain prospect of getting two boats through. Once they arrived at Lysekil all element of surprise would be gone, and the Germans would be fully alerted to what was being attempted. On all subsequent crossings the opposition would intensify.

At 19.40 that evening Binney reluctantly ordered his flotilla to return to Immingham. Reforming into cruising line, they shaped their course for Flamborough Head. But as it happened, most of Binney's arguments against going on were nullified by a factor of which he was unaware. Harry Whitfield, in Gay Viking, having seen and heard nothing further of Binney, was still following his original course. Earlier that day, to growls of disgust and derision from his crew, he had hoisted the Nazi flag, keeping a Red Ensign handy for breaking if necessary. If attacked they would quickly revert to their true colours and defend themselves; but an attempt at deception in these waters seemed worthwhile.

At 13.15 that afternoon they spotted a plane which they identified as hostile, and every man on board went to his action station. The German crew were inquisitive but cautious; they circled Gay Viking for the next twenty-five minutes, and for most of that time they kept discreetly out of range. When they ventured in closer, the silence and tension on Gay Viking became acute, until it dissolved in delighted chuckles as 33-year-old cook-steward Stan Close, manning the twin Vickers on the port wing of the bridge, called out to his skipper: 'Shall I bring him down, sir, or just wing him?' Such confidence was infectious, and the crew breathed more freely. But the orders Whitfield gave were clear: his gunners were not to begin the firing.

The puzzled indecision of the German crew was reflected in their flying: but eventually they seemed to make up their minds, turning purposefully towards the Danish coast as though perhaps to seek a second opinion. From now on, thought Whitfield, they must expect to be attacked at any time. He turned to Brian Reynolds.

'What do we do? Do we carry on—or do we turn back? It's up to us—we can't break wireless silence now.'

'Let's carry on. They don't know who we are.'

The atmosphere of the little ships seems to have permeated Harry Whitfield's personality. Like all the other captains, he was a big ship man, and he acted the part, sober, God-fearing, taciturn. Now for the first time in his seafaring life—or so it seemed to those who knew him—he was letting his hair down. Nevertheless his grunted agreement scarcely hinted at the truth: he had no intention of turning back anyway.

They too were ahead of schedule. 'There's no point in getting too near the Danish or Norwegian coasts before nightfall,' said Reynolds. So they altered course to the north, as Binney had done, and reduced engine revolutions from 1,000 to 800. Visibility was now down to less than a mile, with very low cloud, and a few minutes later, when another German plane appeared out of the mist at low level, it crossed in front of them not more than 300 yards ahead without seeing them, then disappeared into the overcast. It looked, however, as though the hunt was on.

As dusk turned to darkness Gay Viking was some fifteen miles to the east of the flotilla and slightly to the north. The crew had been scanning the horizon the whole afternoon in the hope of picking out the other boats, but visibility never cleared to more than two miles and the flotilla was never close enough to be seen.

At 18.28 Whitfield increased revolutions to 1,350 on the port and centre engines for the run through the Skagerrak; the timing was out of order on the starboard engine and this he restricted to 1,000 revolutions. At the same time the crew donned their exposure suits. These suits, much less cumbersome than those issued to the Rubble and Performance crews, had originally been designed for the Hurricane pilots who were catapulted off the foredecks of merchant vessels in mid-Atlantic to intercept the Focke-Wulf Condors, with no chance of reaching land. 'Naturally,' writes a crew member, 'one went to the "heads" before donning this contraption approaching the Skagerrak, but the tension was such that many of us had to go again shortly afterwards, thus having to repeat the whole procedure.'

By eleven o'clock that night, three hours twenty minutes after the rest of the flotilla had turned back, Gay Viking was in the jaws of the Skagerrak off Hantsholm. Aided by the alertness of the look-outs, Whitfield threaded his way through what he took to be the Danish fishing fleet. He didn't think they had been seen. Steering a course roughly midway between Norway and Denmark, their diesels throbbing cheerfully, they ploughed on between the minefields.

Visibility improved perceptibly during the night, and the look-outs redoubled their vigilance. Every five minutes the radar aerial was cranked and the operator scanned the illuminated sweep of his oscilloscope.

'Nothing on the radar, sir.'

At 03.30 the lights of two more fishing vessels were glimpsed a long way ahead, and Whitfield altered course to pass to the north of them. But nothing showed up on the radar, and presently Whitfield identified the lights as those of the lighthouses at Väderöbod and Hallö; he was in sight of the Swedish coast. Here, as he had been warned, he faced two interception hazards: the Arendal-Hirtshals line patrol, and the convoys that plied between Oslo and northern Denmark. But under the pressures of convoy and escort tasks the patrols had been neglected. Nothing was sighted, and at 04.40 Whitfield stopped off Väderöbod to take bearings; with this whole coastal area fronted by a litter of islands and rocks, he wanted to fix his position.

Before entering Swedish waters he ordered the dumping of all surplus ammunition, retaining only a single pan for each gun; this would enable him to take an additional case of cargo. He also dumped all surplus fuel and fresh water, keeping only enough to get them back home with a small margin. Then, after fixing his position, he headed southwards for the Hallö Light at reduced speed, keeping inside territorial waters and waiting for daylight.

At Hallö pilot station he stopped and signalled for a pilot, but he got no response. A Swedish merchant vessel was also waiting about in the darkness. Although he knew that pilotage was normally compulsory, he decided that it would be dangerous to hang about for long, and as soon as it was light he set course for Lysekil.

Although the port they had chosen was little more than a village, it was one of the centres of the Swedish fishing industry. Built on a promontory shaped like a blister, it boasted two harbours, one north of the promontory, one to the south. Behind the waterfront of the south harbour, where preparations had been made for the boats' arrival, the village piled up on rising ground, dominated by the tall spire of Lysekil church, soaring 295 feet above the fjord. From a vantage point on this rising ground, a small but privileged party had taken up their vigil during the night. The signals sent via SOE channels on the arrival of the boats had not been cancelled, and most of the party, having been driven up from Gothenburg by taxi the previous night, had spent the early hours staring out into the raw October darkness. Among them were Bill Waring and Jack Aird; William

Kjellberg, and Alva Henriksson; Landsfogde Gerhard von Sydow, police superintendent; and Landsfiskal Gunnar Nyblom, mayor of Lysekil. Also present was the local Customs Officer, Helge Fallquist; and there were ambulances to care for the wounded, should there be any. Below them on the quayside, a stack of what were known as 'butter-parcels' lay ringed by barbed wire and hidden and protected by blocks of paving stones. But dawn came and there was still no sign of the boats.

'Chugging through the islands to Lysekil in the morning light,' wrote Whitfield afterwards, 'gave us a wonderful thrill. We had an oversize Red Ensign aft, a small one at the gaff, the Wilson house flags were flying, and the whole ship's company was bursting with pride. We passed two or three open fishing boats and the occupants could hardly believe their eyes, but they stood up in their boats waving and cheering.'

For all its natural solitude and isolation, Lysekil was a lively port, and Whitfield was puzzled by the deserted look of the quayside. In fact he had entered the north harbour. After cruising around for a time he sounded his klaxon, and soon the harbourmaster came out in a pilot boat and guided him round the blister to the other side of the village. Here, overlooked by the house of the German vice-consul, Gay Viking tied up on Andersson quay to the cheers of the little knot of spectators, the first call of a vessel flying the Red Duster in a Swedish port for three and a half years.

First man on board was Customs Officer Fallquist, prepared, with the backing of Landshövding (Governor of the Province) Malte Jacobson, to interpret the regulations with flexibility. 'I remember that among other things we omitted the regulation concerning tonnage,' he said afterwards. 'But it was of course a completely normal commercial transaction, and the German vice-consul, watching every move from his house, could not interfere. The men were packed like herrings in a barrel, and Captain Whitfield had very little room in his narrow, hot cabin. "Have a drink," he said, beaming all over his face, and he offered me a bottle of whisky. Looking out of the cabin window I saw some flashing lights out to sea. It was the German patrols outside the three-mile limit.'

Before leaving Immingham the crews of all five ships had been adjured by Binney to remember that for prestige reasons it was important to create the best possible impression in Sweden. Cleanliness and cheerfulness were the maxims, but the first of these was not easy to achieve. There was no hot water on board for washing, the plywood was inclined to sweat, and ventilation was poor. It was difficult to keep anything or anyone clean owing to the nauseous fumes from the diesels. Even in the moderate weather of this first crossing the motion and the polluted air had caused sea-sickness and fatigue. The quarters were so cramped that it was inhuman to keep the men on board while they were in port, and arrangements had been made by Bill Waring for them to be accommodated at the Stadshotel. Now, as they emerged on to the quayside for their first look at Sweden, while the astonished population of Lysekil swarmed down to the pier to stare back, they looked more like miners than seamen. But this did not seem to detract from their welcome; rather the reverse.

They were taken first to the Russian bathhouse; but since Lysekil was a defended coastal area, prohibited to foreigners, they had to be marched off under armed guard, a process that soon appealed to some of the men's sense of the ridiculous. Meanwhile the cargo of fuel was discharged by local labour and the base engineer party repaired the starboard engine and carried out exhaustive mechanical tests. Then the return cargo was loaded. During the loading, Captain Whitfield put the rest of his crew ashore and continued to accept 'butter-parcels' until he was down to his marks.

Having made their first contact with 'Blondie', the bathing attendant at the bathhouse, the crew were escorted to the hotel, where they had breakfast and then slept, most of them for the first time since leaving the Humber. At tea-time they were introduced to the delights of Lidell's Konditori, where they varied their operational diet of self-heating soups by gorging themselves on Swedish pastries. One man eventually earned himself the soubriquet of 'Creamcake Charlie', becoming known by that name to the townsfolk as well. In the evening they were given a special film show in the local cinema, and then they were escorted back to the hotel, where, with guitar and piano accordion accompaniment, they finished off the day with a sing-song. When they looked out of the windows of the hotel lounge, half the population of Lysekil seemed to be watching and listening. Next morning, 29th October, it was back to the ship.

The planned procedure was for the gunboats to move into Brofjord the day after arrival to lie alongside Dicto and Lionel and wait for suitable weather; but from the hamlet of Lahälla, close to the anchorage of the two merchant vessels, a coded telephone call informed Waring and his staff at the Stadshotel of the forecast prepared by Michael Choyce. To Whitfield it looked extremely favourable; and with his chief engineer now confident of managing a comfortable seventeen and a half knots at 1,300 revolutions, and twenty knots if needed, with very little risk, he decided to sail at dusk. He had already heard rumours, picked up by Intelligence sources, of a German submarine, together with a minelayer, heading up the coast to lie in wait for him. Another rumour was that Lord Haw-Haw had announced the arrival of a British vessel in Sweden but had promised his listeners that it would never get out. It seemed to Whitfield that the sooner he left the better, and Reynolds agreed.

The British had appreciated that the arrival of a flotilla of five boats in a Swedish port could not be kept secret, and that the German vice-consul at Lysekil would immediately inform his Legation; they had therefore agreed with the Swedish Government on a simple press release giving the facts. But the arrival of a single boat was not thought so likely to attract press comment, and no release was made. That morning, however, while Whitfield was getting ready to sail, the German vice-consul, finding all telephone links mysteriously interrupted (by the Swedes), travelled to Gothenburg to report to his Consul-General, and later that day the Swedes intercepted a telephone conversation between the Consul-General and his Legation in Stockholm in which the 'very strange news' was announced that a British motor speed-boat had arrived at Lysekil and had taken on some unknown cargo. 'Were they flying the merchant flag?' asked the Legation. 'Yes.' 'In that case I don't see that we can do much about it.' This conversation, repeated at once by the Swedes to Victor Mallet, showed that on a diplomatic level, at least, the Germans were accepting defeat. But they retaliated at once by suspending the Gothenburg safe-conduct traffic 'for military reasons'; and later that day Berlin warned of an imminent breakout attempt. Troop transport tasks were postponed so that their escorts could be used against possible enemy ships, six patrol vessels were to steam singly at intervals covering the line Hallö-Väderöbod by night and the line Skaw-Oslo fjord by day, and a group of Fleet minesweepers was to patrol northwest of the Skaw by night and farther west in mid-Skaggerak by day. But Whitfield hoped to get clear before the inevitable countermeasures could be implemented.

The afternoon weather report remained favourable, and shortly before the ship was due to sail, five Norwegian seamen were brought from Lionel and taken on board. The previous day, Bill Waring and Jack Aird had boarded Lionel and told the crew that five boats were expected, so there were twenty disgruntled men. The choice was made by drawing lots, but one or two disappointed losers managed to buy themselves back in by means of a hoarded tobacco ration.

At 15.50, with a pilot to see him out of the harbour, Whitfield sailed. Waring then sent a coded departure signal to Gothenburg by telephone, and a message was passed by soE channels to London so that fighter protection could be provided over the North Sea from dawn next day.

As soon as Gay Viking was outside the harbour the pilot authorised Whitfield to extinguish his navigation lights, and he also told the pilot boat to extinguish theirs. The pilot was then dropped.

Whitfield's plan was to leave territorial waters south of Lysekil, on the assumption that the German patrols, with Dicto and Lionel still very much on their minds, would be more likely to concentrate off Brofjord to the north. After steaming up to Hallö for a short period inside territorial waters, he headed south to a point near Maseskär before breaking out into the Skagerrak. The time was then 18.55.

Half an hour after leaving territorial waters the crew saw the lights of a fishing fleet ranged to the north of them in a semi-circle, so they altered course to the south. Once clear of the lights they resumed their south-westerly course, and they saw nothing more until four o'clock next morning, when they passed safely through another fishing fleet. By that time they had reached a point 57.06 North, 06.55 East and were clear of the Skagerrak.

When dawn came they were eighty-five miles from the Norwegian and Danish coasts, but visibility was excellent, with no cloud, and the five Norwegians, acting as look-outs, scanned the horizon for signs of the hostile aircraft that must surely be out looking for them. Even though they had made excellent progress throughout the night their detour had left them slightly short of the rendezvous position, but they began to look hopefully for the promised air escort.

Low cloud and poor visibility had delayed the take-off of the first two Beaufighters, but they reached a point forty miles short of the rendezvous position by nine o'clock and then began searching along Gay Viking's anticipated track. Even in the perfect conditions obtaining the difficulty of locating so small a target as a motor coaster was soon apparent, but a sighting was made at 09.25 and the Beaufighters stayed in company until 10.49. For the rest of the day the look-outs saw no other aircraft, hostile or friendly; but the crew were kept at action stations until midday. Ordinary watches were then resumed, and with a fuel shortage threatened, speed was reduced to 1,000 revolutions.

As the triumphant lone sortie of Gay Viking neared its end, George Binney, safely back at Immingham with the other four boats, was preparing to try again. But his leadership of the first attempt was already coming under scrutiny, and among his critics were C-in-C Nore and DOD(H). Tovey felt that Binney had over-reacted to the fishing vessels, which in his experience did not carry transmitters. And he thought Binney's 'Help' message was premature. Eccles, too, was critical of the 'Help' message, and he thought the resultant alteration to westward was chiefly responsible for the decision to return to the

Humber. The view of the naval staff was clear: the value of even a single cargo of special machinery and ball-bearings was such that the safe arrival of two ships would have more than justified itself. To expect a higher percentage showed an optimism that was scarcely warranted.

The news that Gay Viking had got through to Lysekil had both excited and dismayed Binney. He had wanted to get a maximum load through while surprise could still be achieved. But he had much more faith in the long-term prospects of his blockade-running operations than had the naval staff, and the crews, although disappointed, were behind him. Celebrating the news of the arrival of Gay Viking, they saw in a Grimsby pub the famous Guinness advertisement embodying the toucan. ('How grand to be a toucan, just think what toucan do.') The pub lost its advertisement, but Bridford gained a motto (what one boat could do, two could do), and a mascot, which was good for morale.

* * *

On the morning of 31st October Gay Viking duly arrived back at Immingham, and with a forecast of light southerly winds and favourable weather, Binney decided to sail that day with his three serviceable boats. These were Hopewell (Captain Stokes), Gay Corsair (Captain Jackson), and Master Standfast (Captain Goodman). Each ship was loaded with approximately twenty tons of fuel-oil for transfer to the Dicto. Unfortunately Captain Goodman had slipped and fallen on deck during the first abortive attempt, and his wrist was so badly swollen that he was unfit to sail. At the last moment Binney found himself minus a captain, and he decided to promote the senior mate, 35-year-old G. R. W. (George) Holdsworth. Holdsworth had been with the flotilla from the outset on Gay Corsair and had been fully trained and briefed, but this was his first voyage in command, and he knew none of his crew.

There was a further set-back immediately the flotilla sailed. After passing through Immingham Lock at half-past four that afternoon, Gay Corsair developed trouble with an auxiliary gear-box and Captain Jackson had no alternative but to abandon the voyage. Even the final departure of the other two vessels was delayed by further engine adjustments, but at length the inner channel to Flamborough Head was negotiated and the minefield crossed. Learning from previous experience, they set a north-easterly course to steer clear of the Dogger Bank and thus avoid contact with Danish fishing vessels.

Next day, 1st November, passed without incident. The wind, which was from the south-east, freshened to a good Force 5–6 and the sea was rough, causing great discomfort amongst the crews; but Binney's experience was that so long as these craft could be kept clear of a head sea they could maintain progress without damage even when conditions were moderate to rough. The engines, run at 1,200 revolutions, gave a speed of about sixteen knots. Visibility, clear during the day, deteriorated towards dusk, but no air activity was seen.

Accurate navigation in these small craft was difficult even under good conditions, and with a beam sea Binney knew they might be many miles off their course. He was worried that instead of entering the Skagerrak squarely in the middle as he intended, he might find himself within range of the shore radar stations on either side. The home radio direction-finding stations given to him before sailing proved no help, and Stokes was forced to rely on his gyro compass and his echo-sounder. Dead reckoning put them at about their anticipated dusk position at the mouth of the Skagerrak by 17.30, but in fact they were fifteen miles farther east than they supposed. There was no reason, however, why this should cause any problems, and Binney's main worry was the poor station-keeping of Master Standfast—a fault that most of the captains had exhibited from the start. As big ship men they were nearly all inclined to be obsessed with the collision risk. It was pitch dark, with no moon, and Master Standfast kept her distance throughout the night at about two cables; but fortunately the water was highly phosphorescent and the look-outs on Hopewell had no difficulty in keeping her bow-wave in sight.

Taking advantage of an inward current on the southern side of the strait, Hopewell steered a course about twenty-five miles from the Danish coast and thirty-five from the Norwegian. Soon after midnight Stokes was compelled to slow down temporarily through an air lock in her fuel system, and Master Standfast quickly came into station. The trouble was soon cleared, however, and Stokes then increased to 1,300 revolutions, aiming at a speed of eighteen knots for the last and most dangerous lap of the voyage. Master Standfast immediately fell back to two cables, which worried Binney, but he was reluctant to signal her for fear of disclosing their position.

Two hours later, at 02.30, Swedish coastal lights were sighted from the bridge of Hopewell, Master Standfast at this stage being about 600 yards astern. Stokes was making for Hallö, but Binney, certain that German patrols would be lying in wait for them, suggested a diversion. 'How about going north of Väderöbod?' This, he thought, might avoid the most likely patrol area, the Skaw–Hallö–Väderöbod triangle.

Binney's instinct was right. Five patrol boats were operating singly along the line from Maseskär north to Hallö and beyond, and two

M-class minesweepers were patrolling in mid-Skagerrak north-west of the Skaw; but north of Väderöbod there was nothing.

'I'll have to stop and get some cross-bearings,' said Stokes.

On Master Standfast the officer of the watch was the SOE representative, the heavily bearded Al Brown. Some time earlier George Holdsworth, anxious to fix his precise position, had joined Brown on the bridge. The mate, Tom Jardine, was in the chart room, counting the flashes on the Chernikeff log to get the vessel's speed. As Hopewell was clearly slowing down, Holdsworth gave the order to do the same. Brown slowed to half-speed and waited for further orders. None came, and as he was coming up fast behind Hopewell he stopped engines.

As they overran Hopewell on the starboard side, Hopewell sheered to port. So as not to lose sight of her, Brown ordered 'Hard a'port'. Holdsworth, however, countermanded the order. 'She'll come back this way directly.'

Brown, looking out on the starboard side, was wondering why Hopewell had stopped when Holdsworth, looking out to port, suddenly shouted 'Hard a'starboard! She's coming our way.'

Looking over to port, Brown saw the Hopewell apparently heading south-east. After the correction was made he resumed his look-out to starboard, seeing nothing except the white and red characters of the Väderöbod Light. Shortly afterwards he was amazed to hear Holdsworth say: 'We've lost the Hopewell.' He raked the sea north and east with the night glasses but could see no sign of her.

At this point Jardine came out on to the bridge. 'Why are we stopped?'

'We've lost the Hopewell.'

Holdsworth decided to run for Väderöbod, and he told the helmsman to steer for the light. But he was still not absolutely sure about his position. Jardine and Brown, however, had identified the characters of the light as definitely those of Väderöbod. When the light bore roughly east, Holdsworth stopped the ship and said 'Here we are'.

Fearing that Holdsworth's intention was to heave to until daylight, Brown demurred; with the probability of armed patrol craft nearby, he suggested they run for the Hallö Light. Jardine was of the same opinion, and with Holdsworth agreeing Jardine laid off a course.

Holdsworth rang down for 1,000 revolutions and called to his chief wireless operator, Albert Fox, for an echo-sounding. Brown suggested it would be safer to go faster, but Holdsworth was worried about running aground. A few minutes later Fox called out that the sounder read six feet.

Holdsworth immediately rang the engine astern and stopped the ship. 'There you are,' he said to Brown. 'Nearly on the beach.' There was no lead-line aboard, but a shackle tied to a heaving line produced by the boatswain, Arthur Hannah, found no bottom. According to the chart they were in about eighteen fathoms. Beset by contradictions, and quite properly determined not to risk running aground, Holdsworth called for radio bearings from a shore station. Brown, with the responsibility for fighting the ship, was so perturbed by the risk of attack that he rang for action stations.

'There's a ship coming up astern.'

The warning came from Hannah, in charge of the aft gun. 'Tell the old man it's a Jerry—a Bremen-built bastard.' He had seen hundreds of German trawlers and ice-breakers in his time, and he identified her from her long, undercut bow. But she was not so easily identifiable from the bridge. 'It'll be the Swedish pilot boat,' said Holdsworth. 'I think not,' said Jardine. Holdsworth told the second mate to flash the recognition signal, and this was done.

The vessel swung across the stern of the gunboat and then ran parallel along her starboard side at a distance of 300 yards. Holdsworth hailed her and asked for a pilot boat. When he got no reply the engines were put full ahead. At once the vessel turned and fired a burst with an Oerlikon that was clearly intended as a warning; it was aimed well overhead.

The German patrol vessel Vp 1606, of the 16th Patrol Vessel Flotilla, had picked up the sound of engines on her directional hydrophones and had followed them up at full speed, then lost contact as Master Standfast stopped. But soon, peering into the darkness, the look-outs sighted an unfamiliar silhouette.

When Vp 1606 was exactly amidships it switched on a searchlight, blinding the crew of the gunboat and making identification impossible. As the vessel overtook them, Holdsworth steamed another half-mile and then stopped the ship.

'For God's sake don't let her come alongside,' said Brown.

'What else can we do?'

'Steam off south-east for Hallö and shake him off.'

Captain Holdsworth shook his head. To a seaman of his experience, any high-speed escape through the islands and rocks fronting Lysekil hardly seemed a practicable proposition. At this Brown switched on the navigation lights to show the Swedes—if they were Swedes—that the vessel they had under scrutiny was friendly. Then, to prepare for the obvious alternative, he got the demolition charges out of their box, intending to fit them and stand by. When he got back to the bridge the other vessel had completed a full circuit of the gunboat and

Bob Tanton and the Toucan mascot

Brian Reynolds – the 'Lion'

Cook-steward Stan Close taking a 'cuppa' to the *Gay Viking*'s bridge

Some of the crew of the *Gay Corsair*. Left to right, *standing*: J. Angus (2nd engineer), J. Downey (chief engineer), Tommy Mallory (AB), F. Clarke (AB), Bob Tanton, Ken McNeil (2nd officer), Kenneth Parker (cook-steward), J. Bird (AB), J. Conway (motorman). *Squatting*: Arthur Fray (AB). *Seated*: Laurie Kohler (bos'n)

was lining up exactly parallel on the starboard side, with the two bridges abreast. With its searchlight beam still flooding the gunboat, it was not more than seventy yards away.

The vessel opened fire again, and this time the aim was direct. The first volley hit the wireless mast and smashed the aerials; that was all communication severed. The second volley was aimed at the bridge.

A cannon shell, penetrating the bridge structure, exploded on the bridge itself, throwing Holdsworth and Brown off their feet. Both were seriously hurt. Jardine, pulling out from under the chart table canopy, was hit in the shoulder, and he too went down. Steward Dennis Moore, manning the starboard gun, was also badly hit, and the pan of ammunition on his gun went swivelling round, spraying bullets all over the deck.

As Miller Bennett pressed the trigger of the gun abaft the bridge a shell exploded beneath him. He crawled to the back of the bridge, where he heard groaning. He noticed that the helmsman was lying flat on the grating unharmed; the groaning was coming from the wounded officers. The firing was still going on and he dropped over the back of the bridge to avoid it.

Brown recovered consciousness to find himself draped over the battery box, looking at a hole in the bridge armour plating. He tried to struggle to his feet but his right leg was broken. Then he saw Jardine standing aft of him, his injured arm pumping blood. 'Start her up, Chief!' called Brown, but Jardine, seeing that the steering had been shot away, realised they were finished. 'It's no use Mr. Brown, we're shot to bits.' He turned back towards the patrol vessel, hoping to save further bloodshed. 'Hi, Kamarad!' At this Brown reached up to the engine-room telegraphs and pushed them full ahead. Nothing happened.

As Bennett dropped down on the port side, away from the firing, he found the deck blocked. Someone had inflated a life-raft and it had blown up so quickly it had jammed between the bridge and the stanchions. 'I was scared to death,' he wrote afterwards, 'and so shocked I was gabbling like an idiot. When I calmed down I got into the engine room alley-way, and glancing down I saw two men moving around in a daze. I learned later that the ether bottles for starting the engines had been hit.' He too could hear someone groaning, and in the wireless cabin he found the second operator, Reg Broadly, with a hole in his back the size of a golf ball. He dragged him out on deck and laid him on his belly to apply a field dressing, but as he bent to the task he was prodded in the back by a tommy-gun. The Germans were aboard.

The gunboat crew were bundled roughly on to the trawler, but once on board they were treated correctly, and the wounded were well looked after. Later that day they were put ashore at Frederikshavn, as the captured crews of Performance had been. There they found an armed guard waiting to escort them along the quay. 'You would have thought they'd got Sir George Binney himself,' writes Miller Bennett. And indeed the Germans thought they very probably had. Chief suspect was the bearded Al Brown, who was sent to Berlin for interrogation. But the crew of Master Standfast made a great impression on their captors, who believed they must have been selected very carefully—as indeed they had. 'The prisoners stated that they were not allowed to make any statements,' reported the German naval commander-in-chief. 'No prisoner would give any information about the purpose of the trip.' Accused of piracy and spying, the men of Master Standfast spent some time in solitary confinement before being accorded their normal rights as prisoners-of-war.

Most seriously wounded was the unfortunate George Holdsworth, the last-minute substitute whose voyage had suddenly assumed such nightmare complexity. Puzzled by Binney's unexpected changes of speed and course, and lacking the knowledge of his crew that a captain needs, he had been through a wretched enough experience even before his ship was fired on. He died of his wounds.

*   *   *

After losing contact with Master Standfast, Hopewell continued without incident towards Gulmarfjord, berthing on Andersson quay at 06.15. Binney's first request of Kjellberg was for news of the other vessel; but he had heard no gunfire, and he was not anxious at first. News later filtered through from a Danish pilot that Master Standfast had been captured and towed into Frederikshavn by a German armed trawler, and that ambulances had been at the quayside to meet them.

From other sources Binney learned something of the number of German patrol boats and minesweepers that had been lying off the coast, and he also learned that Commodore Elis Björklund, who had succeeded Akermark as commander of the Swedish Västkustens Marindistrikt, intended to apply a number of restrictions to Hopewell 'for the trouble she has caused', restrictions which could only prejudice her chances of escape. But they were not Government-inspired, and directly Waring referred them to Stockholm they were removed.

There was one matter, however, which the Swedish Government resented: the return of George Binney to Sweden. Waring had told them informally of his proposed visit, and they had raised no immediate objection, but on 4th November Victor Mallet reported as follows :

1. Secretary-General informed me today that his Government were annoyed at the arrival of Sir George Binney at Lysekil. In view of all that the Swedes have done to facilitate Bridford they felt that Binney's presence was a piece of singularly bad taste on the part of those responsible.

2. I hotly argued that as Binney was obviously the moving spirit it was natural that he should take part, and his courageous spirit in doing so was admirable. The Secretary-General admitted admiration for his courage but said that Binney was obviously extremely *non grata* and knew it; he would have been arrested and condemned but for his diplomatic immunity and his return to Sweden in these circumstances was an act of impertinence. He hoped that when once he had left in his ship he would never return during the war.

3. The reason for the Secretary-General's extreme bitterness is undoubtedly because the Swedish Government believe Binney to have been mainly responsible for all their troubles over Lionel and Dicto and for the heavy loss occasioned to them by the three-months' closure of the Gothenburg traffic last spring. I feel sure that nothing I can say will alter their feelings and a further visit from Binney would, in my opinion, prejudice the chance of future friendly co-operation over such operations.

No further visit from Binney, of course, would be possible until he returned home safely from this one. However, the attitude of the civilian authorities towards him at Lysekil remained helpful. They did everything to make the crew of Hopewell, and Binney in particular, welcome, and they did all they could to protect the operation from German interference, arresting a Swedish Nazi who showed more interest in the Hopewell than natural curiosity warranted, and keeping other doubtful characters under surveillance. Although the crew were always escorted to and fro, and the Stadshotel was picketed by police, many kindnesses were shown.

Galvanised by their success in capturing Master Standfast, the Germans increased their vigilance, and the Swedish authorities accepted that Hopewell was being watched too closely to sail direct from Lysekil. They gave permission for her to lie alongside Dicto and Lionel in Brofjord, the solution Binney had always looked for, though on his past form he feared he might be suspected of trying to smuggle arms aboard the two merchantmen. Here they would have direct access to the forecasts of Mike Choyce, who was living as a civilian aboard Dicto.

According to Choyce's reports there was a good prospect of favourable weather on 10th November, and Binney decided to put to sea. At four o'clock that afternoon, with a load of forty-one tons of ball-bearings and six Norwegian escapers from Lionel, and having alerted London by SOE channels, Hopewell took a pilot on board and passed through the boom, to the cheers of the guard ship, whose crew had earlier given them fresh bread and water. From the boom Hopewell sailed north via the inner coastal channels to within ten miles of the Norwegian frontier, where at 20.15 the pilot was dropped. But first the pilot handed over to Stokes his own detailed chart on the promise that Stokes would destroy it as soon as he reached open water.

Crossing Oslo fjord Stokes was soon confronted by a strong head-wind and a high sea. The gunboats were always loggish when fully loaded, and Hopewell pounded so badly that after getting thirty miles out from the coast without seeing any patrols, Stokes was forced to put back. But now, unable to get a positional fix, he had to negotiate the heavily indented coastline without the assistance of the chart, which he had dutifully destroyed. Fortunately the weather was clear. But by the time Hopewell had regained the quayside at Lysekil, her port main gear-box had overheated and seized up, and on closer examination it was found to be beyond repair. This on the face of it meant weeks of delay. Binney had the immediate problem, too, of preventing a series of abortive escort flights by Coastal Command, and a telephone message was quickly passed to Gothenburg in a pre-arranged code and thence to Stockholm and London.

Next Binney sent an urgent request to the Admiralty for a new gear-box to be flown to Sweden. The response was immediate, and Peter Coleridge, his liaison in London, sent the gear-box, which weighed over a ton, north to Leuchars, where it was loaded on to a Dakota and flown direct to Gothenburg, arriving there four days after Binney's request.

Meanwhile Binney had seen an opportunity to show the flag. 'Tommy' Thomas had been flown out with the gear-box, and the repair could quite reasonably have been carried out by the engineers at Lysekil; but by sending Hopewell to Götaverken in Gothenburg Binney would be displaying the Red Ensign there after more than four years' absence. The Swedes, perhaps unaware that the gunboat's journey was not really necessary, agreed, and while Coleridge was completing the transport arrangements, Hopewell sailed under Swedish naval escort for Gothenburg.

It was an eventful journey. Required to put all her ammunition and certain parts of her guns ashore at the naval base at Kalvsund, near the entrance to the Göta river, Hopewell was fired on by the fort while approaching in accordance with instructions, greatly to the embarrassment of the two naval control officers who had been placed on board. There were elements in the Swedish Navy, it seemed, which still bore a grudge. But from that point on the passage up to Gothenburg became a triumphal progress, the workers in the docks and shipyards deserting their tasks to give the Victory sign and to cheer Hopewell to her berth. The restrictions the crew were subject to at Lysekil did not apply at Gothenburg, and wherever they went they were fêted. A natural reticence on the part of survivors draws a curtain over some of the excitements of the week that followed, but of the many notable encounters and confrontations, one took the form of a classic double-take. Seven or eight of the crew of Hopewell passed a similar group on a Gothenburg street, and the two groups were twenty yards apart when both turned round as the penny dropped.

'Bloody Jerries!'

'Bloody British!'

For the next few days the Germans found the competition in Gothenburg just a little too keen; and there were hilarious scenes in cafés when British and German songs vied with each other for musical supremacy. 'It was to their credit,' wrote Binney afterwards, 'that when after six days the time came, on 22nd November, for the crew to return to the austerity of Brofjord, only one member missed the ship.'

When Hopewell had her armaments restored to her on the way out, someone in the Swedish Navy got in a final niggle. Everything had been left out in the rain. A protest lodged through the British Legation drew an expression of the Swedish Navy's regret.

*   *   *

On the other side of the North Sea, the crews of the other three vessels waited impatiently almost throughout November for favourable weather. But at last, on Friday the 26th, the forecast showed signs of improvement, and Brian Reynolds, acting for Binney, consulted the captains and decided to sail. Passing Spurn Light the three ships ran into a long swell, and cutting through the gap in the minefields they began to roll heavily. At midnight they increased to 1,100 revolutions, but at this speed they started to pound badly and seemed likely to suffer damage. 'At 1,000 revs. we had only been making $11\frac{1}{2}$ knots instead of our estimated 14.2,' wrote Reynolds afterwards, 'thus 1,100 would only have given us $12\frac{1}{2}$, which would have been insufficient to reach our evening position. If we had increased sufficiently to give us 15 knots, the speed required, we should have had to go up to 1,200 revs. or more, and at this speed we would certainly have started shipping green seas and have done considerable damage. I consulted with the captain, and owing to the above, and the fact that we would have been poorly placed for dealing with aerial attacks, owing to the violent movement of the ship, and our inability to man the forward Oerlikon owing to green seas, I reluctantly ordered the flotilla to return to base.'

In addition to the rough weather, the flotilla had been beset by communications difficulties, none of its messages being received; and this was typical of many sailings that winter. Less typical was the performance of the engines: all three vessels, despite some superficial damage, were ready to sail again that evening after fourteen hours at sea.

For the crew of Hopewell, still held up in Brofjord, the contrasts of the previous month began to prove almost too much. First had been the long abortive two-way crossing of the North Sea, lasting fifty-one hours, when Hopewell, like all the other ships except Gay Viking, had turned back. Then had come the tensions and fatigue of the trip with Master Standfast. The brief delights of Lysekil had been succeeded by a bleak sojourn in Brofjord and an unsuccessful attempt to break-out, with each man, after the loss of Master Standfast, fully aware of the risks. 'The disappointment of this false start had a marked reaction on the crew,' recorded Binney. The six days in Gothenburg had been exhilarating, but they were poor preparation for the dis-comforts and short rations of Brofjord. Even tobacco and cigarettes ran out. Cream cakes remained plentiful, but they were apt to pall. 'The despondency of our crew,' wrote Binney, 'was great.'

On 30th November Mike Choyce's midday forecast promised reasonable weather in the Skagerrak, but out in the North Atlantic the meteorological picture was uncompromising, with strings of depressions following one another in rapid succession from the west. The problem Choyce had to advise on was whether in his opinion the incidence, direction and force of these depressions and their various fronts gave Hopewell sufficient time to accomplish her 500-mile voyage. There was an obvious danger of being overtaken in the North Sea by conditions that might be destructive to the slender coastal-type craft with its plywood superstructure; but Choyce was able to give Binney a fair idea of what course to steer to avoid the worst of the wind if that happened, and Binney eventually decided to sail that evening. The Admiralty were alerted accordingly.

The boom across the narrows was opened by the Swedes at 16.15, one hour after Binney had given notice of his intention to sail. By that time it was dusk and there was eight-tenths cloud. What Intelligence the Germans had gathered from their capture of Master Standfast Binney could only guess at, but such secrets as his flotilla had had must surely be known, and he had to plan accordingly. The one certain way of alerting the Germans to Hopewell's departure was to employ one of the Lysekil pilots, whose movements were closely watched, so Binney asked Stokes if he was prepared to sail without one, and Stokes agreed.

The plan for the voyage was to give the Hallö Islands a wide berth and to sail down the coast this time to Maseskär, using only the centre engine to reduce noise. They were followed at a cable's length by a Swedish patrol vessel. Finding the coast clear off Maseskär Island, Stokes left territorial waters at about 17.20 and shaped a north-westerly course that would keep him well clear of the Skaw radar station. The wind was light from the north-east, but the swell was uncomfortable and stomachs soon felt queasy.

Binney was taking a calculated risk on the weather, and when it was known in London that he had sailed, the prospects looked so gloomy from that end that a signal ordering Hopewell to turn back was seriously considered. Binney was also taking a risk on his fuel: after the abortive attempt to sail on 10th November, and the voyage to Gothenburg, Hopewell had only 1,920 gallons remaining. There was, too, another and even greater risk, in addition to the regular patrols, which he was mercifully unaware of. 'We ran at 1,250 revolutions giving us (with the set of the current) approximately 17 knots,' wrote Binney afterwards. 'At 23.30 we reckoned that we were off Kristiansand. At this point we encountered a substantial radar echo one mile from our port bow.' Stokes altered course at once, and as Binney wrote afterwards: 'We should have been even more incurious had we then known that German Fleet destroyers were stationed at Kristiansand.'

Early next morning, 1st December, one of the big end bearings in the centre engine broke and Hopewell was forced to run on her two wing engines. Despite good visibility, it was mid-afternoon before the Beaufighters found them. Then, as darkness fell, the port engine gave out, and they continued for the Humber on their one remaining engine. Meanwhile the engineers, who had been working on the centre engine since one o'clock that morning, were greatly handicapped by the rough seas. Signals difficulties as they tried to fix their position in the minefields maintained the tension right to the end, and when they finally reached Albert Dock they had consumed all but 120 gallons of their fuel.

Binney had heard that his visit had upset the Swedes through a

letter from Victor Mallet, delivered to him while he was in Gothenburg. 'I'm sorry you can't come up here,' said Mallet, 'but evidently
someone high up—King or Cabinet—must have got very angry as
Erik Boheman was very cross. However they seem to be getting over
it a bit, and otherwise have been as co-operative as they can.' This,
Binney felt, was likely to be the end of the matter, and on his return
he prepared to accompany the next outward voyage. But on 14th
December came a warning to the Foreign Office from Mallet.

> 1. I have reason to believe that Binney intends to return in
> the next trip of the motor coasters.
> 2. There will certainly be renewed complaints from the
> Swedish Government especially as our inaction over Dicto and
> Lionel is adding to their irritation.

The reference to the two merchantmen was pertinent : with the
supply situation eased for the moment by the two successful MGB
deliveries, there was no immediate need to risk either of these ships or
their crews. For many months the Germans had been busy laying a
new type of mine right across the Skagerrak, paravanes were useless
as a defence against them, and the presence of destroyers at Kristiansand was a further deterrent. The Swedes, having helped the British
with their MGB operation, were hoping for a declaration that Dicto
and Lionel would be laid-up; with that declaration they believed
they could get the Germans to re-open the Gothenburg traffic. Yet
for the British, the final abandonment of any plan to sail Dicto—
Lionel was now conceded to be too slow—had to await the overall
result of Bridford. Encouraged by the comparative success of the first
two trips, Waring had changed his tactics and was sending special
priority material by sea, so that Bridford was running on an exactly
equal footing with the Air Service; but this situation might not last.
The target set was now 400 tons, and with that amount the Ministry
of Supply felt the situation would be reasonably comfortable; but only
eighty tons had been delivered so far, and there was still a long way
to go. Meanwhile the threat posed by Dicto and Lionel would continue to absorb German naval effort in the Skagerrak and keep the
enemy guessing.

All this was very frustrating for the Swedes, and there must have
been some temptation in Britain to give way to them on the Binney
issue as a *douceur*. But Binney was now in London, where he had the
ear of the Foreign Office. With the loss of Master Standfast still
dominating many minds, Binney's infectious confidence was needed
more than ever. He had Mallet's own assurance that Swedish annoy-
ance had been transitory (Mallet had asked him to destroy the letter,

but Binney had not done so), and he had got a great welcome and all the co-operation he wanted in Lysekil. He was also able to give a first-hand account of his reception in Gothenburg. The Foreign Office reply to Mallet put the ball back in his court. 'Unless you are definite that his return would prejudice the success of the operations, we shall not prevent him going again.'

On 19th December Mallet wrote a somewhat petulant reply. 'While I cannot go so far as to assert that Binney's presence would definitely prejudice the success of the operation, I feel certain that his return would be considered in high quarters here to be an act of discourtesy in face of the strong views expressed to me by the Secretary-General reported in my telegram.' This did not entirely accord with his private letter to Binney. 'The Swedes are very punctilious about such matters,' he went on. 'If we let them see we attach no importance to what they say it is always possible that the present favourable atmos-phere in which operations are being conducted may deteriorate.'

Set against the importance of improving the supply of ball-bearings, for which the British regarded Binney as their man, this sounded feeble, and the reply from Anthony Nutting, of the Northern Depart-ment of the Foreign Office, was unequivocal. 'We see no harm in, and will not prevent, Sir George Binney taking part in further MGB expeditions.'

*　　　*　　　*

While Hopewell was at sea on her return voyage, the other three vessels had started out again for Sweden, but Gay Viking and Non-such ran aground in thick fog in the Humber, sustaining considerable damage, and the attempt was abandoned. Two days later, Gay Corsair started out on her own but was forced to return next day through rough weather. With an improved forecast, however, she tried again later that day. Sailing in the late afternoon, she cleared the Humber by dusk and set course for Flamborough Head.

Gay Corsair under Bob Tanton was in some ways the archetype of the Hull–Lysekil MGBs, and Tanton's own puckish personality had a lot to do with it. Tanton had gone to sea at 15 in a South Wales coaling ship—the coffin ships, as they were known—carrying a kit-bag that was as big as he was, and he could still remember his weeping mother and sisters seeing him off. He came from a sheltered home, but ten years earlier his elder brother had run away to sea, and he had determined to emulate him. Conditions on the coaling ship were indescribable, but Tanton had gone against his father's wishes and he couldn't give up. Now, at 34, he could tell anyone on board to do any job because he'd done it himself.

Tanton had collected a colourful bunch around him, many of

whom had sailed with him before. His chief officer, 42-year-old Roger Thornycroft, was an expert handler of this type of boat. The mate, Ken McNeil, had been at nautical school with Tanton in Hull; and twelve of the crew of nineteen were Hull men. 'We weren't like a normal ship's company,' says Tanton, 'we were just a team.' In rough weather the handling of the boat was generally left to Thornycroft. Tanton and McNeil did the navigation. Laurie Kohler, the bos'n, had just got back from the Mediterranean with Tanton when the chance came to join the MGBs. He would have gone anywhere with Tanton. It was Kohler who had bullied young Tanton, years before, into studying for his ticket. There was 'Tiny' McLaren, 6' 3" and broad-shouldered, who would never have his photograph taken; whenever anyone appeared with a camera, McLaren was missing, nourishing the suspicion that he was either a wanted man or a secret agent. There was Arthur Fray, polished and studious, more like a bank clerk than an AB, yet fitting into the picture. There was Eric Hodgson, the first radio officer, already mentioned, who always took a bottle of fruit cordial and a bucket into the wireless room before battening down the hatch up to the bridge when approaching the Skagerrak. The bucket was there in case he was sick, the cordial to relieve the unpleasantness afterwards. And there were the men whom Tanton felt had the worst jobs of all, the engineers and greasers, like Billy Marr of the pleasing light tenor voice, sweating continually, never able to escape the noise and the smell; and the cooks and stewards, like Kenneth 'Ginger' Parker. 'There was only about a square yard of space in the galley to move about in,' writes Parker, 'and much of the food preparation had to be done on No. 2 hatch, which was just outside the galley. This was an uncomfortable job, as one was continually covered in spray, quite cold too. Also the fumes from the engine exhausts would sweep round the housing, making one feel sick as well as being sea-sick. The evening meal had to be cooked before dusk as the galley fire had to be extinguished before darkness in case of sparks coming from the chimney.' During the night it was self-heating soups only. 'Although my job was the coldest,' says Tanton, 'I think it was the best.'

As a big ship man, Tanton had to make important adjustments. His work on Gay Corsair quickly altered his whole outlook on seafaring. Big ship men, he reckoned, only worried when they saw land. Little ship men worried when they didn't. The whole sensation of being at sea was different. The short steep sea that they normally encountered was typical enough, but the effect was quite unlike the pitching and rolling he was used to. The length of the boat just about fitted in between the troughs, and the boat had to leap over each oncoming wave to get into the succeeding trough. 'The boats didn't cut through the water,' says Arthur Fray, 'they bounced, like water-ski-ing.' And always there were the ubiquitous diesel fumes that permeated everything.

Running through the Skagerrak the following night in the darkness, Tanton did not worry about the minefields; but he knew that the sea around them would be strewn with floating mines that had broken adrift, and these were the real danger to the MGBs. During daylight he entered every one he spotted in his log. During the night he tried to forget them. He always hoped that the bow wave would push them aside. But it was just a matter of luck whether you hit one or not. In a boat of this kind, to hit a mine meant certain oblivion. As for navigation, there was so much violent motion on these ships that compasses were never reliable and Tanton swore by his echo-sounder. Leaving the Yorkshire coast there were clearly defined shoals to check by, while the approaches to Sweden were marked by a fifty-fathom line running parallel with the coast. Radar he regarded as liable to induce a false sense of security, but he welcomed it nevertheless. Up there on the bridge in a snowstorm, with one's position uncertain and not a light to be seen, to hear that warm voice coming up from the radio cabin reporting 'Nothing on the radar, sir' was immensely comforting. But it was the echo-sounder he relied on.

The routine at Lysekil was now well established—the police escort, with the police running to keep up with some of the more boisterous crew-members; breakfast at the Stadshotel, served by Edward and Nancy Hegg, the proprietors of the hotel, with special attention from daughter Britt; the sauna bath; the Swedish waitresses, and the cream pastries; the loading of cargo; the cocking of snooks and victory signs, inverted and otherwise, at the house of the German vice-consul; and then the departure for Brofjord. When a German vessel was in, as sometimes happened, they too used the Stadshotel; but the belligerents were kept on different floors. While the British went to the cinema, the Germans went to the sauna, and vice versa, all under police escort, all expertly timed so as never to meet, like the couples in a bedroom farce.

Like her sister ships on the other side of the North Sea, Gay Corsair was delayed for the next three weeks, and the crew were allowed to do some Christmas shopping. Jack Aird, showing some of them round, noticed that even the toy aeroplanes in the shops were beginning to change sides. Then at last, on Christmas Eve, carrying forty tons of ball-bearings, eight Norwegians, Hopewell's damaged gear-box, and Christmas greetings from the whole of Lysekil, Gay Corsair crept through the boom and out into the Skagerrak for the voyage home.

Binney, too, had embarked on a Christmas cruise: twenty-four hours earlier, on 23rd December, he had sailed from Immingham in Hopewell (Stokes), with Gay Viking (Whitfield) and Nonsuch (Jackson) in attendance. The forecast was uncertain, but he was hoping to snatch a fast passage in a brief spell of better weather. All went well until the three boats emerged from the Flamborough mine gap; there they met strong winds which quickly recreated the confused sea that had been a feature of conditions for weeks. The wind rose to Force 6–7 and it became impossible to head the ships into it so as to shape a course that would avoid the Dogger Bank. They proceeded on a north-east-by-north course until the early hours of Christmas Eve, reducing to 1,100 revolutions and then to 1,000, but the motion was such that the crews of all three ships were by then in a state of collapse. The conditions were clearly beyond the capability of men or ships, and Binney ordered a return to the Humber. On the way back Nonsuch broke the crankshaft of her centre engine. 'This engine had not done more than 30 hours running,' wrote Binney, 'and the failure of the crankshaft is inexplicable.'

Heading in the reverse direction, Gay Corsair met the full force of the gale. 'This is the sort of night,' Tanton told Thornycroft, 'when you want to be in the lee of Bum Island.' After searching the chart for this mythical island, Thornycroft caught the twinkle in Tanton's eye. Tanton's reference had been to the comforts of the marriage bed. Radar echoes during the night kept them alert, but dawn on Christmas morning saw them clear of the Skagerrak, and the serving up of a Christmas dinner of bacon sandwiches and mugs of steaming coffee coincided with the arrival of the Beaufighter escort. One of the Norwegian seamen later went on record as having spent 'the finest and happiest Christmas of my life'.

*　　　*　　　*

As Gay Corsair docked, Binney was setting out again in Hopewell, in company with Gay Viking, but without the crippled Nonsuch this time. Strong winds were anticipated, but they were not expected to exceed Force 4–5, and the two ships crossed the North Sea at fourteen to fifteen knots and were approaching their dusk position when Hopewell's centre engine broke down. Her starboard engine was also temporarily out of action with air locks in the fuel system; and soon afterwards her steering gear failed. Binney would normally have turned back, but the wind was now approaching Force 6, and this combined with the swell from the north-west was creating an awkward sea, ruling out any possibility of retreat.

The first essential was to clear the air lock in the fuel system and repair the rudder, and when this had been done, Gay Viking was signalled and told that Hopewell would proceed at 1,250 revolutions on her two wing engines, giving a speed of about fifteen knots, and that after dark in the Skagerrak Whitfield was to use his own discretion as to whether or not he proceeded independently at a faster rate. In fact Whitfield, after discussing the position with Reynolds, tucked in behind Hopewell and prepared to follow her through the night.

The two boats shaped their usual inward course on the southern side of the Skagerrak about twenty-five miles off the Danish coast, the only excitement coming when evasive action was taken opposite Kristiansand as a result of two substantial radar echoes off the starboard bow. Neither of these ships was showing lights and almost certainly they were German patrols. Binney consoled himself with the thought that the only destroyer known to be at Kristiansand, the Hans Lody, was believed to be out of commission. (It wasn't, and it was accompanied by a torpedo-boat and a minelayer; but the Hopewell got through.)

Some hours later, off the Skaw, another series of radar echoes, from ships which were again showing no lights, gave further evidence that German vigilance was increasing. But with the aid of their radars Hopewell and Gay Viking steered clear of trouble and entered Swedish waters six miles north of the Väderöbod Islands at 05.30 that morning, 28th December. They then took the inner route to the Hallö Light. Despite further serious trouble on Hopewell, this time in her starboard gear-box, they berthed at Lysekil at 07.30.

With the interception of Master Standfast in mind, Bill Waring and Jack Aird had delayed their departure from Gothenburg, and that of the shipping agents, in case their movements should alert the Germans to an impending arrival; but they reached Lysekil by taxi just before the gunboats berthed. They were not, however, the first to board Hopewell. As soon as the boats tied up alongside, a Swedish naval control party went aboard with instructions to seal up all guns, ammunition, radio and radar equipment while the boats were in port. Binney did not demur, but he noticed that particular attention was paid to the radar equipment. Some two hours later, while he was ashore talking to Waring, a Swedish naval officer boarded Hopewell and told the first radio officer, a 23-year-old Londoner named Franklin, that he had instructions to remove the radar display tube. Franklin protested, but the Swede, on the pretext that radar valves could be used for transmission and were therefore subject to control, insisted that Franklin hand it over. The Swede then took it with him to a corvette that was also lying alongside the quay. Peter Lawrence, the SOE representative on Hopewell, told Binney of this when he went back on board two minutes later, and as the radar apparatus was of a secret nature, Binney went off to tackle the Swedes and demand the return of the valve. At the same time he asked Waring to protest in the strongest terms to the local magistrate. The magistrate immediately got in touch with the captain of the corvette, and the valve was returned within forty minutes of its confiscation.

This, however, was by no means the end of the harassment the two boats suffered on this visit at the hands of the Swedish Navy. That same afternoon another Swedish officer, a lieutenant-commander this time, boarded Hopewell and told Binney that the Swedish naval authorities still insisted on the removal of the radar tubes from both ships and that he proposed to take them forthwith. 'I've no intention of surrendering them,' said Binney. 'And you've got no authority to remove them. All you can possibly want is to find out how to make them. If there's any more of this nonsense I'll clear Hopewell and Gay Viking from Lysekil immediately and we'll go somewhere else.' The lieutenant-commander affected a show of righteous indignation. 'Surely you don't think that simple, unintelligent Swedish naval officers could be guilty of espionage.' Binney admitted that he was at a disadvantage in that he knew very few Swedish naval officers. 'But I would not have called Count Oxenstierna unintelligent.' (Captain Count Johan Oxenstierna was at that time Swedish naval attaché in London and was well known to Binney.) This riposte so unsettled the Swede that he left the ship, returning within the hour to withdraw his request and apologise. There had been, he said, a misunderstanding, and it would not occur again.

Next morning Mayor Nyblom asked if he could meet Binney on board and be shown over one of the ships. With Hopewell out of action, Binney had transferred to Gay Viking, which was preparing to move up to Brofjord; but he was glad to show Nyblom round. After expressing his regret over the naval incident the mayor assured Binney that he had the goodwill of the authorities and the local inhabitants, and he added that thorough steps were being taken to protect British interests from Nazi agents, both at Lysekil and in Brofjord. This showed the attitude of the civil authorities. But the Swedish Navy still had to be reckoned with. Permission to move Gay Viking to Brofjord had been given, but just before she was due to sail the Swedish lieutenant-commander boarded the vessel, and after expressing the formal regret of the naval authorities for the previous day's incident, he asked permission to accompany Gay Viking to her anchorage and to bring with him the officer of naval control who had seized the valve, together with two Post Office engineers whom he introduced to Binney as experts in the Swedish Radio Service. These men, he said, had been sent up from Gothenburg to instruct the naval control officer as to what instruments he could properly seal and to agree with the gunboat's radar operators where the seals were to be placed. The whole object was to avoid future friction. This seemed reasonable enough and Binney agreed. Gay Viking then sailed for Brofjord, where the Swedes, after arranging the seals, left the ship.

It was later discovered by Henry Denham from one of his Intelligence sources that the two specialists were not Post Office officials at all; they had been sent by the naval authorities from Stockholm, and one of them, named Elmquist, was the head of Svenska Aktiebolaget Trädlöstellegrafi (SATT), a German-controlled subsidiary of the German electrical firm AEG. When Mallet faced Boheman with this, the Secretary-General was horrified; but after enquiry he admitted it was true. He passed on to Mallet the personal apologies of Sweden's long-service Prime Minister, Per Albin Hansson, and the assurance that nothing of the sort would occur again and that heads would roll. In mitigation, Boheman asserted that the subterfuge had been plotted not on behalf of the Germans but for the Swedes' own Board of Military Research.

Since the radar equipment under surveillance, ASV, was antiquated and already in the hands of the Germans, British Intelligence sources were not unduly perturbed, and they made no further protest, regarding the incident as useful ammunition to be used if the Swedes pressed the case they had been urging for the recall of Denham because of his Intelligence work. Denham had built up many valuable contacts in Sweden, and the Foreign Office wanted to keep him there during the prelude to the invasion of Europe.

For the next few days, at the Swedes' insistence, Gay Viking lay alongside the Swedish guard ship just inside Brojford, within a few feet of the jetty, but Binney was able to visit Dicto and Lionel. The crews of these two vessels, having been isolated in the fjord for nearly four months, with no shore leave, had become a prey to doubts and resentments, and were beginning to suspect, with some justice, that they had become no more than pawns in the game. At Waring's request Binney explained to them the importance of what he called the 'Brofjord Front', and particularly of the value of the ships in a 'fleet in being' role. No final decision had been made, he told them; but if the MGB operation continued to be successful, the ships and their crews and cargoes would probably not be risked at this stage of the war. Key men such as masters, chief officers and chief engineers would have to remain in Brofjord for the rest of the winter in case the situation changed, but most of the Norwegians on Lionel would be offered passages to England in the MGBS. This bolstered morale on Dicto and greatly eased the tension on Lionel.

On 31st December Hopewell, although still under repair, followed Gay Viking to Brofjord. Both ships had orders to lie alongside the Swedish corvette. A week later, however, when a full gale developed from the south-west, Stokes and Whitfield expressed anxiety about their anchorage; owing to the continual rolling of the corvette there was considerable danger of damage to the MGBS. Binney requested permission to lie alongside Lionel in the centre of the fjord, and his request was referred back to Gothenburg and approved. Next evening, after the two ships had moved, the approval was withdrawn: the two MGBS could lie nowhere else except alongside the corvette. As the weather was as rough as ever, Binney refused to take the responsibility of instructing his captains to move; and next morning he telephoned to Mallet the text of a protest to be lodged with the Swedish Government. Since he knew that all long-distance calls in Sweden were tapped by the police and immediately reported verbatim to the appropriate Government department, he expected quick action and got it. The Swedish naval headquarters in Stockholm cancelled the order before Mallet had time to lodge a protest.

'Unquestionably,' wrote Binney afterwards, 'somewhere in the senior ranks of the Swedish naval staff there is an element hostile to us, which is possibly a legacy from the Swedish destroyer incident in the Faroes in 1940.' The Head of Military Intelligence in London was more specific. 'The Head of the Swedish Navy is a pro-German admiral,' he wrote, 'and expected changes have not produced the pro-Allied trend looked for.' Happily Binney was able to add that this was very far from the spirit of the officers and crews of the Swedish naval ships with whom he was in daily contact.

Hopewell's repairs could not be completed until spares arrived from England, and Binney decided that Gay Viking should make the passage alone. But strong westerly winds with frequent gales kept her immobile for the first fifteen days of 1944. Meanwhile the civilian authorities continued to show a consideration that amounted to genuine friendship. They had information that the Germans were planning to sabotage Dicto and Lionel at their anchorage, using limpet mines, and they consulted Binney on countermeasures. Binney pointed out that the boom at the mouth of the fjord was unguarded at night and that saboteurs could negotiate it easily enough by carrying a canoe round it on the shore. The Swedes responded by doubling their marine watch and issuing them with tommy-guns, while Binney for his part ordered the doubling of the watch on the two vessels and their illumination by searchlights at night. Another concern of the

civilian authorities was the number of suspect Swedes who were finding reasons for lodging in Lysekil, and to seek a solution the Landsfogde, von Sydow, came up from Gothenburg to see Waring. The
two men inspected a number of ports to the north of Lysekil for use as
an alternative, and Hunnebostrand, a small and isolated port some
fifteen miles distant with reasonable facilities, was settled on.

On 16th January the forecast was for a south-west wind in the
Skagerrak during the night, Force 3–4, with clear visibility. The wind
was expected to rise to Force 5 by next morning, but cloud was
estimated as five-tenths to seven-tenths, with a moderate sea, and on
this forecast Binney resolved to sail. Choyce recommended that if the
seas proved too strong they steer a more southerly course than usual,
where they could expect to find calmer weather. The moon was not
due to rise until 22.40, which meant they would have the benefit of
full darkness until somewhere short of Kristiansand; they reckoned to
be abreast of Kristiansand soon after midnight.

Unknown to Binney, three more destroyers of the 6th Destroyer
Flotilla had been moved to Kristiansand in a determined attempt to
intercept the 'grey ladies', as the Germans called them. When weather
conditions favoured a breakout, Flag Officer Baltic planned to put
them at two hours' notice to sail. Air reconnaissance had disclosed
their presence at Kristiansand six days earlier, but inexplicably the
information had not been passed to Binney.

Carrying a cargo of forty tons of ball-bearings and eight Norwegians, and with a Swedish pilot, Gay Viking left Brofjord at 15.00
that afternoon, 16th January. Followed by a Swedish corvette, Whitfield took the inner route northwards until he was under the lee of
Soteskär Island, where the pilot transferred to the corvette. He then
made for the channel dividing Väderöbod Island from the mainland,
striking out to sea at 17.30 when he was about six miles north of the
Väderöbod Light, shaping a course that would bring him parallel
with the Norwegian shore and about twenty-three miles from it.

The night was clear with surface visibility about a mile. Radar
sweeps were maintained at five-minute intervals to give early warning
of patrol vessels. Meanwhile the swell, and the adverse wind, prevented Whitfield from attempting a higher speed than fifteen to
sixteen knots at 1,200 revolutions. They had been at sea for exactly
an hour when the radar operator reported an echo dead ahead.
Simultaneously a small stationary ship of 5,000 to 6,000 tons, carrying
no lights, was picked out from the bridge a mile distant. As a signalling lamp blinked a challenge at them out of the darkness, Whitfield
turned abruptly through 180 degrees and kept on an opposite course
until he was out of sight of the enemy vessel. He then struck out in a

northerly direction before turning west to resume his course, aiming to pass between the German vessel and the shore. The fact that this would bring him much nearer to the Norwegian coast than usual did not, in the circumstances as he knew them, worry him unduly. Half an hour later an echo showed up again on the port bow, just about where he expected, and this time he was able to avoid contact. The vessel must have been a supply ship heading to or from Oslo.

Whether or not the departure of Gay Viking had been witnessed and recorded, the Germans now knew that a gunboat was escaping through the Skagerrak. When Whitfield heard aeroplane engines overhead an hour later, and realised the plane was circling at not more than a thousand feet, he guessed the *Luftwaffe* were looking for him. Stopping two engines and reducing speed to minimise the phosphorescent wake that might easily be visible from the air, he took evasive action again, and by 19.30 the sound of the plane had died away.

Even so, Gay Viking's situation was precarious in the extreme. Not only did the Admiralty know of the destroyers at Kristiansand, but they also knew that these destroyers would soon be lying in wait for Gay Viking. Yet they could not alert the gunboat to her danger at this stage without compromising their highly secret intercept service.

It had always been accepted that the only vessels that could successfully chase the motor gunboats were destroyers. Now, with Gay Viking running straight into the trap, the operations centres in Britain concerned with the action resigned themselves to the inevitable.

Some time after shaking off the German reconnaissance plane, Whitfield noticed that the Pole Star, which should have been almost abeam to starboard, was actually on his starboard quarter. He looked to see what course the helmsman was steering and found that the gyro compass was behaving erratically. On his present course he was heading obliquely across the Skagerrak towards the minefields off the Danish coast.

Whitfield knew that his location and his cargo combined to render his magnetic compass unreliable, so all he did for the moment was alter course to put the Pole Star back where it should be on his starboard beam and carry on while Brian Reynolds rectified the fault. How long he had been heading across the Skagerrak was uncertain, but he knew he was much too far to the south and that his present course would take him through the minefields. He had to think, too, about his dawn position, and he decided to use the fifty-fathom line on the south side of the Skagerrak as an aid to navigation, relying on his shallow draught to get him through.

With the Pole Star to his right and the fifty-fathom line to his left, Whitfield made good progress until midnight. But as the moon began to rise, the sky, which had been cloudless, became overcast, as Choyce had predicted, completely obscuring the stars. With Reynolds still working on the gyro compass, Whitfield sat like a statue in one fixed position for the next two hours to keep the wind on his face.

At two o'clock that morning, with the wind freshening, Gay Viking was abreast of Kristiansand. 'That's the end of George Binney,' was the verdict pronounced at more than one operations centre. No one suspected that Binney's luck had held yet again and that an enforced detour had taken Gay Viking into an area where destroyers dare not venture.

By daybreak Whitfield estimated that he was no more than fifteen miles short of his anticipated dawn position. Soon afterwards a series of aircraft echoes began to be picked up on the radar, and Binney and Whitfield rightly assumed that these aircraft were looking for them; but with ten-tenths low cloud and visibility of less than a mile, neither man was unduly worried. They did not expect to see friendly aircraft either, and in fact all Beaufighter sorties aimed at locating and protecting Gay Viking were cancelled throughout the day. As often happened on Bridford, weather that suited the gunboats automatically grounded the air escort.

During the afternoon Whitfield reduced speed to improve his slender fuel margin, and at about 07.45 on 18th January the gunboat passed through the Humber boom. It was then, with a group of excited Bridford officers waiting to hear how the gunboat had escaped, that misfortune struck. 'The weather had been foggy throughout the night,' wrote Binney afterwards, 'and there were still patches of fog in the estuary. We were nosing cautiously at 900 revolutions towards Immingham. Close to the Middle Lightship we came into collision with a small coastal steamer which suddenly emerged without navigation lights from a fog patch on our port bow.' The impact removed about thirteen feet of Gay Viking's bows, and although the bulkhead held, it would be a month before she was ready for sea.

When the crew finally got ashore, it was their turn to be astonished. They were entirely ignorant of their fortuitous escape.

*   *   *

On 18th January Bill Waring reported to Mike Wheeler in London on the situation as he saw it at his end. 'The relief which Bridford has brought to the freight position is considerable,' he wrote, 'and instead of steadily accumulating urgently required material with little hope of being able to transport it, things are now on a much more reasonable basis. I feel, therefore, that a preliminary comparison between Bridford and the Air Service is not out of place.' In the six months ending 31st December 1943—a convenient period for comparison, for which figures were available—the Air Service had made 157 flights (129 by Mosquito) and had delivered 110 tons of freight in all. (This included diplomatic freight.) Against this Bridford, in four completed trips so far that season, and despite unlooked-for mechanical set-backs, had delivered 160 tons. Waring did not attempt to cost either operation in terms of kroner or sterling, but he did contrast the losses on the Air Service—two Mosquitoes, two Lodestars, and twenty-three lives—with the losses on Bridford—one motor gunboat, one fatal casualty, and nineteen men taken prisoner. Invaluable as the work of the Air Service was, it had already been eclipsed by Bridford.

Next day, 19th January, Gay Corsair sailed for Sweden under Bob Tanton, and although a faulty fuel feed prevented Tanton from increasing engine revolutions in the Skagerrak, the crew hand-pumped the fuel throughout the night and the gunboat just got into Swedish territorial waters before daylight on the morning of the 21st. The trouble was cleared within a few days, but there followed a long wait in Brofjord due to the weather and the phase of the moon. Recreation for the stranded crews remained hard to find, but the fishing was good, Monopoly, cribbage, pontoon and brag were popular, and tombola (Bingo) evenings on Dicto and Lionel were enlivened by Laurie Kohler's calling of the numbers in English and Norwegian. During this period, in which there were no further sailings from Britain, Hopewell completed her repairs and the two ships finally headed for the boom on the homeward voyage in the last twilight of 16th February.

Before sailing, Stokes and Tanton agreed that they should proceed in company, with Hopewell leading, until they broke through the coastal patrols; they would then sail independently in order to get the best possible speed from each ship. Immediately on setting course they encountered large fleets of fishing vessels, and avoiding them meant either running north, parallel to the enemy patrols, or taking a chance and cutting the patrol line at right angles. The latter course was decided upon.

> All went well [wrote Stokes afterwards] until a searchlight was sighted very fine on our starboard bow. At this time we had fishing vessels on either side. We turned about on a 90 degrees course until the beam was extinguished, and then headed north, through the line of vessels extending between the searchlight and our course. Carrying on until well clear, we gradually edged

round for 'westing' without further trouble, but persistent echoes were recorded on fixed bearings on the starboard quarter.

Wondering if we were being trailed we once turned to starboard, but saw nothing, so turned again to course 233 degrees so as to sail down the edge of the minefield. About an hour after this, at about 22.30, Gay Corsair (who by the way followed our every move very well indeed) parted company and we increased our revolutions to 1,350.

Continuous lines of fishing vessels were passed to port, and one large trawler to starboard, and at times the echoes from it were still received on the starboard quarter by radar. Owing to these persistent echoes we proceeded to haul south, into the minefields, and eventually passed only about 14 miles north of Hantsholm, and lost all echoes.

Once again, but not this time involuntarily, the southern minefield had been used as a means of escape. Next morning RAF Beaufighters reached both vessels at 10.30, and they were unloading their cargoes in Hull on the morning of the 18th. Their arrival meant that individually the gunboats had completed six round trips and brought out over 240 tons of ball-bearings and special machinery; but this was still well below the target of 400 set by the Ministry of Supply, and the nights were shortening. Three days earlier, however, George Binney had left Hull in Nonsuch with Captain Jackson in command on the seventh outward voyage, the first attempt to be made by Nonsuch since she broke a crankshaft on 23rd December. Johnsen, the Norwegian chief officer, had been recalled for other duties, and his place was taken by Captain E. B. ('Ted') Ruffman, who had been wounded at Tobruk and invalided out of the Army. He was farming in Scotland when he heard of the chance to join the gunboats and at once volunteered.

The start was delayed by last-minute mechanical breakdowns, and this forced Jackson to keep up a minimum of 1,200 revolutions to gain a safe dusk position next day. When the time came he was about ten miles short, so he increased speed to 1,250 revolutions, but this brought fuel suction troubles to two engines and the log showed they were making only fifteen knots. To reach their dawn position off Sweden Jackson had to take advantage of the strong inward current on the south side of the Skagerrak, which meant edging in to within seventeen to eighteen miles of the Danish coast and cutting inside the fishing fleet, and they were passing ships continually from Hantsholm to the Skaw. Several times they came under the surveillance of German patrol boats, and one of these chased them for a time; but at

03.00 on the morning of 17th February Jackson increased speed for the run in towards Lysekil, finally berthing at 07.40. Apart from fuel suction trouble, engine repairs were light, and by nightfall another forty tons of cargo had been loaded, partly ball-bearings but including further items of machinery essential for the manufacture of ball-bearings in Britain. Next morning, 18 February, with Hopewell and Gay Corsair now unloading in Albert Dock, Nonsuch left Lysekil for Brofjord to study the weather charts and embark her quota of Norwegian refugees.

For once there was difficulty over a refugee who had been promised a passage: after the promise was made it was discovered that he had earned the nickname of the 'Butcher of Trondheim' because of his Resistance activities, and the Gestapo were most anxious to find him. Binney was warned against giving the man passage for fear the entire crew would be compromised if the gunboat were caught. His solution was to lend the man a lethal pill. If Nonsuch were captured, the man must swallow the pill and jump overboard. This he undertook to do.

The fate of Nonsuch on that seventh return voyage thus had more than average significance for one Norwegian refugee. But at least he was given no time to brood. Choyce pronounced the weather favourable, and at six o'clock that evening the gunboat left Brofjord. A smoking bonfire high up on a hillside overlooking the fjord suggested some primitive form of signal, but Waring investigated and found it had been lit by the children of a farmer.

Half an hour later, Jackson left coastal waters about five miles south of the Hallö Light. Strong searchlights were playing to and fro off Maseskär, but their beams swept high over the top of Nonsuch. Meanwhile Jackson was repeatedly forced to take evasive action to avoid ships that were carrying no lights. He kept slightly to the Danish side of the Skagerrak and experienced no further trouble, emerging into the North Sea at 01.30 next morning nineteen miles north of Hantsholm. By 04.00 he had left the Danish fishing fleet behind, and at dawn he was only ten miles short of his standard position. Soon after midday he was picked up by three Beaufighters. But even this trip, the fastest round trip yet achieved on Bridford, was not completed without the intrusion of mechanical disaster; at 14.10 that afternoon Nonsuch broke the crankshaft on her port engine, the second broken crankshaft she had suffered, and she also ran one of her big end bearings. This was her only successful voyage. Although a great many of the delays that winter were due to the weather, many more round trips might have been accomplished but for the chronic mechanical faults that dogged all the ships. This trip, however, with its cargo of special material, was designated 'the most valuable so far made on Operation Bridford'.

They had now delivered 280 tons; but the nights were shrinking fast, and the prospects of reaching the target before the spring were diminishing. Indeed, a move was afoot to wind up the operation altogether. 'In view of our engine disabilities,' wrote Binney, 'our sponsors were seriously thinking of calling off further voyages.' Time and again there had been breakdowns in dangerous waters, and it seemed too much to hope that the luck would hold. But Binney was determined to fulfil the task he had been set, and as soon as repairs to the other three ships had been completed he planned a final attempt to round off the season by hitting the target.

By the first week in March, Hopewell, Gay Viking and Gay Corsair were all ready to put to sea; and on 6th March the weather prospects were reported to be fair. The full moon was only two days off, but since they had always avoided the full moon period in the past, Binney believed that the enemy might be less vigilant at that time. Admiral Tovey agreed with him, and the three ships left Hull at 16.15 that day, with Hopewell, the flagship, leading, Gay Corsair in the middle, and Whitfield in Gay Viking in his old place as Tail-end Charlie. Binney's only concession to the prospect of moonlight in the Skagerrak lay in an order he issued that if any of the ships were sighted by enemy aircraft during the North Sea crossing they would all return to the Humber.

Five hours after sailing, Binney's hopes of a triumphant conclusion to the winter's operations received a savage blow. Passing through the minefield off Flamborough Head, Hopewell broke the crankshaft of her centre engine and Ginger Stokes had no alternative but to return. Before he did so, however, Gay Corsair closed him under the expertise of Bob Tanton and the commodore threw his briefcase aboard before jumping across.

The two remaining vessels continued through the minefield at 1,000 revolutions, increasing to 1,150 at dawn. There was a moderate northerly breeze and slight sea and swell, but the cloud, although extensive, was neither thick nor low enough to give much protection from enemy aircraft. At 07.17 a machine flew dead overhead heading eastwards, and everyone took it for granted that a sighting was inevitable. But just as the RAF Beaufighter crews searched so often in vain, so the German crew appeared not to have seen them.

It was dusk at 18.30 [wrote Binney afterwards]: dead calm, strong moon and clear sky. We increased to 1,250 revolutions, shaping a course which would bring us through the centre of the

Skagerrak. At 20.40 we stopped as Gay Viking was experiencing some engine trouble. She came alongside. Fortunately the trouble was of a minor character. At 22.30 we were abeam of Kristian-sand in brilliant moonlight, our hull showing a very clear silhouette. The visibility was estimated as 5 miles. Fortunately at 01.30 we ran into a dense belt of fog which enveloped us right through to the Swedish coast.

Bob Tanton, too, has vivid memories of this final outward voyage. 'Captain Whitfield followed me for many miles through dense freez-ing fog and was still sitting on my stern when we picked up Hallö Lighthouse in the cold grey dawn right on the place and time where we hoped to be. The Whitfield stock was very high on Gay Corsair that morning.'

As the voyage had not been as exhausting as most, and as the fog-belt seemed likely to hold, Binney looked for a chance to return to Britain that night, and Choyce approved. Gay Viking needed a day or two for repairs, but Gay Corsair's engines needed only minor adjustment, and loading was completed by 16.00. Unfortunately Tanton was held up by the usual last-minute engine frustrations and he was unable to sail before 19.25; as he left territorial waters the moon was already bright. The indications of fog, however, were still strong.

Almost at once, off the Hallö Islands, Tanton had to take evasive action, but he had spotted the approaching vessels in good time and Gay Corsair got through unseen. At 20.15 he increased to 1,250 revolutions. 'For no particular reason,' he said afterwards, 'my thoughts were on a bottle of Blue Label Bass and my local in Hull. But this comfortable vision was soon shattered.' Four miles on their starboard bow a 12,000-ton merchantman, escorted by three E-boats or gunboats, was southward-bound from Oslo fjord; Tanton was alerted to their presence by the sound of propellers thrashing near at hand and getting closer. He began to take avoiding action, but as he did so, at about 21.30 and twenty-three miles west-south-west of the Hallö Light, the input shaft of the gear-box on Gay Corsair's centre engine fractured itself with a ghastly clatter, splitting the casing and causing a fire in the engine room. The fire was quickly extinguished, but the engines had to be stopped meanwhile. 'This was an interesting interlude,' says Tanton, 'during which our immobility and helplessness were not fully realised by the enemy until the final silhouette appeared on our port quarter and passed us at speed some distance off. This was undoubtedly one of the escort vessels of the E-boat type, and either he failed to see us or he mistook us for one of the escort.'

Limping back towards Lysekil, keeping a wary eye on the convoy and again slipping through the coastal patrols, they berthed soon after midnight. Closer investigation next morning revealed a damaged or fractured crankshaft in addition to the broken gear-box, totally beyond repair. At this late stage in the winter, Binney decided they would have to rely on the two wing engines to see them home. He didn't intend Gay Corsair to be stuck in Brofjord all summer. It was fortunate that it was the centre engine, which would least affect their speed.

The damage had another disagreeable consequence; they would have to unload some of the cargo to reduce the strain on the other two engines. They watched dejectedly while twelve and a half tons of ball-bearings were deposited back on Andersson quay.

After a diver had removed the centre propeller, they ran a series of engine trials in Gulmarfjord to check the engine performance in relation to displacement and speed. The results showed they could still expect, within their temperature limits, a speed slightly in excess of sixteen knots at 1,250 revolutions, graduating down to just over thirteen at 1,050. Deciding that this was satisfactory, they sailed through the boom into Brofjord to rejoin Gay Viking, whose repairs had been completed meanwhile.

They now had to wait a further week for favourable weather, and on 15th March they were visited by Peter Tennant, press attaché to the Legation in Stockholm and a fervent supporter of Binney. Since this would be the last voyage of the winter, Tennant was keen to release a story on Bridford to the press as soon as it was safely completed. He felt that, besides having good propaganda value, the release would serve two other important purposes. It would counter the wilder type of rumour that was circulating in Sweden, and it would be very much in the interests of the crew of Master Standfast, whose capture in the course of a normal Merchant Navy voyage could be stressed.

Binney, thoroughly in agreement with Tennant, added some reasons of his own. Publicity would make it more difficult for the Swedes to withdraw facilities already granted, which might become important next winter. The prestige of the Merchant Navy, and especially the morale of the Bridford crews, many of whom he planned to put up for decorations, would be enhanced by such a release. The boost to morale would be timely if, as seemed possible, there was a need to keep them together as a unit. As for the security angle, he was still prepared to rely on exaggerating the speed of the ships.

Choyce came up with a better forecast next day, 16th March, but it was now so late in the season that darkness would not be absolute until after 20.00, which meant beginning the voyage in daylight. Binney, however, refused to be deterred by this. After embarking the usual quota of Norwegian volunteers they left Brofjord in a welcome spate of snow flurries and at once made northwards up the coast towards Soteskär Island. As they emerged from territorial waters at 19.15 the snow-belt suddenly failed them and they found themselves approaching the German patrol area in clear daylight. But the Binney luck still held: a pronounced wall or front of thick black low-lying cloud ran parallel to them, and by taking cover in the edge of this wall they were able to keep more or less to their course without much fear of being seen.

Daylight died hard and it was not until 20.30 that all traces of the afterglow were gone. Shaping a course down the middle of the Skagerrak at 1,250 revolutions, hoping to pass Kristiansand before the moon was high, they settled down to the last voyage home.

Because of Gay Corsair's precarious engine position the two captains had agreed that she could not afford to linger in enemy waters, and when, at about one o'clock that morning, Gay Viking had to slow down through fuel suction trouble, Tanton pressed on alone. From that point on the two ships lost contact. But by 02.00, when the moonlight became strong and searching, the radar echoes ceased and both captains believed they were just about clear of the most dangerous area.

At 03.15 on Gay Corsair the radar operator reported a single substantial echo dead astern and rapidly overtaking; this was just about the time and place where a destroyer from Kristiansand might catch them up, and all guns were immediately manned. As each man stood tensely at his action station, expecting to be illuminated by a star shell from a destroyer at any moment, a solitary aircraft lumbered right over the top of them at little more than mast height, its silhouette instantly recognisable as an RAF Wellington, returning from a mine-laying operation. The RAF, about which harsh things were sometimes said when air escorts failed to arrive, were never more popular than at that moment.

When first light came at 05.50, neither boat was more than forty-five miles from the Danish or Norwegian coasts; but there was a tracery of coastal fog all round them, and a low cloud ceiling, so the galley fires were lit and a meal prepared. Later, as the sky cleared, the prestige of the RAF dropped as the Beaufighters were looked for in vain; and there was more trouble for both vessels as Gay Corsair broke her starboard crankshaft and Gay Viking her main gear-box input shaft on the port engine. Yet despite these and other set-backs, complicated by a bank of dense fog off the Yorkshire coast, the two vessels berthed in Albert Dock on the morning of 18th March within two hours of each other, bringing another sixty-seven and a half tons of urgently needed ball-bearings to Britain.

*　　*　　*

After the Rubble operation, Binney had been prevented by illness from writing a full report straight away, and the same thing happened after Bridford; but this time his collapse was more serious. It took the form of a heart attack, and meant that his activities would be considerably curtailed for some time. In view of the pressures he had lived under that winter, and indeed almost continuously since 1940, this was hardly surprising. In addition to numerous false starts in the gunboats he had actually completed four round trips to and from Sweden, more than anyone else except a 41-year-old South African greaser named Ernest Schaper and a 23-year-old New Zealand AB named John Valentine, the only 'foreigners' on Bridford, who completed the same number. As with Rubble and Performance, he could have done nothing without loyal support in London and Sweden, to say nothing of the fanatical comradeship of his crews: but as with those other operations, the mountains were moved by George Binney, and this was recognised in the award of the DSO.

A breakdown of the actual weight of materials delivered by the four gunboats, covering machine tools, high-speed steels, spare parts, and electrical and measuring equipment, as well as the preponderant cargo of ball- and roller-bearings, showed a total of 347 tons. Taking precisely the same period this time—November 1943 to March 1944 —the Air Service to and from Stockholm had carried eighty-eight tons. Essential as the work of the Air Service had always been in backing up Binney's blockade-running operations, it could never cope with the tonnages required, nor could it carry some of the bulkier items. After the operation Sir Andrew Duncan, the man who had originally appointed Binney to Scandinavia and who was now Minister of Supply, told the Minister of War Transport:

> This operation gives us a substantial part of the equipment for a vital new ball-bearing factory which we are putting up, and which should enable us to maintain our own supply of ball-bearings. There is no need for me to exaggerate the importance of this.

The immediate significance was possibly even greater. In those vital months of preparation for the invasion of Europe, Britain's special ball-bearing needs were largely met by the little ships operating out of the Humber.

Postscript to Bridford

There was one more blockade-running operation through the Skagerrak before the war ended, and had it not been for his illness George Binney would have led it. It was at his house at 17 Porchester Terrace in the first week of August 1944 that an informal meeting was held to formulate plans, and although medical advice was that he must not take part in any operational work for some time, he stubbornly held out against it. 'The doctor only won after a hard battle,' wrote Brian Reynolds later. But Binney remained to give his advice on all matters connected with the operation, and he had a natural deputy in Reynolds, whose appointment as commodore was agreed.

Two months before this meeting, the invasion of Europe had begun, and one of the tasks given to Special Operations Executive was to direct and support every form of sabotage to cut the enemy's communications in the occupied countries. So intensive did the campaign become that in Denmark, at least, the supply of demolition material ran out. Small quantities were then delivered by air, but these operations, besides being inadequate, exposed those who took part in them to unacceptable risks. The planners of SOE Headquarters turned to George Binney.

Three of the original motor gunboats, Hopewell, Nonsuch, and later Gay Viking, were allocated to the operation, which was code-named 'Moonshine', and the captains recalled were Harry Whitfield, 'Ginger' Stokes and 'Jacko' Jackson. Chief Officers—Lord Fitzwilliam (Peter Lawrence), Ted Ruffman, and a new man, J. B. 'Jim' Woodeson, shot in the sciatic nerve during the North African campaign and like Ruffman invalided out—were again appointed, and many of the original crew-men returned with the ships. Bill Waring was made responsible for the handling of the cargoes on the Swedish side, Wilson's were appointed agents, and Peter Coleridge again acted as liaison in England. Victor Mallet was put in the picture but was instructed to say nothing to the Swedish Foreign Office other than to warn Erik Boheman at the appropriate time that motor coaster operations for the purpose of bringing further supplies of ball-bearings to Britain were about to restart. This was a cover story that was easily substantiated, as the ball-bearing situation had deteriorated as a consequence of the flying-bomb assault and further dislocation was expected through the V2 rocket.

There was some doubt as to the guise that Reynolds, alias Bingham, should assume as leader. He could still not return to Sweden as Reynolds because of his gun-running activities in Performance. For the

Bridford operation, as Bingham, he had grown a beard, and no one had recognised him. It was decided to award him a temporary commission as Lieutenant-Commander Brian Bingham, RNR, which would ease his problems in the event of capture; and he was to shave off his beard. Curiously enough this seems to have proved an adequate disguise. Either that or the Swedes winked at it.

The luck and resolution that had helped to make Bridford such a success, and the hazards that had been overcome by the crews, were emphasised by the experience on Moonshine, when, from an initial attempt in September 1944 right through to January 1945, not a single vessel got through to Sweden. Two ships got within 125 miles of the Swedish coast before being forced back by headwinds, and the weather frustrated the flotilla continually; but the most irritating delays were those caused by fogs and tides in the Humber. Accordingly in the New Year the three boats were transferred to Aberdeen, and it was from there, on 13th January 1945, that the only successful voyage on Operation Moonshine was made.

All three ships crossed safely to Lysekil, where they discharged their carefully camouflaged cargo for onward transmission by clandestine means to Denmark. They then continued to Gothenburg for servicing as planned. The Germans had long since abandoned their standing Skagerrak patrols and there had been very little danger of interception. But other hazards remained, as was to be shown on the return voyage.

One natural hazard that had particularly troubled newcomer Jim Woodeson was the extreme cold, which he had felt acutely in his game leg. His ordinary black leather boots, to which calipers had been fitted, gave little protection. The last thing he did before sailing for home was to swop boots with Ted Ruffman, who had a pair of waterproof canvas boots with fleece linings. Woodeson had tried them on earlier and found that, besides keeping his feet warm, they gave his leg enough support to enable him to walk.

Ruffman donned Woodeson's boots in exchange. Unlike Woodeson he could move around freely and keep the circulation going.

Choosing Hunnebostrand as an alternative departure point, after loading at Lysekil, the three ships took advantage of a fog-bank to sail at 16.30 on 5th February, thus gaining what amounted to an extra hour of darkness for the run. At 20.30 Nonsuch ran clear of the other two boats as they turned to avoid some fishing vessels, and from that point on she continued alone, reaching her dawn position an hour before sunrise and being spotted by two Beaufighters at 09.30 on the 6th. For Hopewell and Gay Viking, however, the night did not go so well.

For the last few hours before losing sight of Nonsuch, Jackson or Hopewell had been without gyro compass, log and echo-sounder; all had broken down and all failed to respond to the coaxings of the crew. With his steel cargo Jackson could not rely on his magnetic compass; but none of this mattered so long as he could keep track of Nonsuch's wake. Now with Nonsuch gone he needed a pilot, and he signalled Gay Viking by lamp to come through to take the lead.

The moon was not yet up, and the night was dark. Visibility was poor with fog patches and drizzle, and there was sufficient swell to cause difficulty in steering. Even the close station-keeping that had been attempted so far had not succeeded in keeping all three ships together. The only things visible from the bridge of Hopewell had been the bow wave of Gay Viking and the wake of Nonsuch, and this had not proved enough.

There was an obvious danger that in manoeuvring to change places, Hopewell would lose Gay Viking as well. This was appreciated by Stokes, who aimed to pass to port of Hopewell as close as safety considerations allowed.

The difficulty of station-keeping in darkness with no lights on the one hand, and the risk of collision on the other, had been opposing factors that the men of the motor gunboats had always had to weigh. The loss of Master Standfast had been directly attributable to this dilemma. Now, on what was to prove the last voyage of the Little Ships, the same problem was to provoke another disaster.

Standing to the right of Stokes on the bridge was Ted Ruffman, and he strained his eyes to starboard for a sight of Hopewell as they began to overtake. Suddenly he saw a torpedo-like track running towards him. Stokes saw it in the same moment and his reaction was instantaneous.

'Hard a'port!'

On Hopewell, Captain Jackson and the mate, Ken McNeil, had seen Hopewell about to pass them, and they reduced speed. Suddenly it seemed to them, as they themselves yawed to port, that Gay Viking yawed to starboard.

'Hard a'starboard! Get that wheel over!'

On Gay Viking, Stokes and Ruffman now realised that what they had taken for a torpedo track was the bow wave of an oncoming vessel, the white foam of which was visible for only a few seconds. There was no time for the helm action taken to have any marked effect on either ship. Hopewell's bow tore into Gay Viking and gouged out a great section of the starboard side of her engine room, and as the two ships reeled away from each other, Gay Viking started to submerge like a crash-diving submarine.

Leaving the bridge to find out the extent of the damage, Ruffman met Chief Engineer Love as he emerged from below, and the two men stuck their heads through the engine-room hatch to be met by a frightening sight. About half the starboard side of the engine-room compartment had gone, and their torches shone straight through this gaping hole and out into the heaving Skagerrak. When Stokes realised what the situation was he ordered the crew to their boat stations.

'Will you stand by?' Stokes called across to Hopewell on the loud-hailer.

Hopewell, her bow stove in on the port side, was taking water rapidly too. They were still less than a hundred miles from Sweden and some distance short of Kristiansand, and the risk of interception was considerable; but Jackson decided without hesitation that his first priority must be the rescue of Gay Viking's crew.

'Yes.'

Using five circular rubber dinghies, four men to a dinghy, the evacuation was begun. The plan was that the last of the dinghies, carrying three men only, would stand in closer to the ship than the others to pick up the last man to leave, Ted Ruffman, whose responsibility it was to blow up the vessel.

Having helped launch the dinghies, in which the entire crew escaped, Ruffman turned back from the rail and mounted the ladder back to the bridge. To scuttle the ship he had to insert an ordinary power plug into a socket on the bridge bulkhead and pull out a pin similar to that in a hand grenade. He would then have three and a half minutes to get clear.

He thrust the plug into the socket, but before he pulled the pin he did three things. First he jammed the bridge door open with a steel helmet. Then he took off Jim Woodeson's beautiful leather boots with the caliper fittings; it was a pity, but they were far too heavy to take into the water. Finally he shouted across to Ginger Stokes in the dinghy that he was about to pull the pin. As soon as he had done so he raced off the bridge.

As he turned to step backwards down the vertical ladder the ship rolled and his left hip struck hard against the steel stanchion of the bridge rail. The jar dislodged the torch from the pocket of his life-jacket and it fell the length of its cord, about three feet, before looping itself round the bridge rail. At the very moment when his urgent need was to be off the ship and away, he was attached to it as securely as a climber to a belay.

He had no knife to cut the cord, and no light by which to unravel it. He tugged at it frantically, but it held. Then he thought of a remedy —to throw himself backwards off the bridge to the main deck, a drop of about eight feet. His weight, he calculated, would tear the cord free from the life-jacket.

He jumped; but as he did so he felt the life-jacket being wrenched from his shoulders. He landed on the deck stripped of any form of buoyancy.

He knew he wouldn't survive long in the water without something to keep him afloat. Looking round despairingly, he spotted an old ring lifebelt on the guard rail. Seizing it greedily, he threw it into the water and jumped in after it.

The shock of that first plunge was such that he hung on grimly to the lifebelt for several seconds. Then, driven by the fear of imminent explosion behind him, he swam faster than ever before, pushing the lifebelt ahead of him.

He reached the dinghy safely and was hauled aboard. Seconds later the scuttling charges went up.

As they came up with the Hopewell, her spray strake fouled the dinghy and punctured it. Thrown once again into the water, Ruffman struggled with the others to a rope ladder amidships. As he hung there exhausted, Jim Woodeson leaned out over the rail and shone a torch on him. 'Ah, it's you, Ted,' he said. 'Have you got my boots?' Ruffman wasn't going to answer that one until he'd been hauled aboard. But as they heaved him off the ladder, Woodeson learned the truth. 'My God!' he shouted, half-choked with conflicting emotions. 'You've lost them! You've lost my bloody boots!'

*   *   *

Returning to Sweden overloaded and in a crippled state, the Hopewell was lucky to limp across the Oslo–Frederikshavn shipping lane without being seen. They were allowed by the Swedes to proceed direct to Gothenburg without dismantling guns or disgorging ammunition, and a message was awaiting 'Bingham' there from the Chief of the Swedish Naval Staff asking whether everything possible was being done for them, 'otherwise he would attend to the matter personally'.

Sweden's attitudes, naturally enough, had changed dramatically as the war moved towards its climax. A complete embargo on steel exports to Germany had been secured, one of the negotiators being Bill Waring; all special facilities of an unneutral nature previously afforded to the Germans had been withdrawn; and the concessions that were granted now were all in favour of the Allies. When Hopewell was ready to leave, Commodore Björklund gave orders that on no account was the guard ship or any other naval vessel to follow her into outer territorial waters and thus risk drawing the attention of the

Nancy Hegg

Ted Ruffman

Unloading at Lysekil

'Harry Whitfield's stock was high that morning.' Looking aft from the *Gay Corsair*

'Ginger' Stokes and Brian Reynolds on the bridge of *Nonsuch*, with *Hopewell* to starboard

Germans. Remembering all the bitter battles fought by George Binney over issues like this, the new orders drew wry smiles from old hands like Waring and 'Bingham'.

Despite the loss of Gay Viking it had been a successful trip.* On the outward run the three ships had carried over a thousand carbines and just under a thousand Sten guns (the latter complete with four magazines each), four Bren guns, four bazookas, 120 bazooka rockets, and about $2\frac{1}{4}$ million rounds of ammunition, mostly 9 millimetre, for the Danish Resistance. And on the return run Nonsuch and Hopewell carried over sixty-three tons of special steel cargo between them, more than a third of which was conveyor band steel, a much-needed material that was then only obtainable in Sweden.

Three successful outward voyages, two successful homeward: that was the disappointing tally of Operation Moonshine. Yet for the whole of that winter of 1944–45, determined efforts were being made to get through, as many as twenty abortive attempts being mounted. These failures took more out of the crews than many a successful voyage, even when the mental strain of a dash through the Skagerrak is taken into account. The men would return wet and dispirited after long hours at sea, nearly always suffering from the after-effects of severe sea-sickness, and at the end of that winter Brian Reynolds wrote a moving tribute to them. 'It was significant of the enthusiasm they displayed in everything connected with the operation that they never lost their keenness to see the job through. We had only one instance of a man wishing to leave during the whole winter out of a company of sixty officers and men.'

Much as all these men admired Brian Reynolds, it was George Binney who had originally chosen them, and they never forgot it. 'By the time we got to sea for that first voyage,' remembers Bob Tanton, 'we were all prepared to go to the moon.' Binney's pugnacious and piratical spirit permeated the ships to the end.

For Brian Reynolds an obvious question mark remained: could George Binney have done better? Had they been exceptionally lucky the previous winter on Bridford, and exceptionally unlucky on Moonshine? After his years with Binney, Reynolds was well aware of the part that luck played in such enterprises, and of the way that some men made their own luck. But his final summary is worth repeating. 'Looking back on the operation I hope I can say that on only one occasion was I doubtful as to whether I made the right decision. In

* How tough these little ships were was shown when Gay Viking survived her attempted scuttling and was captured and later refitted. As recently as 1970 she was reported to be operating in the Bahamas as 'Bahama Viking'.

making these decisions I always tried to keep before my mind the one and only rule I think one must stick to in any operation: Is it vital? If it is, then all and every risk must be taken to carry it out. Moonshine was not vital, only very important, therefore one had to try to stick to the limits laid down for the operation. Men's lives, and ships, were at stake, and their loss would not have justified the potential results.

'In the category of vital operations I would put Rubble and Performance,' he concluded. 'In these I think a policy of stake-all was more than justified.' Not far short of these two operations came Bridford.

Throughout all these operations, both of the big ships and of the little ships, there was one ever-present danger that all except the tanker Storsten escaped: mines. Scarcely a moment of the many hours spent in the Skagerrak was free from the fear of them, particularly of drifting mines. Even when loaded, the motor gunboats with their five-foot draught had seemed invulnerable to them, yet the crews knew well enough that this was not so. The dangers they had undergone were emphasised with brutal force two days after VE Day when a naval motor gunboat of exactly the same type, paying an official visit to Gothenburg as a gesture to the Swedes for their co-operation and to arrange for the final removal of Dicto and Lionel, disappeared in the Skagerrak. Four days later, two survivors were picked up in a pitiful state from a Carley float; but for the rest of the crew, the luck that had held for them right through the war had run out.

Among those who died were Captain Herbert 'Jacko' Jackson and Lieutenant-Commander Brian Bingham, once better known as Sylvanus Brian John Reynolds, one of the best-loved of all the characters associated with Binney in the blockade-running operations through the Skagerrak. 'Brian was no dare-devil,' said one of his Commando comrades. 'Risk was a commodity which he measured coolly and carefully.' It was a tragic irony that this man who had risked so much since volunteering to fight in Finland in 1939, yet whose judgment of what was acceptable in the way of risk for himself and his fellows was so finely tuned, should lose his life on so comparatively unimportant a mission.

The second of Binney's chief lieutenants, Bill Waring, also lost his life in tragic circumstances, in an air disaster in 1962. But Binney himself recovered from his heart attack to live a full and active life. Born in 1900, he died in 1972.

Partly because of the secrecy with which his wartime operations and behind-the-scenes battles have been cloaked, the extent of

Binney's achievement has remained little known. Indeed there is evidence of suppression. One of the most bizarre features is the treatment of the Rubble operation in Volume I of the official history, *The War at Sea, 1939–1945*, published in 1956 by Her Majesty's Stationery Office, in which the historian wrote of the 'bold and careful planning which it [Rubble] involved and the courage and determination of the Norwegians to whom its success was due'. There was no mention of the British crews, or of George Binney. Such a travesty of the truth in an official history was infuriating to Binney and many others, and to rectify the injustice Binney immediately sought permission to publish his own factual account. 'This,' he wrote later, 'was officially refused by letter, on the grounds that Rubble was a secret operation and that the authorities considered it unwise to disclose the methods employed for its use.' They suggested, according to Binney, that such information might be 'valuable to a potential enemy of the United Kingdom'.

A later edition of Volume I of the official history was amended to pay tribute to the 'courage and determination of the British and Norwegian crews'; but there was still no mention of Binney. Even Volume II, which gave a brief account of Operation Performance, failed to mention Binney, and it was not until Volume III that his name was linked with these operations.

The historian himself, Captain S. W. Roskill, admitted his error 'with a good grace', according to Binney; and recently he disclosed that, for passages which might be thought likely to cause problems with foreign countries or give them offence, he was 'required to consult the Foreign Office'. But he denied that there was any censorship and insisted on taking full responsibility for omissions. Here his memory would appear to be at fault, as on 28th January 1967 he gave Binney a different explanation—one that differed, too, from the grounds for avoiding disclosure that were given to Binney by officialdom. 'I remember that at the time I wrote Volume I, I was asked not to mention your name because it was considered that your business position might be compromised if your nefarious wartime activities had been revealed.' Did the same apply six years later to Volume II? And why was Binney not consulted? 'I have an idea I did try to contact you,' wrote Roskill, 'but you were abroad.'

These differing explanations and excuses only tend to confirm that a special embargo of some sort was indeed placed on the release of details of the Skagerrak operations, and of Binney's part in them, in addition to the automatic withholding of secret documents under what was then the fifty-year rule. The true reasons for such an embargo are more likely to have been:

1. To avoid embarrassing the Norwegians. (Sensitive over the Norwegian seamen who opted out of Rubble and who left some of the Norwegian ships to be manned by British crews, they could not easily forget the events that led, in Performance, to the sinking of six of their ships and the capture and victimisation of over 250 of their loyal subjects.)

2. To avoid embarrassing the Swedes.

3. To preserve the level of security under which all wartime SOE operations were conducted.

4. To protect those who took part, or failed to take part, in the various operations.

5. To protect those non-combatants and neutrals who opposed or failed to give full backing to Binney's schemes.

Even now there are files dealing with these operations which are under an embargo of up to seventy-five years. But when the documents came up for consideration under the 1967 Act of Parliament which promulgated the new thirty-year rule, the vast majority of them were released to the Public Record Office in London. This, poignantly, was in 1972, the year of Binney's death.

With wartime secrecy thus perpetuated over the years, even many of the people who served and worked with Binney at critical times knew little of his real stature. It is only since his death that this has emerged.

Addresses at memorial services are apt to develop into eulogies, but for one distinguished diplomat at least—Sir Archibald Ross, who served for a time with Binney at the Legation in Stockholm and who later became Britain's Ambassador to Sweden—the short history of Binney's life given on that occasion (by Sir Peter Tennant) was a revelation. 'He was a man,' Ross said afterwards, 'of whom I had no conception.'

The men who really found out about Binney were the men who joined him from Hälsingmo, the Norwegians and the Swedes who took part in his blockade-running operations, and the men of the Little Ships. They were never in any doubt.

SOURCES

Among the documents which I have drawn on particularly for background detail are Chapter 17 of Erik Boheman's book *På Vagt*, published in Stockholm in 1964; 'Running the Blockade', an unpublished manuscript by the late H.W.A. 'Bill' Waring; *Svensk Utrikespolitik 1939–1945* (Swedish Foreign Policy 1939–1945), by Dr Wilhelm M. Carlgren, translated for me by Anthony Arfwedson; The Struggle About the Kvarstad Ships – What the Bonn Files Relate (a series of five articles by Sverre Hartmann); A Report on Operation Performance and Imprisonment Thereafter, by Leonard Sandberg, Oslo, 6th December 1945; *The Gothenburg Traffic*, Swedish safe-conduct shipping during the Second World War, by Nicolaus Rockberger (Stockholm, 1973); *Kvarstadbåtene*, by Alf Pahlow Andresen and Helge Stray Johansen, published in Oslo by Johan Grundt Tanum in 1949 and translated for me by Jack Aird, and on which the authors generously allowed me to draw; the unpublished memoirs of Anne Waring; and two unpublished manuscripts by George Binney, entitled 'Skagerrak Grand Slam' and 'Irate Pirate'.

I have received invaluable help from the Naval Historical Branch of the Ministry of Defence, especially in the provision of a summary of German records; and most important of all has been the access I have had to documents released to the Public Record Office.

General

J. C. Aird; Terge Baalsrud, Editor, The Norwegian Journal of Commerce and Shipping; Colonel Andrew Croft, D.S.O.; Captain Henry Denham, C.M.G., R.N. (Retd.); C. W. Kjellberg, Wilson and Co., Gothenburg; Sir Martin Lindsay of Dowhill, C.B.E., D.S.O.; Lars G. Malmer, Press Relations Manager, S.K.F., Gothenburg; Harald Meltzer; Sir Archibald Ross; Sir Edward Senior; Mrs. Stina Siberg; H. N. Sporborg, C.M.G.; Sir Peter Tennant; Mrs. Anne Waring; the late Sir Charles Wheeler.

Among other documents and papers consulted the following may be mentioned:

Lecture to Swedish-British Society on the wartime blockade of the Skagerrak, by Sir George Binney, 9th February 1948.

The SKF History; and Some Notes on SKF in Sweden during the Second World War, 1939–1945.

Everyman's History of the Sea War, Volume II, by A. C. Hardy (Nicholson and Watson, 1949).

The Blockade Runners, article by A. Cecil Hampshire in the *Nautical Magazine* for November 1973.

On Hazardous Service, by A. Cecil Hampshire (Kimber, 1974)

English, Swedish and Norwegian newspapers.

Royal Norwegian Embassy, London.

Royal Swedish Embassy, London.
Unpublished memoirs of the late Sir Victor Mallet, by kind permission of John V. G. Mallet.

Rubble

M. Bain; Mrs. Thelma H. Davis; Captain W. J. Escudier, O.B.E.; William W. Henry; and Captain Carl Jensen, O.B.E.

Performance

F. Wessel Berg; Finn Bie; Henry Brym; H. B. Christoffersen; Colonel Björn Egge; Finn Haneberg; Peter Jebsen; Colonel and Mrs. Joar Krohn; Gunnar Melle; Kristen Sandaas (whose comprehensive study of the reasons for the failure of W/T communications on Dicto removed all doubts and uncertainties on that score); David Somerville; and Arne Sörbye.

An account of the sinking of Skytteren, written by the late W. 'Bill'. Hateley, and made available to me by courtesy of his widow, Mrs. W. Hateley.

'Were we Neutral? Should the Norwegian Ships have been Sunk?' Text of an open letter to Admiral Tamm by A. Cervin, *Göteborgs-Tidningen*, 5th March 1946.

Bridford

Bill Beavis; H. Miller Bennett; Report from A. E. Reynolds Brown and letters written by him in captivity; James D. Ferguson, N. E. Scottish Correspondent, Aviation News; Terje Fredh, Editor, Lysekil Bohus-läningen, and author of the booklet *Kullagertrafiken* (The Blockade Runners), Lysekil, 1975; Arthur Fray, B.E.M.; Raymond Hobley; Eric Hodgson, M.B.E.; Mrs. M. M. Holdsworth; G. M. Hudson; Captain A. T. Jardine; Laurie Kohler, B.E.M.; Captain K. H. McNeil; Captain Tom Mallory, B.E.M.; Captain J. K. Marrow, M.B.E.; Graham Nixon; Kenneth Parker, B.E.M.; Gilbert Richardson; E. B. Ruffman, D.S.C.: Jack Scott; Captain D. A. Stokes, O.B.E.; Captain R. W. Tanton, O.B.E.; Roger Thornycroft; and Captain B. W. Waldie, M.B.E.

An account by the late Captain H. W. Whitfield, O.B.E., of the first MGB crossing.

Ellerman's Wilson Line Ltd., Hull, for much practical help.

British Coaster, 1939–1945, the Official Story (H.M.S.O., 1947).

'Master Standfast', article in *The Navy* by Jack Dusty.

Documents Studied at Public Record Office

Foreign Office Files

FO 371/29424, 29426–8, 29666, 32812–3, 32815–7, 32820–1, 33075; 33082, 36872–3, 43215, 43454, 48049, 48064.

FO 837/816, 822, 831, 834, 836, 841, 851, 854, 862–3, 866, 872, 880.

Admiralty Files

ADM 1/12448, 12657, 12820, 13402, 16252, 16361.

SOURCES

ADM 199/393, 429, 552.

Air Ministry Files

AIR 15/610

R.A.F. Squadron Operations Record Books

48, 224, 235, 248, 254, 269, 320, 404, 608; and No. 4 (Coastal) Operational Training Unit.

INDEX

Ships are listed under Merchant Ships and Warships. Ranks and titles are those current at the time.

INDEX